Michał Kalecki in the 21st Century

Palgrave Studies in the History of Economic Thought Series

Palgrave Studies in the History of Economic Thought publishes contributions by leading scholars, illuminating key events, theories and individuals that have had a lasting impact on the development of modern-day economics. The topics covered include the development of economies, institutions and theories.

Titles include:

Jan Toporowski and Łukasz Mamica (editors)
MICHAL KALECKI IN THE 21ST CENTURY

Tadeusz Kowalik
ROSA LUXEMBURG THEORY OF ACCUMULATION AND IMPERIALISM

Riccardo Bellofiore, Ewa Karwowski and Jan Toporowski (editors)
ECONOMIC CRISIS AND POLITICAL ECONOMY
Volume 2 of Essays in Honour of Tadeusz Kowalik

Riccardo Bellofiore, Ewa Karwowski and Jan Toporowski (editors)
THE LEGACY OF ROSA LUXEMBURG, OSKAR LANGE AND MICHAŁ KALECKI
Volume 1 of Essays in Honour of Tadeusz Kowalik

Timothy Shenk
MAURICE DOBB: Political Economist

Jan Toporowski
MICHAŁ KALECKI: AN INTELLECTUAL BIOGRAPHY
Volume 1 Rondezvous in Cambridge 1899–1939

Forthcoming titles:

Anthony Thirlwall (editor)
ESSAYS ON KEYNESIAN AND KALDORIAN ECONOMICS

Jan Toporowski
MICHAŁ KALECKI: AN INTELLECTUAL BIOGRAPHY
Volume 2 1939–1970

The full list of titles available is on the website:
www.palgrave.com/economics

Palgrave Studies in the History of Economic Thought
Series Standing Order ISBN 978–1–137–35018–3
(outside North America only)

You can receive future titles in this series as they are published by placing a standing order. Please contact your bookseller or, in case of difficulty, write to us at the address below with your name and address, the title of the series and the ISBN quoted above.

Customer Services Department, Macmillan Distribution Ltd, Houndmills, Basingstoke, Hampshire RG21 6XS, England

---

Michał Kalecki in the 21st Century

Edited by

Jan Toporowski
School of Oriental and African Studies, University of London, UK

Łukasz Mamica
Cracow University of Economics, Poland

palgrave
macmillan

First published 2015 by
PALGRAVE MACMILLAN

Palgrave Macmillan in the UK is an imprint of Macmillan Publishers Limited, registered in England, company number 785998, of Houndmills, Basingstoke, Hampshire RG21 6XS.

Palgrave Macmillan in the US is a division of St Martin's Press LLC, 175 Fifth Avenue, New York, NY 10010.

Palgrave Macmillan is the global academic imprint of the above companies and has companies and representatives throughout the world.

Palgrave® and Macmillan® are registered trademarks in the United States, the United Kingdom, Europe and other countries.

ISBN: 978–1–137–42827–1

This book is printed on paper suitable for recycling and made from fully managed and sustained forest sources. Logging, pulping and manufacturing processes are expected to conform to the environmental regulations of the country of origin.

A catalogue record for this book is available from the British Library.

A catalog record for this book is available from the Library of Congress.

Transferred to Digital Printing in 2014

Contents

List of Figures vii

List of Tables ix

Notes on Contributors x

Introduction 1
Łukasz Mamica and Jan Toporowski

Part I Kalecki and Macroeconomics

1 The Failure of Economic Planning: The Role of the Fel'dman Model and Kalecki's Critique 9
Peter Kriesler and G. C. Harcourt

2 Are Rigid Prices the Cause of Unemployment? 29
Jerzy Osiatyński

3 Kalecki and Post-Keynesian Economics 51
Marc Lavoie

4 Effective Demand and Path Dependence in Short- and Long-Run Growth 68
Amit Bhaduri

5 Kaleckian Traverse, Socialist Planning and Hayekian Objections 80
Roni Demirbag and Joseph Halevi

6 The Impact of Innovations on Investments and Economic Growth in the Thought of Kalecki 99
Łukasz Mamica

7 'Dr Kalecki' on Mr Keynes 108
Hanna Szymborska and Jan Toporowski

Part II Kalecki and Crisis in the 21st Century

8 Michał Kalecki's Capitalist Dynamics from Today's Perspective 119
D. Mario Nuti

9 Kalecki's Profits Equation after 80 years 131
Kazimierz Łaski and Herbert Walther

10 Kalecki and Kowalik on the Dilemma of 'Crucial Reform' in the United States and Poland 157
Gary A. Dymski

11 A Kaleckian Perspective on Changes in the Aggregate Income Distribution in the US 182
Tracy Mott and Mark Evers

12 Addressing the 'Great Recession' Using Kalecki's Macroeconomic Analysis 198
Malcolm Sawyer

13 Economic Policies for Exit from Crisis, in a Post-Kaleckian Model 212
Edwin Le Heron

14 Firm Heterogeneity, Finance and Development: A Kaleckian Perspective 239
Jago Penrose

15 The Kalecki-Steindl Theory of Financial Fragility 252
Jan Toporowski

Index 265

List of Figures

1.1	Growth rate of net output as a function of the degree of industrialization	14
1.2	The choice of technique in China	20
7.1	Determination of short-run equilibrium in Kalecki's interpretation	110
7.2	Impact of an increase in capitalist expenditure on the short-run equilibrium in Kalecki's interpretation	111
9.1	Lowering the wage share	138
9.2	The Kaleckian cross	139
9.3	US sectoral financial balances	147
9.4	The uses of gross corporate profits	151
9.5	Increasing income inequality in the US	152
10.1	Annual US unemployment rates in post-1980 expansions, trough to peak (truncated at 6 years)	169
10.2	Annual US long-term unemployment rates in post-1980 expansions, trough to peak (truncated at 6 years)	170
10.3	Annual percentage changes in components of US GDP growth, 1992–2010	171
10.4	Annual Polish unemployment rates in post-1990 expansions, trough to peak	176
10.5	Annual Polish labour-force participation rates in post-1990 expansions, trough to peak	176
10.6	Annual Polish youth unemployment rates in post-1990 expansions, trough to peak	177
10.7	Annual Polish long-term unemployment rates in post-1990 expansions, trough to peak	177
10.8	Annual percentage changes in components of Polish GDP growth, 1992–2010	178
11.1	Degree of unionization	188
11.2	NIPA mark-up	192
11.3	BLS mark-up	192
11.4	BLS and mixed mark-up comparison	193
11.5	Real corporate dividends	195
13.1	Inflation curve	226
13.2	Inflation and state of confidence of firms and banks in France effects on the economic growth	227

13.3 Three hypotheses for fiscal policy 229
13.4 Better income distribution effects on economic growth 230
13.5 Lower wages effects on economic growth 231
15.1 Household saving & firms' retained profits in industrial capitalism 256
15.2 Household saving & firms' retained profits in financialized capitalism 262

List of Tables

11.1 Labour Income and Productivity in the US 185
11.2 Unemployment in the United States 186
11.3 The Mark-up in the United States 190

Notes on Contributors

Amit Bhaduri is Emeritus Professor of Economics at the Jawaharlal Nehru University, Delhi, India.

Roni Demirbag is Lecturer at the Department of Political Economy at the University of Sydney, NSW Australia.

Gary A. Dymski is Professor of Applied Economics at the University of Leeds, UK.

Mark Evers is Adjunct Professor in the Economics Department, University of Denver, USA.

Joseph Halevi is Senior Lecturer in the Department of Political Economy in the University of Sydney. He is also a member of CRIISEA at the Université de Picardie, Amiens France and of the International University College, Turin Italy.

G.C. Harcourt is Visiting Professorial Fellow at the University of New South Wales, Australia, Emeritus Reader in the History of Economic Theory at the University of Cambridge, UK, and Emeritus Professor of Economics at the University of Adelaide, Australia.

Peter Kriesler is Associate Professor of Economics at the University of New SouthWales, Australia.

Marc Lavoie is Professor in the Department of Economics at the University of Ottawa, Canada, and IMK research fellow at the Institut für Makroökonomie in Düsseldorf, Germany.

Edwin Le Heron is Associate Professor in Economics at the Bordeaux Institute of Political Sciences, France, and Researcher at GREThA of the University of Bordeaux.

Kazimierz Łaski is Emeritus Professor of Economics at the University of Linz, Austria, and the Vienna Institute for International Economic Studies.

Łukasz Mamica is Associate Professor in the Department of Public Economy and Administration, Cracow University of Economics, Poland.

Tracy Mott is Associate Professor in the Economics Department, University of Denver, USA.

D. Mario Nuti is Professor of Comparative Economic Systems at the University of Rome 'La Sapienza'.

Jerzy Osiatyński is a member of the Monetary Policy Committee of the National Bank of Poland, Professor of Economics at the University of Bielsko-Biała, and Professor of Economics at the Institute of Economics of the Polish Academy of Sciences; from 2007 to 2013 he chaired the Institute's Board of Studies. He edited the *Collected Works of Michał Kalecki*.

Jago Penrose is Economic Adviser to the UK Government at the Department of Transport in London.

Malcolm Sawyer is Emeritus Professor of Economics, University of Leeds, UK.

Hanna Szymborska is a postgraduate student in the Department of Economics, University of Leeds.

Jan Toporowski is Professor of Economics and Finance at the School of Oriental and African Studies, University of London, and Visiting Professor of Economics at the University of Bergamo, and International University College, Turin.

Herbert Walther is Professor of Economics and Director of the Institute of Labour Economics at the Vienna University of Economics and Business.

Introduction

Łukasz Mamica and Jan Toporowski

The Polish economist Michał Kalecki (1899–1970) needs little introduction to English-speaking economists because of his widely acknowledged co-authorship of the Keynesian Revolution in economic theory and policy, and because his theory of the business cycle seems especially appropriate to analysing the instability of capitalism in the 21st century. Quite how much his theory is as widely understood is another matter. While his aphorisms have caught the mood of the new century, for example 'the social function of the doctrine of "sound finance" is to make the level of employment dependent on the state of confidence', recently cited by Paul Krugman (Krugman and Wells 2012), his theory is much less well-known, often hidden by rather forbidding mathematics, and more difficult to read than the engaging John Maynard Keynes.

Michał Kalecki was born at the end of the 19th century in the Polish manufacturing city of Łódź, where his father, Abram Kalecki, owned a small spinning mill. Business in Łódź did not do well in the opening years of the 20th century, and the whole city was wracked by civil and industrial unrest when the 1905 Revolution broke out. Abram Kalecki went out of business in 1910. His son completed his secondary education during the First World War and started to study engineering at the Polytechnic in Gdańsk. Economic conditions in independent Poland did not recover, and Michał had to give up his studies to help support his father. He dabbled in business journalism and through this finally obtained employment in 1929 in the *Instytut Badań Koniunktur Gospodarczych i Cen* (Institute for the Study of Business Cycles and Prices), a Government-financed business research institute. It was there, in 1933, that Kalecki published his model of the business cycle, a model that he presented at a conference of the newly formed Econometric Society in Leiden.

In 1936, Kalecki left Poland on a Rockefeller Foundation Fellowship that took him initially to Stockholm, and then to London, where he met Keynes and was rapidly integrated in Keynes's circle of sympathizers and friends in Cambridge, including Joan Robinson, Richard Kahn, Piero Sraffa and Maurice Dobb. Keynes assisted him arranging a further scholarship and finally, in 1939, a job as a statistician on a project at Cambridge, looking at industrial cycles in the UK. Shortly after the outbreak of the Second World War, Kalecki transferred to the Institute of Statistics at Oxford University, where he engaged in work on War finance and post-War economic policy.

After the Second World War, Kalecki went to work briefly for the International Labour Office and then at the United Nations Secretariat in New York. In 1955 he returned to Poland, where he extended the range of his research to developing countries and the economic problems of socialism. His criticism of economic policy in his home country was not well-taken. In 1968, his theories were denounced, his associates removed from their positions, and many of those associates were driven into exile.

Kalecki died in 1970. His rehabilitation started soon after with a project to publish his collected works in Polish, under the editorship of Jerzy Osiatyński, a contributor to this volume. An English edition of the collected works was published by Clarendon Press, Oxford, in the 1990s. There is now a considerable literature on Kalecki's theories, much of it concerned with comparisons with Keynes's analysis in the *General Theory*. An intellectual biography is in the process of publication, with a first volume published in 2013 (Toporowski, 2013). But there is also increasing interest in applying Kalecki's analysis to the problems of 21st-century capitalism, where that analysis seems especially appropriate to the conditions not only of seemingly intractable mass unemployment that Keynes's work was supposed to deal with, but also inequality, instability and debt difficulties that feature largely in Kalecki's work.

The transformation of Poland from Communism to free market capitalism was accompanied by particularly virulent and widespread unemployment and economic instability. It is not really surprising, therefore, that after a period of neglect, Polish economists are returning to the study of Kalecki. In 1999, Kalecki's centenary was celebrated by a conference at the Polish Academy of Sciences (Sadowski and Szeworski, 2004). The present volume adds the experience of the 21st century to the existing literature on Kalecki, that is the most recent developments in economic theory, the widespread economic crisis that has affected Europe and North America through most of the century that we have experienced, and the distinctive role of finance in that crisis.

In October 2012, the European Association for Evolutionary Political Economy held its annual conference at the Cracow University of Economics. Professor Jerzy Hausner and Dr Łukasz Mamica organized special sessions devoted to the work of Kalecki and applications of his theories. Most of the papers that appear in this volume were presented during those sessions. The conference itself took place only months after the death of Tadeusz Kowalik, one of Kalecki's closest associates during the last ten years of Kalecki's life. It is not surprising therefore that many of the authors in this volume have chosen also to commemorate Kalecki's friend and co-author.

Given this background, the papers in this volume fall naturally into two parts. The first part discusses Kalecki's macroeconomics. In this part Peter Kriesler and Geoffrey Harcourt examine the role of the Fel'dman model, which focused on autarkic growth, with an emphasis on industrialization, in determining the 'method' of economic planning. They analyse the influence of this model on subsequent Soviet planning. This chapter refers to Michał Kalecki's critique of this model, especially of the mechanical use of the model as a solution to the development problem. Peter Kriesler and G.C. Harcourt treat the Fel'dman model as partly responsible for the collapse of the USSR and the European 'socialist' economies. A key chapter by Jerzy Osiatyński analyses the respective theories of Kalecki and Keynes on the relationship between rigid wages and unemployment. They both showed that cuts in money wages can be compensated by reductions of prices, or would result in a reduction of aggregate demand, and consequently employment. The reduction of wages in relation to rising labour productivity has a temporary positive impact on the competitive position of exporters but affects adversely the markets of importers. The practical consequences of this process are painfully visible in the Southern European countries of the European Monetary Union.

Marc Lavoie then stresses the importance of Michał Kalecki in Post-Keynesian economics. He refers to the fundamental ideas of Kalecki on the evolution of economic crisis, focussing on income distribution, his profit equations and the lack of confidence associated with a recession that would drive up the interest rates on private debt. Marc Lavoie shows that many of Kalecki's ideas are still crucial for understanding the global financial crisis mechanism, especially the need for liquid assets and the role played by liquidity preference. This is followed by Amit Bhaduri's examination of Kalecki's theory of output and profit determination. Bhaduri argues that the succession of short runs (caused by problems of demand) create a path dependent growth process affecting the trajectory of the economy to or away from long-run equilibrium. The chapter shows that, even in a one-good model, variations in the level of aggregate demand affect the time structure of the capital stock, exhibiting some properties of path dependence. He links the level of aggregate demand to the supply potential of the economy through a path-dependent time structure of the capital stock.

This analysis is further developed by Roni Demirbag and Joseph Halevi in their consideration of the relationship between Kalecki's macrodynamics and the method of the 'traverse'. They argue that all short- and long-term macroeconomic adjustments (outside the case of a deep depression) should be thought of as Kalecki-Kaldor-Lowe-type traverses. Demirbag and Halevi treat socialist planning (as envisioned by Kalecki himself) as the only meaningful institutional, and hence policy, framework in which traverses can be successfully completed. They discuss also Hayek's objections to socialist planning to show some form of socialist planning as the only viable option in maintaining full employment. Łukasz Mamica extends the discussion to analyse the impact of innovations on investments and economic growth in the thought of Michał Kalecki. He stress that Kalecki treated technical progress as a factor of long-run investment and supporting long-run expansionary trends. According to Kalecki the innovation process is a chain of short-term decisions of entrepreneurs concerning their innovative activities, and technical progress does not increase output but save labour.

Finally in this section, Hanna Szymborska and Jan Toporowski analyse Kalecki's interpretation of the *General Theory*, contained in his review of the Keynes book from 1936 (and, until 1982, available only in Polish). Kalecki presented there a simple exposition of Keynes's view of the determination of output and employment, the basic composition of aggregate demand and the distribution of income. Szymborska and Toporowski stress that Kalecki identified the key weaknesses and inconsistencies in Keynes's theory, while recognizing its seminal refutation of 'classical' theory.

The second part of the volume connects Kalecki's theories of the business cycle with the crises of the 21st century. In this part Domenico Mario Nuti, who was present at Kalecki's lectures in Warsaw 50 years ago, refers to his model based on the political economy of government fiscal policy and of capitalists' behaviour. This model is analysed taking into account globalization of labour markets, stronger pressure on the sustainability of sovereign government debt and the diminished credibility of achieving full employment. Mario Nuti's chapter is an important voice in the discussion concerning the role and consequences of fiscal consolidation officially recommended by the International Monetary Fund.

Kazimierz Łaski and Herbert Walther then develop Kalecki's argument that private investment determines private savings. They argue that the short lag between investment decisions and expenditures is an essential element of any meaningful interpretation of his profits equation. According to them, demographic ageing in Western economies causes an excess of desired long-term household savings over investment. This imbalance can be eliminated by accepting the necessity of a permanent primary public deficit or active redistributive policies (or both of these policies). Gary Dymski analyses the work of Michał Kalecki and Tadeusz Kowalik on the challenge of the 'crucial reform', the name given by them to political agreements between capitalists and workers allowing sustained growth and rising wages. Dymski presents reasons for the failure of 'crucial reforms' in both capitalist and socialist economic systems. The ideas developed by Kalecki and Kowalik are presented as illuminating the current Eurozone crisis, where conflict between state and capital as well as between state and markets can be observed.

Tracy Mott and Mark Evers refer to Kalecki's taxonomy of factors affecting aggregate income distribution in the US. Their analysis shows that distributional changes in the American economy since 1983 can be attributed to a rise in the aggregate mark-up. The rise in this mark-up is due to overhead salary compensation rising at the expense of the real wage income of production and non-supervisory workers. These processes are connected also with growth in real terms (with the exception of the 2007–2009 time period), stock prices and dividend payments in the analysed period. Malcolm Sawyer analyses Michał Kalecki's use of budget deficits and other policies to reach full employment. He explains Kalecki's arguments against fiscal consolidation and for a positive role of redistribution from higher- to lower-incomes as ways of increasing consumption out of a given national income. Malcolm Sawyer agrees with Kalecki's scepticism about the existence of mechanisms which would readily bring savings behaviour and investment decisions to equality. In conclusion he stresses that fundamental reforms, proposed by Kalecki as necessary, are more remote than ever.

In his chapter, Edwin Le Heron explains the latest financial crisis through a Kaleckian analysis of the behaviour of private banks, the financial risks of firms and banks, and the psychological variables along with the state of confidence of private sectors. In the case of France, Edwin Le Heron assumes that financial crisis essentially involves a fall in the state of confidence of the economic agents that afterwards depressed the real economy. He warns against the policies of lowering wages and proposes instead a better income distribution as the best solution to restore confidence and economic growth without worsening public debt.

The last two chapters examine the particular developments of Kalecki's theories that were made by his friend and co-worker Joseph Steindl. In the first, Jago Penrose shows the consequences of heterogeneous financing, funding and liquidity strategies of firms, as put forward by Michał Kalecki and later Joseph Steindl. Financial institutions have a strong impact on these strategies. Jago Penrose presents the policy dilemma of solving the problem of capital financing in developing countries and shows how in South-East Asia public financing of large firms may have a positive role in the absence of a developed financial sector. Finally, Jan Toporowski explains Kalecki's and Steindl's modelling of the financial fragility of companies through a circular flow of income analysis. He highlights the role of household saving as a factor in the macroeconomics of Kalecki and in precipitating financial crises. Macroeconomic imbalances in a credit-based capitalist economy work themselves out through the constraints that debts impose upon firms and households, although this process does not necessarily result in equilibrium.

The editors of this volume are grateful to Taiba Batook and Ania Wronski in helping to prepare this volume for publication. The financial support of the Polish central bank, the Narodowy Bank Polski, for the publication of this volume and the Kalecki sessions in Kraków in October 2012 is also gratefully acknowledged.

References

Krugman, P. and Wells, R. (2012) Economy killers: Inequality and GOP ignorance, *Salon*, April 15.

Sadowski, Z.L. and Szeworski, A. (eds) (2004) *Kalecki's Economics Today*, London: Routledge.

Toporowski, J. (2013) *Michał Kalecki: An Intellectual Biography, Volume 1: Rendezvous in Cambridge 1899–1939*, Basingstoke: Palgrave.

Part I

Kalecki and Macroeconomics

1
The Failure of Economic Planning: The Role of the Fel'dman Model and Kalecki's Critique

Peter Kriesler and G. C. Harcourt

> The 'purposive' man is always trying to secure a spurious and delusive immortality for his actions by pushing his interest in them forward into time. He does not love his cat, but his cat's kittens; nor, in truth, the kittens, but only the kittens' kittens, and so on forward for ever to the end of catdom. For him jam is not jam unless it is a case of jam tomorrow and never jam today. Thus by pushing his jam always forward into the future, he strives to secure for his act of boiling it an immortality. (Keynes 1972, p. 330)

1.1 Introduction

In the 1920s, Soviet economists began to develop growth theory with the specific aim of facilitating the planning of their economy. Their work differed from that of most 20th-century economists because it was not aimed at academic economists but, rather, at politicians, bureaucrats and others involved in the machinery of planning. This meant that, although the work was often not as technical as the authors may have liked, it strongly related to the actual economy that they were attempting to model.

At the end of the 1920s, there was a debate about what are the appropriate goals for economic planning.[1] The growth model developed by Fel'dman was regarded as the most important to emerge from that debate.[2]

Fel'dman's initial training was as an electrical engineer, but he was involved with the Soviet Planning Agency, Gosplan, from 1923 to

1931. The growth model for which he is best known was part of a report to:

> the Commission for the General Plan of the Gosplan of the USSR, concerning the question of the interrelationship of the rate of growth of reproduction of individual sectors of the economy among themselves and of the structure of the reproduction process as a whole. (Note of the editor of *Planovoe khoziaistvo,* Fel'dman 1928a, p. 174n.)

The Fel'dman model played an important role in influencing Soviet policy:

> [It] expresses the foundations of the Soviet strategy for economic growth until the mid-1950s, based on priority for heavy industry and production goods; the same strategy was passively followed by the other socialist countries of Eastern Europe after the war. (Nove and Nuti 1972a, p. 13)

The priority given to heavy industry that emerged from the model played an important role in subsequent thinking about economic planning. The model has often been labelled as a 'structural' model because it was not just concerned with the absolute sizes of output and of investment, but is also with their composition. According to the model, the structure and composition of national output and, in particular, of investment will have as significant an influence on the rate of growth as their absolute values. The division of investment between capital goods for the consumer sector and for the capital goods producing sector is seen to be the key structural policy variable. Using this variable, Fel'dman developed an analysis of growth that foreshadowed the major western growth theories.[3]

This chapter examines the role of the Fel'dman model in determining the 'method' of economic planning, rather than with the environment in which it was developed or with the precise mechanics of the model *per se*. Rather, it is concerned with the influence of the model on subsequent Soviet planning and with the main criticisms of the model, particularly those by Michał Kalecki. The model has become synonymous with a way of thinking and of looking at the question of economic growth which manifested itself in the attitude stressing the absolute priority of industrialization and investment in heavy industrial capital/high capital intensity, at the expense of present consumption. Due to the role of the Fel'dman model in Soviet thinking and its strong association with Stalinism and Stalinist policies, providing a theoretical justification for heavy industrialization policy, it provides a good starting point for understanding some of the failures of economic planning in Eastern Europe, and for rethinking future roles for economic planning.

The next section of this chapter examines the Fel'dman model, outlining its salient features, first in a closed economy environment, and, in the following section, opening the model to trade. In the next section, some of the criticisms and extensions of the model are discussed. Problems relating to the Fel'dman model with respect to choice of technique are then examined. Kalecki's critique and his concept of a 'government decision function' as a response to these problems are discussed subsequently.

1.2 The Fel'dman model

Underlying the Fel'dman model is an attempt to use the Marxian reproduction schemas to analyse long-run growth. As a result, there was some modification to the original formulation of the schemas, as Fel'dman abstracted from short-run crises in order to focus on the longer-run problems of capacity growth. In particular, concern with longer-term growth issues allowed him to abstract from shorter-run problems associated with realization of the surplus.[4]

In the Marxian reproduction model, Department 1 produces capital goods for the economy, and Department 2 produces consumption goods. Department 1 provides Department 2 with fixed and circulating capital. In the case of simple reproduction (no growth), this is done in order to maintain existing production levels, in other words, to cover replacement. In the case of expanded reproduction, additional capital needs to be provided in order to enable the economy to expand.

> This gives rise to the idea of dividing the capital of sector A into two sections, of which one supplies sector B with the means of production required to sustain output at a given level, and the other supplies all industries in both sectors with additional capital to enable reproduction to expand. (Fel'dman 1928a, p. 176)

As a result, Fel'dman reformulated the model so that the output of each sector was determined solely by their final products. This meant that sector B not only included all consumption goods but also the capital used in producing those consumption goods.

> The value of the output of sector B can include only the value of raw materials and that portion of the equipment and producers' goods actually used up in the production of consumer goods.... Thus the wear and tear of productive equipment in sector B must, by definition, be made good within that sector.... [P]roduction must be divided into *sector B*, capable of maintaining consumption at a given level even with a cessation of the inflow of producers' and consumers' goods from *sector A*, which provides both sector B and itself with all the capital required for expansion of reproduction.

Thus, starting from Marx's division, we have arrived at a new division which corresponds, however, to another division, the Marxian simple and expanded reproduction, the 'production of income' and 'the production of capital'.

> The only criterion for classifying production into the proposed sectors is whether it serves *to increase capital*... or only *to maintain consumption* at a given level. (Fel'dman 1928a, p. 177–178; emphasis in original)

Sector B produces consumption goods for the economy and also what is needed to replace depreciation of both fixed and circulating capital (although Fel'dman later assumed away deprecation of fixed capital). This means that, in the case of simple reproduction, the economy would only need sector B, while the output of sector A is solely aimed at accumulation. So we are dealing with vertically integrated sectors.[5]

Sector A produces capital goods for itself and for any expansion in the consumption goods sector. Fel'dman assumed that, before they are installed, capital goods are malleable and can be installed in either sector. Once the capital is installed, however, it is no longer malleable and cannot, therefore, be shifted between sectors, that is:

> A rolling mill cannot, so to speak, be constructed with the aid of a weaving loom, nor can a rolling pin be adapted for the production of cloth. (Fel'dman 1928a, p. 189)[6]

Fel'dman developed his model at various stages of abstraction. In expositing the analysis it is important to distinguish between analytically fundamental assumptions and those used to simplify the analysis. According to Fel'dman, the fundamental assumptions are constant returns to scale, given prices, the independence of production from consumption, and the absence of lags and any bottlenecks except in the production of capital.[7]

For simplicity, Fel'dman assumed that there was no depreciation of capital, that the supply of labour was infinitely elastic and that he was modelling a closed economy with no government sector.[8] Although Fel'dman considers the implications of relaxing all these assumptions, except the last one, the economists who utilized the insights of the model, for various purposes, ignored the important possibilities of either labour shortages or international trade.

The essence of the model lies in the distinction between capital goods used to produce more capital goods and capital goods used in the consumption goods sector, which is embodied in the ratio:

$$I_k = K_u/K_p$$

where K_u = capital goods in the producer goods sector
K_p = capital goods in the consumer goods sector
I_k reflects the 'index of industrialization'.

While I_k is given at any point of time, it will change over time as a result of a changing composition of investment, which was seen as the key policy variable affecting the long-run rate of growth of the economy. The allocation of the output of sector A between the two types of capital goods is the means by which policy influences the growth rate. The larger the proportion of sector A's output which is ploughed back into sector A, the higher the subsequent growth rate of the economy will be. However, this results in less of sector A's output being allocated to sector B, which reduces the economy's ability to provide consumption goods in the near future. This means that, as a result of the assumption of the full employment of all resources, higher growth rates come at the expense of lower consumption levels.

> The rate of *increase* in the growth-rate depended on the rate of increase in the proportionate size of the capital-goods sector, and hence on the proportionate allocation of current investment between the two sectors. (Dobb 1967 p. 110 emphasis in original)

In other words, the higher the proportion of the capital stock devoted to production of capital goods, the higher the growth rate of the economy. This is captured in the fundamental equation:

$$D' = S \,.\, D_u / D$$

where D′ = rate of growth of net output
S = effectiveness of capital utilization which is the inverse of the capital/output ratio
D = net output
D_u = output of capital goods sector, that is, accumulation

The rate of growth of output is determined by the effectiveness of the utilization of the capital stock and the proportion of total output devoted to the capital goods sector. The larger the ratio D_u / D, the higher the growth rate will be.

Fel'dman argues that the ratio I_k, which is a reflection of D_u / D, determines the possible rates of growth of the economy and illustrates this in the figure reproduced below.

In Figure 1.1 the curve also indicates how the rate of growth of income increases as a function of the industrialization of the country at every stage of development, for the ratio K_u/K_p is undoubtedly one of the primary indicators of the level of industrialization of the country, by virtue of the constantly increasing significance of industry in the contemporary economy. Thus an increase in the rate of growth of income demands considerable industrialization.... heavy industry, machine building, electrification (Fel'dman 1928a, p. 194).

This illustrates the core proposition of the Fel'dman model, that to increase an economy's rate of growth, there must be an increase in its level of industrialization. This requires a switch of resources away from

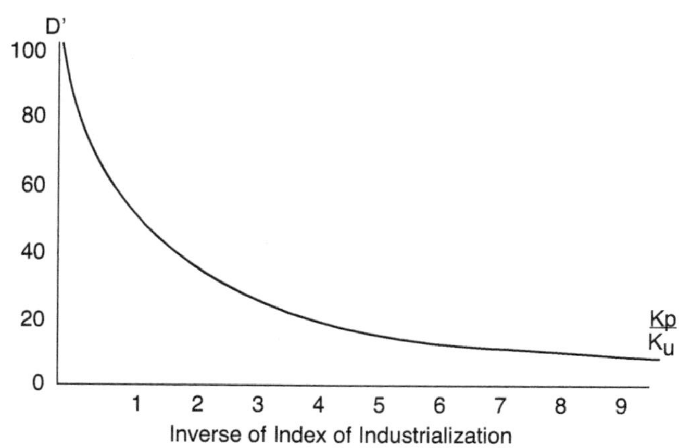

Figure 1.1 Growth rate of net output as a function of the degree of industrialization
Source: Fel'dman (1928a).

the production of capital for consumption goods, in order to augment production of capital for the production of additional capital. As a result, there will be an immediate short-run fall in the production of consumption goods, due to the relative decline of the capital stock of that sector. However, since the economy is now growing at a higher rate of growth, eventually, consumption will attain a higher level than it otherwise would have. The trade-off between consumption and growth is, according to the model, only an issue in the short term. Of course, it is never clear for how long this short term will last. In the meantime, as the quote at the beginning of the paper indicates, 'it is a case of jam tomorrow and never jam today'.

Contrary to the popular perception that the model advocates growth at the expense of consumption, it is an attempt to describe the conditions necessary to increase the long-run growth of consumption.[9] It is important to note that Fel'dman makes clear, right from the outset of his argument, that he sees increased consumption as the overall goal of economic growth:

> The primary objective of this work is to determine the potential volume of consumption of the masses, and its rate of growth as a function of the structure of the economy. (Fel'dman 1928a p. 174)

As will be discussed below, it was the use of the model by planners which led to increased consumption being permanently postponed (always jam tomorrow).

It is important to note that the Fel'dman model was designed to deal with growth under specific social and historical circumstances. This partially explains the subsequent use of the model. Dobb argued that the model is specific to a particular stage in the development process, where the main bottleneck on economic growth is the lack of development of heavy industry.[10] This is important because it explains the model's lack of flexibility in explaining other necessary aspects of the development process.

To illustrate the model's specificity, consider the results of its stress on industrialization. Relatively more resources are utilized by the investment goods sector, which leads to an increase in total employment with a much smaller change in the output of consumption goods. This, in turn, will lead to a fall in the real wage. It follows that the process is limited, in that there will be some minimum below which the real wage cannot fall.[11] In addition, the larger the size of the investment goods sector relative to the consumption goods sector, the smaller the effect of any further increase in its relative size on the growth rate of consumption goods will be.[12] This means that the heavy industry strategy, with progressively more resources going to that sector, can only be a useful strategy for a finite period. In particular, Dobb locates its optimal use in the early stages of development, where the economy has an excess supply of labour and a shortage of capital. This corresponds to Lewis's discussion of the development process and its key reliance on industrialization.[13] Planning serves the function of facilitating the development process and avoiding some of the problems associated with reliance on markets. However, as the growth process continues and absorbs more labour, eventually a labour shortage will ensue, and at this point the strategy will need to be changed. This is analogous to Lewis's argument that, once labour surpluses are absorbed by the development process, the problems associated with duality and underdevelopment have been overcome.

Even before absolute labour shortages are incurred, the model's shortcomings become apparent. The assumption of fixed prices limits the ability of the model to explain allocative processes. This, coupled with the 'short-run' fall in production of consumption, promotes the use of queuing as an allocative method, although this may not be the most desirable. A case may be made for arguing that the Soviets deliberately eschewed the pricing mechanism as an allocative device for consumption goods in particular, due to an assumption of inelastic demand for these goods. Further implications of the fixed price assumption are discussed in the next section.

1.3 Opening the model to trade

Underlying the formal part of Fel'dman's model is the belief that capital goods production is the main bottleneck to economic growth.[14] One criticism of the model is that this bottleneck is the result of the closed economy assumption. Fel'dman considered the situation 'under free external relations',[15] where he seems to come close to a statement of comparative advantage:

> Under these conditions it is advantageous to export what is produced with maximum efficiency, and to import what is produced with minimum efficiency. (Fel'dman 1928b, p. 325)

The open economy model modified the results, in that it allowed higher levels of consumption to the extent that the effectiveness of the capital used for the production of exports was greater than the capital which would have been used to produce the imported goods. However, due to 'capitalist encirclement', it was the closed economy model which was the most applicable to the Soviet Union. Unsal (1990–1991) attempted to give international trade a more prominent role in the analysis. He showed there are two possible industrialization strategies which will lead to higher growth rates of consumption. The first is the Fel'dman policy of priority to heavy industry, while the second, more closely aligned to the Kaldorian notion of export-led growth, requires a 'policy of outward-looking priority growth of the consumer-goods sector' (Unsal 1990–1991, p. 398). This latter policy is limited by the potential market for exports, as well as the likely long-run changes in the terms of trade. Halevi criticizes the Unsal argument on two grounds. First, it ignores the constraint on export earnings of a country in the early stages of industrialization. Second, it ignores the issue of structural dependence. Importing capital goods for the production of exports limits the domestic economy's ability to develop a capital goods industry independent of its trading partners, which will, therefore, provide an external limit to growth.[16] In other words, by concentrating on static comparative advantage it ignores potential problems arising from dynamic comparative advantage.[17]

1.4 Evaluation of the model

It has long been known that the fundamental equation of the Fel'dman model is formally identical to the Harrod growth-equation.[18] Domar reworked the Fel'dman equations to show that 'his results are essentially similar and reducible to those since developed in the West' (Domar 1957, p. 225).[19]

The strong similarities of the Fel'dman model with Austrian models are interesting. For Fel'dman, as for the Austrians, 'consumption was the sole purpose of production' (Domar 1957, p. 245). The important link is with the reward for postponing consumption. For both, the more that present consumption is postponed, the greater will be future consumption. For Fel'dman this is the result of more capital goods being placed in the capital goods sector, reducing current consumption, but increasing the potential rate of growth of consumption. The overall effect is to increase the economy's level of industrialization. The analogy for the Austrians is that, by postponing present consumption, resources can be used to increase the degree-of-roundaboutness, which will reap rewards in the future. This will lead to an increase in the economy's average period of production which is akin to an increase in the level of industrialization.

As a planning model, the Fel'dman model was criticized for being too abstract to allow definite policy guidelines:

> [F]rom a model like Fel'dman's almost any rate of growth could be derived on paper, provided the capital coefficients were low enough and the propensity to save (or I_k) high enough. They certainly failed to realize that these parameters, and particularly the capital coefficients, were mere abstractions, useful (I trust) in theoretical work, but full of innumerable and well-hidden implications regarding the actual working of the economic mechanism, and that the whole problem of economic development lies not in the algebraic manipulations which Fel'dman carried out in such detail, but in overcoming the immense administrative, technological and human obstacles which a rapid industrialization of a backward peasant economy was bound to create. (Domar 1957, pp. 256–257)

The main policy implication of the Fel'dman model, and the one which was to have the greatest impact on Soviet planners, is the importance of investment in heavy industry. The basic proposition is that by planning investment, and leaving consumption as a residual, despite an initial contraction in the production of consumption goods as resources are moved to the capital goods sector, eventually a higher rate of growth would result, which would lead to higher consumption levels at some future date. Among some planners this became a way of thinking, the justification for an ideological push for industrialization. This was reinforced by another advantage of planning capital production, namely, that any attempt to plan consumption production would require the planners to take into considerations consumers' tastes, a difficult task at the best of times, that is further discussed below.

The problem with planning investment was that it required capital goods to be efficiently utilized, and planners to be realistic in their goals. If either of these conditions were not met, then it was consumption, the residual, which would suffer. When planners attempted to implement the conclusions of the model, they found that the time horizon for the sacrifice of consumption had been grossly underestimated. In other words, it was always 'jam tomorrow, and never jam today'.

Further, if the ultimate aim is to increase consumption, by ignoring it initially, there is no guarantee that the resulting structure of capital goods will deliver the preferred consumption, since there is no way to incorporate consumers' tastes. In the model there is no differentiation between types of consumption goods; the possibility that industrialization will lead to the production of inappropriate consumption goods is not considered. Moreover, without some feedback mechanism from consumers to those in charge of investment, there is no guarantee that the consumption goods that are produced will be suitable and match demand. So, even if 'jam today' ever eventuated, there was no mechanism to ensure that it was the jam that people actually wanted.

An extremely important limitation of the model, despite Fel'dman's attempt to explain it away, is the lack of any analysis of value or price. In a multisectoral model, price will change as a result of the growth process, and this will have important ramifications outside steady state analysis.[20] This reduces the relevance of the model to a two-good case, with vertically integrated capital goods and consumption goods sectors. As a result, within the model the problem alluded to above, that the structure of capital goods and consumption goods may not suit the needs of the economy, is assumed away. Ignoring consumption today means that the model does not consider any mechanism to ensure that the capital structure resulting from the industrialization process is appropriate to deliver the preferred consumption goods. In addition, there is no analysis to ensure that the most appropriate capital is being laid down. To incorporate this would require some acknowledgment and consideration of the problem of technical progress, which is not considered. As a result, the model implicitly relies on the existence of a reserve army of consumers that is willing to accept any consumer goods that the capital structure eventually churns out, and on the ability of planners to perform the same function as prices in signalling producers as to the appropriate goods to produce.

The absence of any feedback mechanism within the model also created an economy resistant to change. Absence of markets and choice for final consumption goods removes any discipline on planners. There was nothing to alleviate the tendency to push for growth for its own sake, ignoring the needs of the consumers. There was no discipline to ensure that the economy was not being run for the sake of the planners and the political stability of the state, rather than for the welfare of the consumers. This is reflected in the choice of technique problem discussed in the next section.

1.5 Choice of technique

Many of the criticisms that can be made of the Fel'dman model and the practice of planning have as their base the writings of Dobb, Kalecki, Sen and Joan Robinson in the 1950s on the appropriate choice of technique of production to be reflected in accumulation in developing economies. Dobb (1955) and Sen (1960) had the Stalinist model of the accelerated development of heavy industry at the back of their heads and so concentrated on maximizing the surplus extracted for accumulation. (Sen also showed that the choice of technique chosen was affected by the length of the planning period adopted – the greater it was, the more capital-intensive would be the technique chosen.) Kalecki and Joan Robinson dissented from this view because it played down employment creation now and implied never jam today, only in a tomorrow that never comes.

The Poznan riots in Poland in 1956 which Joan Robinson witnessed firsthand reinforced her view. Kalecki (1955) argued that full employment and gently rising consumption standards should have priority over surplus creation for accumulation. Like Joan Robinson, who may well have been influenced by him on this, he advocated a choice of technique which allowed greater employment creation but a smaller surplus than that implied by the Dobb–Sen rule.

In a lecture that Joan Robinson gave on her second visit to China in 1957 (see Tahir et al. 2002, pp. 271–273), she illuminated what was involved by a simple diagram (see Figure 1.2).

O/C is output per unit of investment, measured on the vertical axis, and L/C is employment per unit of investment, measured on the

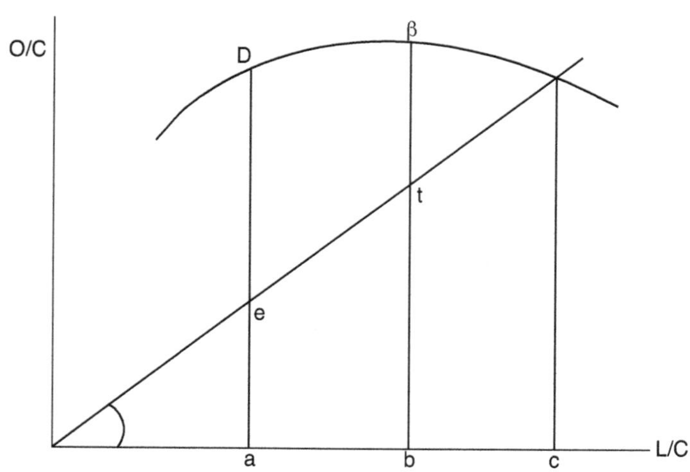

Figure 1.2 The choice of technique in China

horizontal axis. The angle subtended by the straight line through the origin reflects the ruling wage rate determined by unlimited supplies of labour in the subsistence sector. The curve shows the known technical possibilities at a moment in time.

β technique is the one argued for by Kalecki and Joan Robinson, then ruling in China. It gives a surplus of fβ and a level of employment ab (Figure 1.2) greater than does the Dobb–Sen rule which maximizes the surplus eD but creates less employment.

The problem of how to convey the appropriate technique to the planners was specifically addressed by Kalecki, and is discussed in the next section.

1.6 Kalecki's critique of the Fel'dman model

> Kalecki was fighting a dogma. (Nuti 1989, p. 333)

Kalecki, while sharing some of the views underlying the Fel'dman model, nevertheless had serious reservations about its more mechanistic implications for policy. Kalecki's understanding of the development process shares some of the vision of Fel'dman. In particular, Kalecki also located the key to development in the shortage of productive capital:

> The crucial problem of the underdeveloped economies is different from that of the developed countries. This is not to deny that in an underdeveloped economy there may be a deficiency of effective demand. There are many instances of countries whose capital equipment, meager though it is, will nevertheless be underutilized. However, as contrasted with developed economies, even if this equipment is fully utilized, it is still not capable of absorbing all available labour, as a result of which the standard of living is very low... the main problem here being the deficiency of productive capacity rather than the anomaly of its underutilization.... The crucial problem facing the underdeveloped countries is thus to increase investment considerably, not for the sake of generating effective demand, as was the case in an underemployed developed economy, but for the sake of accelerating the expansion of productive capacity indispensable for the rapid growth of the national income. (Kalecki 1976, pp. 23–24)[21]

For Kalecki the capital stock in a less-developed economy is insufficient to fully employ the whole labour force. The resultant surplus labour can only be absorbed by industrialization. Dobb had a similar interpretation of the Fel'dman model, arguing that it was applicable for a specific stage of development, in particular for economies with low levels of industrialization and surplus labour resulting from the inability of the capital stock to absorb the workforce.

Kalecki, however, was critical of the mechanical use of the model as a solution to the development problem. He focused on the long-term nature of the model so that the costs imposed on the economy in terms of reduced consumption were not dealt with. The trade-off between higher growth rates and reduced short-term consumption imposed a burden on policy makers, which, according to Kalecki, gave an incentive to be overly optimistic in planning forecasts, as a way of minimizing this problem. In particular, the role of short-term factors such as bottlenecks in particular sectors, as well as limited natural resources and long construction times, provided important limitations to the potential growth rate of the economy as a whole. Since these were ignored in the Fel'dman model, they contributed to the problems of planning. Pressure to meet output quotas also meant that the most appropriate capital was not always produced and made for an emphasis on the quantity rather than quality produced. In addition, over-optimistic forecasts meant that many of the output requirements of the plan could not be achieved, and it was likely that it would be consumption that suffered as a result:

> The greater the increase in national income, the greater is the investment required to bring it about. The greater the ratio of this increase to the level of national income, the greater is the share of productive investment in national income. Precisely because of this, and although in the longer term the cumulative effect of higher growth rates has a positive effect on living standards, in the short term that situation is reversed. The faster growth requires a greater proportion of current national income to be set aside for investment, and hence has a detrimental effect on consumption.
>
> The setting of the growth rate in the long-term plan is therefore a compromise between consumption in the short and the long terms...a faster growth rate effects an increase in the share of investment in national income, which in turn affects living standards in the short term.
>
> It is apparent from this how difficult the decision over the economic growth rate is. The harmful consequences for living standards in the near future of a high long-term growth rate must be borne in mind when making this decision. It is precisely this difficulty that is the reason for drawing up unrealistically optimistic plans which

> constitute, as it were, a flight into the realms of fantasy, away from the arduous dilemma of consumption in the short and long terms. (Kalecki 1986, pp. 69–70)

It was as a result of this type of consideration that Kalecki derived the concept of the 'government decision' function, as a panacea to the mechanistic approach of the Fel'dman type policy strategy of industrialization. The underlying rationale of the government decision function was to show that 'the procedure for the rational determination by the economic authorities of their target rate of economic growth' (Osiatyński 1988, p. 101) requires a balance of the benefits of increased growth with the cost involved in decreased consumption. Although Kalecki derived such functions under a range of assumptions, he was careful to argue that they cannot be drawn in any precise manner, as they are only illustrative,[22] and therefore do not allow mechanistic determination by economic policy makers.[23] Importantly, Kalecki used this function to show that the optimal rate of growth is much lower as a result of considering consumption during the adjustment period.[24] The decision function provides a framework in which the long-term benefits of an industrialization strategy could be balanced with the short-term costs. Importantly, Kalecki showed that the planning decision is not a purely mechanical economic decision, as implied by the Fel'dman model, but has important political elements:

> The trade-off between consumption in the near and the more distant future is seen by Kalecki as a basic contradiction in a socialist economy....The solution to this contradiction implies necessarily a political compromise as the appropriate decisions cannot be reduced to pure economic considerations. Kalecki illustrates this process of decision making by confronting the 'government decision curve'...with objective possibilities. The whole concept reminds us once more that economic answers are nothing but political questions. (Laski 1987, p. 12)

It is important to note that this analysis could only provide a partial solution to problems associated with planning. The government decision function forced the planning body to make explicit the trade-off underlying its decisions. There was no guarantee that the 'utility' of the masses would be an important consideration in that decision. If, for example, the ability to control was seen as the most important consideration, then the trade-off would be formulated in a very different light, such as the minimum level of consumption good production needed to achieve political stability. In contrast, a well-thought out decision rule could lead to the appropriate choice of technique as outlined in the previous section.

1.7 Conclusion

One important consideration thrown up by this discussion is the limitation of the Fel'dman model due to its implicit assumption that there was only one potential development path. In other words, the model focused on autarkic growth, with an emphasis on industrialization. This ignores the possibility of tying development into trade via, for example, export-led growth or a policy of import substitution. In addition, by attempting to maximize accumulation at the expense of present consumption, the model had no degrees of freedom to allow for the inevitable errors of planning, bad harvests, etc.

Kalecki's innovation of the government decision function can be seen as a deliberate antidote to this way of thinking, although it very much depends on the exact nature of that function. Despite the fact that the exact details of Kalecki's specification were not discussed, the underlying principle that there is a limitation on the degree to which present consumption (jam today) can be postponed in favour of future returns has important ramifications for the planning process. In particular, it requires planners both to acknowledge explicitly the trade-off which they are imposing, as well as making some allowance for satisfaction of present needs. As such, it presents a potential antidote to the industrialization imperative implied by the Fel'dman model.

The Fel'dman model, particularly as amended by Kalecki, indicated one way in which a less-developed economy, in the Kalecki/Kaldor sense, can industrialize. It represents an important alternate path to the market-orientated one analysed by Lewis (1954). However, just as the Lewis model ceases to be relevant when the economy has developed sufficiently, so that the two sectors (agriculture and manufacturing) are the same level of development and the dual nature of the economy has been overcome, so the Fel'dman model would become less relevant under the same circumstances. Once the initial stage of development has been achieved, in which basic production of commodities like steel has been established, detailed planning cannot cope with the emerging complex demands for consumption goods. This major problem was one which Galbraith, in particular, stressed as being a serious limitation of Soviet planning:

> Galbraith had noted, ... said, the difficulty that planned and command systems have 'in dealing with the almost infinitely numerous, diverse, diversely styled and changing products of the modern consumer economy, products that Soviet citizens seek to have. (Crook 2006)

This chapter highlights two important reasons for the collapse of the USSR and the European 'socialist' economies. First, by sticking rigidly to the essential aspects of the Fel'dman model in their economic planning, the authorities alienated the general population by increasing investment and the level of industrialization at the expense of consumption (always jam tomorrow). Second, the consumption goods that were produced were not necessarily the ones that were wanted by the consumers – there was no mechanism for ensuring that today's jam is the desired one.

Acknowledgements

We would like to thank Geoff Fishburn and Craig Freedman of UNSW and Bruce MacFarlane for their helpful comments on an earlier version of this paper.

Notes

1. The Soviet debates of the 1920s; they are reviewed in Nov (1989) Chapter 5.
2. See Nove (1989) p. 123.
3. The distinction between capital goods in the consumption goods sector and in the capital goods producing sector is particularly important for the structural growth analysis associated with Adolph Lowe – see, for example, Lowe (1976).
4. There are clear parallels with Fel'dman's modifications of Marx's analysis in order to ignore short-run problems to concentrate on long-run growth, and the similar modifications by Harrod and Domar to Keynes, to concentrate on a long-run formulation of growth. Therefore, as Domar and others have noted, it is not surprising that there are many similarities in the conclusions of the models (Domar 1957).
5. See Unsal (1990–1991).
6. In other words, the model depicts capital as 'putty-clay'. It is important to note that Fel'dman's distinction is analytical rather than empirical. For a discussion of the problems with making this distinction operational, see Clark (1974), pp. 227–228. Lowe 1976 makes the same assumption.
7. See Domar (1957), p. 229 and Al'ter & Pochkin (1968), pp. 8–9.
8. In a Soviet type economy, it is not clear how one would think about a separate government sector.

9. cf. Dobb (1967) pp. 109–110
10. Dobb (1967), p. 112
11. See Dobb (1967), p. 114. This minimum corresponds to the subsistence wage of the classical economists and Marx.
12. Ibid.
13. See Lewis (1954) and Kriesler (2013)
14. cf. Ellman (1989), p. 145
15. Fel'dman (1928b), pp. 323–327
16. Halevi (1992), p. 451
17. Unsal makes a further, though somewhat misguided criticism: '[T]he model does not provide a basis for the priority given to heavy industry. Since capital goods output is unrealistically assumed to be malleable, no distinction is made between capital goods used in the production of consumer goods and those used in the production of more capital goods. So there is no place for heavy industry in this class of model. Therefore, although the Fel'dman model is generally accepted as presenting the theoretical foundation of the industrialization policy pursued in the socialist countries…it is indeed far from able to do so' (Unsal 1990–1991, p.393).
18. See, for example Dobb (1967), p. 110.
19. However, for a criticism of Domar's representation of the Fel'dman model, see Clark (1974), p. 226.
20. See Dixon (1988), p. 138n.
21. Kaldor, in a number of places, argued similarly. He distinguished between what he calls Marxian and Keynesian unemployment. For Marx there is always an excess supply of labour, what he called the 'reserve army of the unemployed' which continually exerted downward pressure on wages. In the early stage of development of capitalism, competition forced the capitalists to reinvest most of their profits, as otherwise they would lose out in the competitive struggle. At this stage of development, employment depends on capital accumulation. As capitalism develops, both the demand and supply of labour grow. As the pace of accumulation increases, so the demand for labour grows at a faster rate than the supply, eventually 'extinguishing' the reserve army. Labour becomes scarce. When this happens, downward pressure on wages is halted, and they rise, causing profits to fall. This reduces growth and demand. According to Kaldor, this happens in the later stages of capitalism, when the Keynesian explanation of unemployment comes into its own. See Kriesler 2013.
22. Kalecki (1972), pp. 35–36.
23. Osiatyński (1988), p. 103
24. Kalecki (1972), p. 69.

References

Al'ter, L. & Pochkin, P. (1968) 'The first Soviet model of economic growth', *Problems of Economics*, 11(9): 3–13.

Clark, D. L. (1974) *Studies in the Origins and Development of Growth Theory, 1925–1950*, unpublished Ph.D. thesis in the Faculty of Economics, University of Sydney.

Crook, O. (2006) 'John Kenneth Galbraith, revisited' *The Atlantic* (May) http://www.theatlantic.com/magazine/archive/2006/05/john-kenneth-galbraith-revisited/304935/.

Dixon, R. (1988) *Production, Distribution and Value: A Marxian Approach*, Brighton, Sussex: Wheatsheaf Books
Dobb, M. H. (1955), *On Economic Theory and Socialism*, London: Routledge and Keegan Paul.
Dobb, M. H. (1967) *Capitalism, Development and Planning*, London: Routledge & Kegan Paul.
Domar, E. D. (1957) 'A Soviet model of growth' in his *Essays in the Theory of Economic Growth*, New York: Oxford University Press.
Ellman, M. (1987) 'Fel'dman' in J. Eatwell, M. Milgate & P. Newman (eds) *The New Palgrave Dictionary of Economics*, Vol. 2, London: Macmillan.
Ellman, M. (1989, 2nd edn) *Socialist Planning*, Cambridge: Cambridge University Press.
Fel'dman, G. A. (1928a) 'On the theory of growth rates of national income I' reprinted in Spulber (1964).
Fel'dman, G. A. (1928b) 'On the theory of growth rates of national income II' reprinted in Spulber (1964).
Fel'dman, G. A. (1928c) 'The analytical method of constructing perspective plans' reprinted in Spulber (1964).
Halevi, J. (1992) 'Asian capitalist accumulation: from sectoral to vertical integration', *Journal of Contemporary Asia*, 22(4): 444–470.
Kaldor, N. (1960) 'The characteristics of economic development' and 'Capitalist evolution in the light of Keynesian economics' in his *Essays on Economic Stability and Growth*, London: Duckworth.
Kalecki, M. (1955). 'The problem of financing Indian economic development', *Indian Economic Review*, 2: 1–22.
Kalecki, M. (1972) *Selected Essays on The Economic Growth of the Socialist and the Mixed Economy*, Cambridge: Cambridge University Press.
Kalecki, M. (1976) *Essays on Developing Economies*, Brighton, Sussex: Wheatsheaf Books.
Kalecki, M. (1986) *Selected Essays on Economic Planning* (edited and translated by Jan Toporowski), Cambridge: Cambridge University Press.
Keynes, J. M. (1972) *The Collected Writings of: Vol. IX Essays in Persuasion*, London: Macmillan.
Kriesler, P. (2013) 'Post-Keynesian Perspectives on economic development and growth' in *The Oxford Handbook of Post-Keynesian Economics*, Vol. 1, edited by G.C. Harcourt and P. Kriesler, Oxford: Oxford University Press.
Laski, K. (1987) 'Michał Kalecki' in J. Eatwell, M. Milgate & P. Newman (eds) *The New Palgrave Dictionary of Economics*, Vol. 3, London: Macmillan.
Lewis, W. A. (1954). 'Economic development with unlimited supplies of labour', *The Manchester School of Economic and Social Studies*, 22: 139–191.
Lowe, A. (1976) *The Path of Economic Growth*, Cambridge: Cambridge University Press
Nove, A. (1989 2nd ed.) *An Economic History of the U.S.S.R.*, Harmondsworth: Penguin Books.
Nove, A. & Nuti, D. (1972a) 'Introduction' in Nove & Nuti (1972b).
Nove, A. & Nuti, D. (eds) (1972b) *Socialist Economics*, Harmondsworth: Penguin Books.
Nuti, M. (1989) 'Michal Kalecki's contribution to the theory and practice of socialist planning' in M. Sebastiani (ed.), *Kalecki's Relevance Today*, London: Macmillan.

Osiatyński, J. (1988) *Michal Kalecki on a Socialist Economy* (translated by Jan Toporowski), London: Macmillan.
Sen, A. K. (1960), *Choice of Techniques: An Aspect of the Theory of Planned Economic Development*, Oxford: Basil Blackwell.
Spulber, F. (ed.) (1964) *Foundations of Soviet Strategy for Economic Growth: Selected Soviet Essays 1924–1930*, Bloomington: Indiana University Press.
Tahir, P., Harcourt, G. C., & Kerr, P. (2000), 'On Joan Robinson and China' in P. Kerr (ed.) with the collaboration of G.C. Harcourt, *Joan Robinson. Critical Assessments of Leading Economists*, Vol. V, London: Routledge.
Unsal, E. M. (1990–1991) 'The heavy industry priority in Socialist economic planning', *Science and Society*, 32(3): 288–299.

2
Are Rigid Prices the Cause of Unemployment?*

Jerzy Osiatyński

2.1 Summary

The view of old and new mainstream economics that rigid wages are the single most important cause of unemployment rests on the assumptions of declining marginal productivity of factors of production and the substitution hypothesis which makes the entrepreneurs chose more labour-intensive techniques of production when wages fall in relation to the cost of capital. Kalecki and Keynes opposed that view and demonstrated that when the economy operates below full employment of factors of production, cuts in money wages either would have to be offset by corresponding reductions of prices to leave the purchasing power of worker households unaffected, or would result in a reduction of aggregate demand, and therefore of total output and employment. Notwithstanding some significant differences in their respective theories, both Kalecki and Keynes show that after cutting wages throughout the economy, capitalists have no reasons either to increase investments – since their additional profits take the form of accumulation of stocks of unsold consumer goods, and their capital equipment continues to idle below full capacity output – or to raise their consumption, which in turn largely depends on their profits. When imperfect competition and cartelized sectors are allowed for, reduction of wages reduces employment and output even more than under free competition.

In an open economy, as pointed out by Kalecki and Keynes, reduction of wages in relation to rising labour productivity improves the competitive position of exporters vis-à-vis their trading partners and stimulates net exports of merchandise and domestic unemployment. That policy, pursued in the years of Kalecki and Keynes and now, is not a lasting solution to unemployment, since running chronic export surpluses involves chronic current account deficit of creditor countries which ultimately can no longer service their debts as is presently seen in the Euro zone system.

2.2 The key assumptions of effective demand theory

The reference point of this paper will be the key assumptions of Michał Kalecki's theory and only those of John Maynard Keynes's *General Theory* that are different to Kalecki's. However, the importance of any new theory consists in what it rejects from the hitherto accepted ideas, and not only in what it proposes instead. Accordingly, one macro- and two microeconomic hypotheses will be briefly discussed since they constitute the foundation on which the paradigm of the old and new mainstream economics is founded.

The key macroeconomic hypothesis of mainstream economics is that under a free competition regime the unhindered operation of market mechanisms produces a strong tendency to equilibrium of supply and demand at full employment of factors of production. Therefore, cyclical fluctuations caused by shocks in the supply and demand must be, 'naturally', short-lasting and shallow. The crisis will soon 'blow over' and, as soon as it completes its role of 'purging' the exuberances of the previous boom and the least efficient producers are eliminated (Schumpeter's 'creative destruction'), the business upswing will start automatically.[1] The two microeconomic assumptions on which this construct rests are: (i) the rising marginal costs hypothesis and (ii) the substitution of factors of production hypothesis, the rates of substitution being decided by the respective relative prices of factors of production. Within that paradigm of economic theorizing, at least since the times of Say's Law, the problem of insufficient aggregate demand does not appear. Unemployment is caused by too high wages in relation to the marginal product of labour (under rising marginal costs, or declining marginal productivity hypotheses), that is, by an inflexible labour market. If wages were reduced, more labour-intensive techniques of production would be chosen (substitution hypothesis) and the total supply of labour would be absorbed.

The essential macroeconomic postulate of the effective demand theory relates to the modus operandi of a market economy. That economy is assumed to operate as a rule below full capacity use of factors of production and to have no in-built mechanism that would automatically assure full use of those factors or push the economy in this direction.

Therefore aggregate output and employment are determined not by aggregate supply, but by aggregate demand. Moreover, since, roughly speaking, workers spend what they earn, it is the capitalists' spending on investment and on their consumption that decides their profits (and not conversely). Given the distribution of national income between wages and profits, capitalists' expenditure on gross capital formation and on their consumption decides the respective volumes of total output and employment.

Kalecki's key microeconomic postulate is that unit variable costs (called prime costs at the time) are constant until output expands to capacity use of factors of production. Thus, his aggregate supply curve runs parallel to the abscissa axis or only slightly rises due to rising raw materials prices, and it shoots nearly vertically upwards at full employment output or close to it, when, for example, the night shift is introduced (hence Kalecki's aggregate supply function is of a reversed L-shape). Second, Kalecki also rejected the neoclassical economics' postulate that entrepreneurs maximize their profits in the strict sense of the term[2] because this would require knowledge of not only their marginal costs, which of course they know, but also of their marginal revenue, which in turn would require them to know the marginal elasticity of demand for their produce. The latter they cannot know.

Kalecki's rejection of rising marginal costs and of strict profit maximization under perfect competition made his theory radically differ from the dominant mainstream economics, but also in some respects from Keynes's *General Theory*. Keynes, who was brought up in the tradition of economic thinking of Alfred Marshall and his predecessors in the Faculty of Economics of Cambridge University, found it rather difficult to discard fully the concept of general equilibrium. His Preface to the *General Theory* ends with the often quoted phrase to the account that the difficulty in understanding the main message of his book lies 'not in the new ideas, but in escaping from the old ones, which ramify, for those brought up as most of us have been, into every corner of our minds'.[3] According to Joan Robinson, one of Keynes's closest collaborators and friends, the difficulty Keynes alludes to relates among others to the relation of prices to wages. She thought Keynes's argument on that point at least unclear (while in Kalecki's theory it did not appear at all). The reason was, she argued, that 'Keynes relied upon a rather vague sort of Marshallian concept of competition, with short-period diminishing returns, so that an increase in employment is accompanied by a fall in real wages for workers already employed'.[4]

2.3 Kalecki and Keynes on rigid wages and unemployment: Kalecki 1932–1939

The question of relationship between money wages and employment during the 1929–1933 world crisis went far beyond mere dispute in economic theory. It was of imminent practical significance since reductions of wages were commonplace. In Poland and elsewhere, the crisis was countered mainly with deflationary policy, the key instrument of which were wage reductions, although initially the Polish government was opposed to wage cuts and aimed to keep wage rates more or less at their 1928 level.[5] Owing to this policy, until 1932, money wages of industrial workers and wages of government employees did not fall in Poland below their 1928 respective levels. However, large reductions in money wages were made in the following years, reaching their bottom in 1936 when money wages of industrial workers were a mere 80 per cent and those of white-collar workers only 71.2 per cent of their respective 1928 wage rates. The fall of money wages was in Poland sharper and was halted later than in other countries. In the 1936–1939 business upswing not even once did wages reach their pre-crisis rates.[6]

Kalecki joined the discussion on the results of wage reductions in two press articles published in 1932, and then, in a more systematic way, in his 1933 *Essay on the Business Cycle Theory* and in his 1935 paper 'The Essence of the Business Upswing'.[7] Where does the idea that wage cuts, through reducing costs of production, will ultimately terminate the crisis come from – asks Kalecki in the last of those papers. And he replies: 'One of the main features of the capitalist system is the fact that what is to the advantage of a single entrepreneur does not necessarily benefit all entrepreneurs as a class. If one entrepreneur reduces wages, he is able, ceteris paribus, to expand production, but once all entrepreneurs do the same thing, the result will be entirely different'.[8]

In his 1932 article, Kalecki (1932a) uses a simplified two-sector model of a closed economy which produces 100 units of output per month, of which the first sector produces 20 units of investment goods and the second produces 80 units of consumer goods, of which 60 units represent the wage bill of both sectors. Since workers are assumed not to save, 60 units produced in the consumption sector represent also workers' consumption. The remaining 20 consumption units represent the consumption of entrepreneurs. Together with 20 units of investment goods, entrepreneurs' profits are 40 units of total output. If wage rates in that economy were reduced by, say 1/5, consumption of workers would fall by 12 units, that is, to 48 units. If prices did not change, for total output to remain unchanged, entrepreneurs' profits would have to rise to 52 units. To simplify the argument, let us additionally assume that entrepreneurs continue to divide their incomes between investment and consumption in the same proportion as before the wage cut. Then the new equilibrium position would require that their consumption would have to increases to 26 units and so would have to raise their gross investment expenditure. The aggregate output of the consumer sector would therefore have to shrink to 74 units, and that of the investment goods sector would have to increase to 26 units.

However, such an adjustment of output to new distribution of income between profits and wages would not happen. First, following the new income distribution, incomes of producers of consumer goods have increased, hence they have no reason to *reduce* their output. Second, since in the crisis phase of the business cycle factors of production are far from fully utilized, there is no reason to increase investments. Thus a disproportion between output structure and income distribution will make part of incomes of entrepreneurs of the consumer goods sector (6 units) take the form of increased stocks of unsold goods. These stocks wouldn't appear if the wage cuts were followed by an immediate reduction of prices of consumer goods so as to enable workers to purchase for their 48 units of income all 54 units of consumer goods intended for them. But that price reduction necessary to restore equilibrium would take time. In the meantime the purchasing power of workers' incomes would be reduced, and part of entrepreneurs' income would be tied up in a rise of unwanted stocks which would not only discourage them from undertaking new investments but could make them even reduce their investments. Thus a reduction of wages would by no means help to reduce employment and may even add to unemployment.

As regards the reduction in workers' wages – Kalecki concluded in the second of the two above-mentioned articles – 'owing to the domestic market shrinking... this either causes a fall in prices or an accumulation of stocks (or both). In other words, profits either do not rise at all, or are realized in the form of stocks.... In these conditions the cheapening of labour cannot stimulate the establishment of new firms.'[9]

Kalecki's *Essay on the Business Cycle Theory* outlined a macroeconomic theory of business fluctuations in a market economy using as a baseline a model of a closed economy. Given the distribution of national income between wages and gross profits, the arguments of the entrepreneurs' investment decision function determine cyclical fluctuations of output and employment. Therefore, he argues, 'capitalists are unable to increase their share of social income... during the downswing by reducing workers' wages, and workers are unable to increase their share of social income during the upswing by raising them'.[10]

How is that possible? How in practice is the *independence* of national income distribution from changes in the wage rates possible in the course of the cycle? If capitalists reduce wages during the business crisis –Kalecki explains – then their gross real profits do not increase because the volume of their capital accumulation is already determined by their past investment decisions, and their gross profits are proportional to the sum of their gross capital accumulation and the constant part of their consumption. Thus, under free competition, cuts in wages, which reduce workers' demand for consumer goods, must be followed by corresponding falls of prices of consumer goods that would completely offset any advantages gained by capitalists as a whole. Indeed unemployment may actually increase. 'Obviously' – noted Kalecki – 'it is only *total* gross profits which remain constant following wage reductions; however, there will unquestionably be shifts in the share of profits between individual groups of capitalists. With wage reductions in one branch, the profits of capitalists in that branch increase; at the same time, however, other capitalists lose an amount equal to the sum earned by those who lowered wages'.[11]

What is the impact of wage cuts on employment when the free competition assumption is replaced by some form of monopoly competition, which Kalecki calls a partly or wholly 'cartelized economy'? As in a free competition economy, in a cartelized economy the volume of gross capital accumulation is determined by past investment decisions, and therefore a partly or wholly cartelized economy will be subject to analogous cyclical fluctuations. However, in that case, unlike in a free competition economy, together with wage cuts workers' real incomes will be reduced.[12]

It is noteworthy that in his 1933 *Essay*, Kalecki accounted for the consequences of wage cuts for improving the competitive edge of home producers against their foreign competitors, and thereby achieving export surpluses and increasing employment. In an open economy, Kalecki argued, wage cuts 'will unquestionably cause a shift in the distribution of social income between capitalists and workers. The accumulation of capital can be realized in that case not only in the form of production of investment goods, as in our closed system, but also a foreign trade surplus'.[13] And he continued: 'In an open system, increasing profits by rising prices or reducing wage rates is unquestionably possible, since increased profits can be realized then as an export surplus'.[14] He saw export surplus not merely as the end-result of autonomously determined foreign trade turnovers, but as yet another instrument, next to the rate of exchange depreciations, of the 'beggar your neighbour' policy.

In the post-crisis years in Poland, government aimed at improving work conditions, standardizing the length of working week, improving collective agreements, etc. – all in the name of 'social peace'. Although those actions were rather inconsistent and accompanied by anti-strike legislation and regulations limiting the freedom of action of trade unions,[15] and notwithstanding very low wage rates in 1936–1939, well below their pre-crisis levels, that government intervention was strongly opposed by economists and met with a campaign of warnings against the consequences of any such 'reckless reforms'. This was the background for a pamphlet by Jan Wątecki, *Rigid Wages as a Cause of Unemployment.*[16] In 1939 the Institute for Social Problems (in Warsaw) published Kalecki's study, 'Money and real wages',[17] the first part of which discussed the 'classical' theory of money and real wages, and the ideas of Wątecki's pamphlet especially, and the second part examined empirical data on the dynamics of wage rates and employment in Poland in 1928–1937.

In the theoretical part of his 1939 study, Kalecki improved his earlier explanation for rejecting the key assumptions of 'classical' economics – that is, of rising marginal costs and free competition – and elaborated on the consequences of their replacement with the assumptions of constant unit prime costs over the relevant range of output changes, and of imperfect competition. He also no longer argued that in an open economy wage cuts, through their improving competitiveness of exports, would necessarily raise employment or the real wage bill. He now replaced the two-sector economic model used in his 1932 publications with a three-sector one, which greatly facilitates his proving the proposition that wage cuts cannot increase employment or national income.

In his three-sector model, the first sector produces investment goods, the second – goods and services consumed by capitalists, and the third – goods and services consumed by workers. To simplify his argument, Kalecki started with a few restrictive assumptions that do not affect his final conclusions and subsequently are all relaxed. His assumptions include: (i) free competition, (ii) workers (including salary earners) do not save, (iii) all wage rates always change in the same proportion, (iv) the propensity to save of entrepreneurs is the same as that of rentiers, and (v) the rate of interest is kept unchanged.[18]

Wage goods are in part sold to and consumed by workers of sector 3 who produce them, and the rest is sold to workers employed in sectors 1 and 2. That surplus of wage goods represents the profits of capitalists in sector 1 (all expressed at constant prices). Thus their profits depend on the volume of employment in sectors 1 and 2. At the same time the profits of capitalists earned in the latter two sectors are also determined by employment in those sectors. Thus we get a national income equation on one side of which we have the sum of incomes, that is, of capitalists' profits and of wages, and on its other side the sum of expenditures on gross capital formation, on capitalists' consumption and on consumption of workers. Since workers are assumed not to save, we get Kalecki's renowned profit equation whereby the sum of output of investment goods and of goods consumed by capitalists determines their aggregate profits.

What happens should all wages be reduced? If, after succeeding in cutting wages, capitalists immediately increased their consumption or investments, in expectation of higher profits, employment in those sectors would increase accordingly, thus generating higher profits. In that case the reduction in real wages would indeed be accompanied by a corresponding rise of employment that would match the rise in capitalists spending on investments and on their consumption.

> Such a state of affairs is, however, extremely unlikely. First, entrepreneurs will in general not hurry with new investment orders simply on the strength of a successful wage reduction, but will rather wait until the expectations of higher profitability have been realized. Should they even give new orders at once, the technical time-lag between investment orders and the actual production of investment goods would prevent the latter from increasing immediately. ... The position as regards capitalist consumption is similar, in that it is actual rather than expected income which influences the capitalist standard of living, and ... even this influence operates with considerable delay.[19]

Since a wage reduction cannot make capitalist consumption and investments increase immediately after it is effected, their profits also will not increase. And if neither capitalist consumption and investments, nor their profits change right after the wage cuts, they will also fail to increase later on. In conclusion Kalecki writes:

> We attempted to show that the reduction of wages in a closed system does not lead to an increase in production; that in conditions of perfect competition the level of production remains unchanged, while prices decline in the same proportion as wages; however, under existing conditions of monopoly or imperfect competition a reduction of money wages tends to cause a decline in real wages associated with a decrease in employment. Moreover, it appears that in such a system there is in general no reason – in spite of widespread belief to the contrary – for the decline in production to be accompanied by

> an increase in real wages or vice versa. The analysis of the problem in an open system shows that even in such a case the reduction of wages does not necessarily lead to an increase in employment, and the prospects of raising the aggregate real income of the working class are even dimmer. In particular, under the system of high and rising tariffs it is very likely that a reduction of wages will have an adverse effect upon employment also in an open economy.... The slogan 'Rigid wages as a cause of unemployment' – under which title a book by Mr. Wątecki has been recently published in Poland – proves in the light of the above analysis to be entirely unfounded.[20]

In the statistical part of his study Kalecki examined the changes in unit costs, prices and wages in the Polish industry in 1928–1937 to test the thesis of 'classical' economics that a rise in employment is linked with falling real wages. The thesis followed the assumption of declining marginal productivity of factors of production. Kalecki found no such relationship in the examined data and wrote:

> It is immediately clear that the 'classical' theory is not supported by the results of our statistical enquiry. It will be seen that the decline in production and employment is accompanied by an increase in the prices of 'finished industrial products' in relation to prime costs, and conversely. But this phenomenon, which is in disagreement with the law of 'increasing marginal costs', can be easily explained by our hypothesis: by the constancy of marginal costs over the relevant range of output [changes], and by the 'degree of monopoly' increasing in a slump due to the 'rigidity' of prices, and decreasing in a boom. Contrary to the accepted opinion, the ratio of prices to prime costs 'improves' in the depression! It does not follow, of course, that profitability is high: the effect of the drop in sales outweighs by far the advantage from the increased ratio of prices to prime costs.[21]

In conclusion of both his statistical enquiry and the whole 1939 study on changes of money and real wages, Kalecki wrote: 'It appears also most unlikely that the considerable cuts in money wages which took place in Poland during the downswing had any mitigation affect upon the latter. This again is in accord with our approach to the problem of reduction of money wages'.[22]

In 1939 Kalecki's *Essays in the Theory of Economic Fluctuations* were also published. This included the analytical part of his 'Money and real wages'. The *Essays* were an important volume for Kalecki, who spelled out there the basic assumptions of his business cycle and economic dynamics theory, as well as of his theory of national income distribution. He also defined the relationships between his version of the effective demand theory and that of Keynes. No wonder that in his Preface to the Polish edition of 'Money and real wages' Kalecki introduced it as an attempt to critically examine the 'classical' theory of money and real wages, taking as starting point Keynes's theory of wages as well as some of his own papers published in Poland and abroad. This was shortly followed by and even stronger statement of the affinity between Keynes's and his own theory in the Introduction to Kalecki's 1939 study included in his *Essays*: 'We intend in this essay to discuss at some length the Keynesian theory of wages. We are limiting ourselves to the consideration of a closed economy, for this is the only case to which the Keynesian argument fully applies'.[23] What was then the essence of Keynes's theory of wages?

2.4 Keynes: 1930–1936–1939

Charter 19 of Keynes's *General Theory* explains why reductions in money wages, recommended by 'classical' economics as a policy instrument to raise employment and stimulate the economy, may fail to achieve those aims because of the impact of wage cuts on aggregate demand and other economic factors affecting aggregate consumption and investments. Like Kalecki, Keynes started by investigating whether a wage reduction may have an impact on rising employment either directly, that is, in the short-run, or indirectly, that is in the long-run. In both cases he assumes that: (a) the propensity to consume, (b) the schedule of the marginal efficiency of capital and (c) the rate of interest are all given and do not change. In the preceding chapters of his *General Theory* Keynes demonstrates that 'the volume of employment is uniquely correlated with the volume of effective demand... [and the latter] being the sum of the expected consumption and the expected investment, cannot change, if the propensity to consume, the schedule of marginal efficiency of capital and the rate of interest are all unchanged'.[24] Would, then, asks Keynes, a reduction in money wages result in reducing unemployment, in the favourable case to this view, that is, when entrepreneurs from the outset expect the wage cuts to bring this result? And he replies:

> It is indeed not unlikely that the individual entrepreneur, seeing his own costs reduced, will overlook at the outset the repercussions on the demand for his product and will act on the assumption that he will be able to sell at a profit a larger output than before.

> If, then, entrepreneurs generally act on this expectation, will they in fact succeed in increasing their profits? Only if the community's marginal propensity to consume is equal to unity, so that there is no gap between the increment of income and the increment of consumption; or if there is an increase in investment, corresponding to the gap between the increment of income and the increment of consumption, which will only occur if the schedule of marginal efficiencies of capital has increased relatively to the rate of interest. Thus the proceeds realised from the increased output will disappoint the entrepreneurs and employment will fall back again to its previous figure, unless the marginal propensity to consume is equal to unity or the reduction in money-wages has had the effect of increasing the schedule of marginal efficiencies of capital relatively to the rate of interest and hence the amount of investment.[25]

Would, then, the repercussions of wage cuts for the above mentioned (a), (b) and (c) positively affect employment in the long-run? Keynes examined a number of such possible repercussions, of which, in an open economy, some are related to improvement of the competitive edge of home producers against their foreign competitors, which in turn may favour investment. However, regarding factors affecting the domestic market, he was rather sceptical whether changes in the distribution of national income between wages and profits, even when perceived as of lasting nature, may increase propensity to consume or investments. This made him believe that: 'with the actual practices and institutions of the contemporary world it is more expedient to aim at a rigid money-wage policy than at a flexible policy responding by easy stages to changes in the amount of unemployment',[26] and to the conclusion that 'to suppose that a flexible wage policy is a right and proper adjunct of a system which on the whole is one of laissez-faire, is the opposite of the truth. It is only in a highly authoritarian society, where sudden, substantial, all-round changes could be decreed that a flexible wage-policy could function with success.'[27]

Keynes's *Collected Writings* include many of his economic policy statements, memoranda, press articles and voluminous correspondence from the years long preceding the publication of his *General Theory*. These univocally evidence his critical view regarding the policy of wage cuts as an instrument to reduce unemployment during the business crisis. Already in 1930 he argued, for instance, that an overall cut in money wages will merely reduce the purchasing power of the community as a whole, and would not increase employment.[28] In the context of Kalecki's theory, it is noteworthy that notwithstanding Keynes's criticism, until his aforementioned rejoinder to Dunlop, Keynes defended the assumption of rising marginal costs. It is only in his 1939 paper where, together with the defence of the assumption, the first signs of him changing his mind may be seen:

> It seems we have been living all these years on a generalisation which held good, by exception in the years 1880–1886, which was the formative period in Marshall's thought on this matter, but has never once held good in the fifty years since he crystalised it... it had the tendency to offset the influence of the main forces which I was discussing and made it necessary for me to introduce qualifications which I need not have troubled with if I could have adopted the contrary generalisation (i.e. of a positive relation between employment and the real wage)... the practical case for a planned employment policy is considerably reinforced – because not reduction in the real wage is implied.[29]

Their respective theoretical arguments led both, Kalecki and Keynes, in their economic policy recommendations to reject the view that the cause of unemployment is rigid wages and prices. They thought the deficiency of effective demand the main cause of unemployment. In their respective advice regarding the bridging of the gap between the actual and the full employment volume of effective demand, they differed insofar that Kalecki considered direct public investment and changing income distribution towards low-income groups of primary importance.[30] Keynes, on the other hand, defined the causes of unemployment rather in terms of a too high liquidity preference of the savers compared to 'animal spirits' of potential investors, and consequently he sought the remedy in the system of operation of financial markets and the determinants of private savings.[31]

Some followers of the line of thought embedded in Kalecki's and Keynes's writings on the effects of reductions of money wages on employment distinguished the dual role of wages and profits in a market economy. Wages are, on the one hand, a cost of production. But, on the other hand, they represent purchasing power of worker households. Since the propensity to save out of profits is higher than that out of wages, any shift in income distribution towards profits reduces aggregate demand. On the other hand, that shift improves the ability to finance investment projects. Moreover, the higher are past and present-day profits, the higher the expectations of future profitability of investment projects, which in turn positively affects investment decisions.[32] Keynes and Kalecki emphasized the negative impact of reduced money wages on aggregate demand and thereby on total output and employment. Bhaduri and Marglin considered the case when a redistribution of income from wages to profits may be dominated by either of the two effects, that is, by the depressing impact of reduced aggregate demand or the encouraging investments effects of increasing unit profit margins. The scenario when the reduced consumption and aggregate demand effect dominates the other they call 'the consumption- or the wage-led growth path'. When the improved profitability effect dominates, they call it 'the investment- or the profit-led growth path'. Any comprehensive discussion of that line of development of Keynes's and Kalecki's ideas goes beyond the scope of this paper. It should only be noted, however, that – in line with Kalecki's argument presented above – capitalists' profits are determined by their past investment decisions and their consumption. Therefore, even if a reduction of wage rates was successfully introduced throughout the economy, this would not cause capitalists to expand their investments or consumption since their increased profits would at best take the form of unsold inventories which would hardly induce their new investment decisions. Therefore, on the ground of Kalecki's theory, the profit-led growth scenario appears illusory.

2.5 Can internal deflation solve the unemployment problem?

As it was noticed above, already in the early 1930s Kalecki and Keynes discussed the repercussions of wage cuts in relation to labour productivity in an open economy. Next to the rate of exchange manipulations, this additional instrument of 'beggar-the-neighbour' policy became in the past two decades or so a new line of defence for the claim that in a global economy wage reductions help increase employment through strengthening the competitive position of the trading partner who cuts wages. However, for such a policy to succeed two conditions need to be met. First, there must be countries willing to absorb the export surpluses of their trading partners which use internal deflation policy to export their unemployment along with their merchandise. If all trading partners run that policy on the same scale, none would enjoy unemployment reduction while all would suffer a reduction of output and employment.[33] Second, the success of this policy requires either fixed or administered exchange rates (as, say, in China), or a monetary union (as in the Euro zone). Otherwise countries seeking to balance chronic deficits in their current accounts, and thereby restoring their competitive edge, would need periodic devaluations (or crawling depreciations). The policy of internal deflation has been run for a long time by Germany (followed by Austria, Holland and Finland). However, in 2000–2007 in Germany it hardly brought any meaningful reduction of unemployment.[34]

The question of whether 'internal devaluation' can achieve its purpose requires answering two other questions: (i) what are its other macroeconomic repercussions, and (ii) what are its political and economic premises and implications?

The very ability of 'internal devaluation' to meet its purpose is doubtful. Considering that an export surplus represents at best a few per cent of GDP, and consumption expenditure constitutes about 60–70 per cent of GDP, effective demand losses due to wage cuts can hardly be offset by increased net exports. Germany, which has followed such a policy within the Euro zone in the ten years until 2010, recorded only a very moderate GDP growth rate which improved only in the last 2–3 years.[35] This supports Kalecki's opinion that the policy of 'beggaring one's neighbour' through wage cuts may bring only meagre reductions in unemployment, it will hardly affect investment and capitalists' consumption and thus will depress the GDP growth rate. Moreover, when GDP growth is small and that of labour productivity is large, the room for increased employment is also small. This seems to tally with economic developments in Germany in the examined period of time.

Furthermore, Germany's expansion of export surpluses was financed with its commercial re-financing credits granted generously to countries which absorbed those surpluses since exports of those countries were too small to pay for German and other countries' net exports. However, for countries with constant export surpluses to ever see their credits paid back, would require that the presently export-deficit countries start enjoying export surpluses in the future, that is, that there will be sale markets for their produce. For otherwise German credits granted to Greece will have to be written-off the books of German banks and paid by German taxpayers.[36] Therefore a question arises whether in the first ten years since the Euro zone was founded only Greece lived beyond its means, spending German credits which most likely it would not be able to pay back, or whether also Germany did not live beyond its means granting credits to Greece to enable it to finance Germany's export surpluses and thereby reduce German unemployment.[37]

Regarding the political and economic premises and implications of internal deflation, the question arises whether the transferring abroad of domestic unemployment does not harm other countries, especially when it is done within the common space of balanced foreign trade turnovers, as in the European Union. Achieving permanent export surpluses must imply that a country enjoying them at some stage should start running import surpluses, or else the debtor country (countries) would never be able to pay back the received refinancing credits that had helped it (them) to finance its (their) import surpluses. Otherwise the creditor country which solves its unemployment problem at the expense of the debtor country eventually will have to carry the financial burden of this policy. Thus, the beggar-my-neighbour policy by means of internal deflation leads to no lasting solution of the unemployment problem, the latter calling for economic policy instruments operating inside the country, not outside it. Moreover, living beyond means both of the debtor and of the creditor country ultimately will be expensive for each of them and may well undermine the foundations of economic and political solidarity on which the European Community was established.

There are many post-Keynesian studies which demonstrate that when the propensity to save of the private sector is greater than its propensity to invest, and the current account is balanced, the most important way to absorb the surplus of private savings are budget deficits, and by no means wage reductions. Moreover, they also show that chronic budget deficits in the largest capitalist countries and over very long periods of time are not, or not only, the result of loose and expansive fiscal and monetary policies. If it had not been for those persistent deficits, those economies would shrink, and the savings 'surplus' would by no means remain on the account of households and private firms, but would not have ever appeared since there would not be the incomes sufficient to generate those savings. In the absence of public deficits, the equilibrium between private savings and private investments is re-established through economic recession: output and employment would fall until households' and firms' savings taken together sufficiently decline.[38]

How is it possible to finance the cost of servicing the rising public debt without undermining the confidence in the financial markets regarding the ability of a debtor country to meet financial obligations that may be cumulatively increasing due to rising risk premiums together with increasing the public debt/GDP ratios? Again, any attempt at comprehensively answering this question goes beyond the scope of this paper. Let me therefore make only a few sketchy observations. Kalecki assumed that the supply of credit is sufficiently elastic to meet increased demand of the private sector without raising interest rates. Then, he argued,

> if some capitalists increase their investments by using for this purpose their liquid reserves, the profits of other capitalists will rise *pro tanto*, and thus the liquid reserves invested will pass into possession of the latter. If additional investment is financed by bank credit, the spending of the amounts in question will cause equal amounts of saved profits to accumulate as bank deposits. The investing capitalists will thus find it possible to float bonds to the same extent, and thus to repay the bank credits. ... One important consequence of the above is that the rate of interest cannot be determined by the demand for and the supply of new capital because investment 'finances itself'.[39]

Keynes's position was similar: stimulating private investments or expansion of public capital outlays would not raise short- nor long-term interest rates in the phase of business crisis, and he also assumed an elastic supply of money.

Kalecki's and Keynes's ideas were subsequently elaborated on and developed into what is presently called the modern functional theory of finance. It differentiates, in the fiat money system, between servicing the private and the public debt and stresses the capacity of the state to meet its financial obligations through emission of money. Abba Lerner's 'classic' formulation of the theory of functional finance rests on its two laws.[40] According to the first, government spending is limited by full employment of factors of production, and not by government ability to finance its spending. Taxes should be levied only with a view to limiting aggregate private demand when in the boom phase of the business cycle a shortage of production capacity could cause inflation. They are not needed, however, to provide means for financing public spending because, in difference from settling private claims, the government may meet its obligations thorough money printing. This need not give rise to acceleration of inflation as long as factors of production are far from fully used.

The second law deals with the rate on government debt, needed mainly to stimulate sufficient private investments to guarantee full employment.

The government should borrow money only if it is desirable that the public should have less money and more government bonds, for these are the effects of government borrowing. This might be desirable if otherwise the rate of interest would be reduced too low (by attempts on the part of the holders of the cash to lend it out) and induce too much investments, thus bringing about inflation. Conversely, the government should lend money (or repay some of its debt) only if it is desirable to increase the money or to reduce the quantity of government bonds in the hands of the public.[41]

Lerner's concern here is clear: the expected profitability of fixed capital outlays must be sufficiently higher than the rate of interest on borrowed capital (a similar approach to the role of the rate of interest can be found in Keynes and Kalecki).

Does printing money needed to finance government spending beyond its revenue necessarily lead to increased inflation? First, in accordance with mainstream economics, when the supply of money rises in step with GDP and the demand for money on the part of the private sector, it by no means adds to inflation. Why then does a rise in demand for money, which in a multiplier process leads to an increment in GDP, when originating in the private sector is not supposed to increase inflation, but when originating in the public sector is believed to add to inflation? Second, what is under discussion here is the replacement – in the phase of a business depression – of a shrinking demand of the private sector by an increased demand of the government sector. Therefore, especially when the aggregate effective demand does not necessarily rise, but merely its expanding part in the public sector substitutes for its shrinking part in the private sector, it would not give rise to additional inflationary pressures, the more so that in the crisis phase of the cycle the economy operates well if output and employment were below full capacity. Moreover, even in the boom, the economy rarely reaches full employment of factors of production, and therefore even then financing the policy of full employment by increasing the supply of credit via the banking system does not need to increase prices.

2.6 Conclusion

In a closed market economy operating excess capacity and unemployment, successful cuts in money wages would reduce purchasing power of workers but give no reasons for entrepreneurs to increase their consumption and, the more so, their investment decisions. Entrepreneurs have no good causes to increase their consumption seeing that part of their profits takes the form of unwanted increase in stocks of unsold goods that workers cannot buy for their reduced wages. Nor will investment increase in an environment of falling rates of use of the already existing capital equipment. In order to break that deflationary-recession vicious circle, public spending must increase without an accompanying rise of taxation – which proposition is incompatible with the agreement of the advocates of wage cuts, lest the single result of wage reduction was a further decline of output and employment.

In an open economy, as pointed out by Kalecki and Keynes in the early 1930s, and practiced among others by some EU member-countries, wage reductions improve their competitive position against that of their trading partners, thereby allowing the wage-reducing countries to export part of their unemployment. Had such a policy been followed by all countries in the world in the same proportion, they would have to export their unemployment to other planets. If wage cuts are effected by some member-countries of the European Union, the aggregate current account balance of which oscillates around 1 per cent of its total GDP, this must undermine their long-term functioning, especially in the case of the Euro zone member countries.[42] Moreover, as it was shown above, such a form of 'beggar-my-neighbour' policy sooner or later would make the chronic current account deficit countries unable to service the refinancing credits granted to them, and ultimately those credits would have to be written-off from the assets of the export surplus countries.

Notes

*High School of Finance and Law in Bielsko Biała and Institute of Economics of the Polish Academy of Sciences. Contribution in the Session, 'Kalecki Today', of the 24th Annual EAEPE Conference on 'Economic Policy in Times of Crisis', Cracow, 18–20 October 2012. The author is grateful to Professor Kazimierz Łaski for his most helpful comments on an earlier version of this essay.

1. See Osiatyński, in Kalecki, 1990, p. 442.
2. See Kalecki, 1954/1991, p. 210.
3. Keynes, 1936, p. viii.
4. Robinson, 1964, p. 339; see also Mitchell, 2012b. Diminishing returns imply rising marginal costs, that is, rising prices, and falling real wage rates, when output and employment rise. The difficulty with Keynes's formulation boils down to its being open to reinterpretation that may appear consistent with his argument, but in fact puts it back to the bed-rock of neoclassical economics. Since, in line with those assumptions, in equilibrium the wage rate must equal the marginal product of labour, distribution of national income between wages and profits appears to be determined by marginal productivity of factors of production, and thus, it is argued, in the general case the marginal productivity of labour, and the wage rate equal to it, co-determine aggregate employment. This difficulty might have followed from Keynes's attempt to reconcile his effective demand theory with rising marginal costs and with the substitution of factors of production hypotheses of the mainstream economics of his time.
5. See Knakiewicz, 1967, pp. 316–317 (in Polish).
6. See ibid., cf. Osiatyński, in Kalecki, 1991, p. 518.
7. See Kalecki, 1932a/1990, 1932b/1990, 1933a/1990 and 1935/1990.
8. Kalecki, 1935/1990, p. 188. It is indeed difficult to give a clearer message regarding the difference between the micro- and the macroeconomic analysis

of the problem under examination. A macro-economist or an economic policy-maker, when assessing the consequences of wage cuts, must take into account their demand feed-backs for the economy as a whole, a feed-back which an individual entrepreneur may well neglect. Hence the scope of analysis of the former must be far broader than that of the latter.

9. Kalecki, 1932b/1990, p. 52.
10. Kalecki (1933a/1990) p. 100. This conclusion was ill received by the Polish Marxists (see Osiatyński, in Kalecki, 1990, p. 478) who were rightly concerned by its implication for trade union strike actions in the course of business crises, but who overlooked the implied importance of the trade unions' fight for an increased share of wages in gross national income which increased total output and employment, and at the same time damped business fluctuations.
11. Kalecki, 1933a/1990, p. 100, emphasis MK.
12. See Kalecki, 1933a/1990, p. 108.
13. Kalecki, 1933a/1990, p. 101.
14. Kalecki, 1933a/1990, p. 108.
15. See Święcicki, 1960, pp. 325 et seq. (in Polish).
16. See Wątecki, 1938 (in Polish).
17. See Kalecki, 1939c/1991.
18. See Kalecki, 1939a/1990; 1939b, p. 274.
19. Kalecki, 1939a/1990, p. 276.
20. Kalecki, 1939c/1991, pp. 38–39.
21. Kalecki, 1939c/1991, pp. 45–46. Kalecki's concept of the 'degree of monopoly' was his theoretical device to determine national income distribution between profits and wages. More or less at the same time Keynes's hypothesis that real wages change in the course of a business cycle in the opposite direction as output, employment and money wages was put in question by Dunlop (1938) and Tarshis (1939) who studied the US data, and Hall and Hitch (1939) with respect to British industry. The data examined by Keynes in his rejoinder to Dunlop (see Keynes, 1939), as well as subsequent empirical studies rather supported the thesis that in the course of the cycle changes in real wages are insignificant and irregular (see Osiatyński, in Kalecki, 1991, p. 505 and pp. 504–510 for a review of that debate).
22. Kalecki, 1939c/1991, p. 50.
23. Kalecki, 1939b, p. 75.
24. Keynes, 1936, p. 260–261.
25. Keynes, 1936, p. 261.
26. Keynes, 1936, pp. 265–266.
27. Keynes, 1936, p. 269; see also Terzi, 2010.
28. See Keynes, 1930/1972, p. 128.
29. Keynes, 1939, p. 38; see also Mitchell, 2012.
30. This is seen especially in his 1944 study 'Three Ways to Full Employment' (in: *The Economics of Full Employment: Six Studies in Applied Economics*, see Kalecki, 1944/1990) that was highly appreciated by Keynes. In his letter to Kalecki of 30 December 1944 Keynes wrote: 'Thank you for the "Economics of Full Employment"; which reached me, as it were, as a Christmas present. I found it a most excellent and instructive volume.... Your own contribution seems to me most striking and original... also most beautifully compressed' (Osiatyński, in Kalecki, 1990, p. 579).

31. For elaboration of that view, see Davidson, 2009, p. 20.
32. See Marglin and Bhaduri, 1988; Bhaduri and Marglin, 1990; and Bhaduri, 2008.
33. Moreover, in the extreme case, this policy requires that wage rate country-differences did not exceed their differences in labour productivity (expressed in terms of output per hour), which might imply the necessity to reduce wage rates, say, in Germany or the US, to the wage rates in, say, China, taking into account the differences between hourly labour productivity in those countries.
34. As a matter of fact, Germany introduced this policy since the very beginning of the European integration, when its unemployment was relatively high and to combat it successive government programmes: Hartz I, II, III, etc., were introduced. At its peak, in 2007, Germany's export surplus was close to 8 per cent of its GDP (see Flassbeck, 2007, 2012; Flassbeck and Spiecker, 2011; Łaski, 2012; Łaski and Podkaminer, 2012).
35. See Łaski, 2012. Another consequence of this policy is rising household income inequalities to the favour of income groups with high propensity to save, which adds to depressing GDP growth rates.
36. Germany is used here – for the purposes of the presently discussed question – as a representative EU chronic export surplus country in its turnovers with the other EU member countries, and Greece as a representative EU chronic export deficit country. Foreign trade within the EU as a whole is in equilibrium since its balance as a rule does not exceed 1 per cent of the EU GDP.
37. For a more extensive discussion of his question, and of the implications of investing the German savings, say to benefit future German generations, in refinancing credits granted to Greek banks, see Łaski, 2012, p. 20.
38. See Łaski, 2009; Sawyer, 2010; Łaski and Podkaminer, 2012; Łaski, 2012; Palley, 2009; see also Mitchell, 2012a.
39. Kalecki, 1954/1991, p. 244.
40. See Lerner, 1943/1983; see also Davidson, 2009, Ch. 5; Musgrave, 2010 and 2011; Mitchell, 2010.
41. Lerner, 1943/1983, pp. 299–300. Having read Lerner's paper Keynes wrote to James Meade that 'Lerner's argument is impeccable. But, heaven help anyone who tries to put it across the plain man at this stage of the evolution of ideas' (quote after Terzi, 2010, pp. 14–15). According to Musgrave, 'Keynes and Lerner both believed that extra government net spending was needed in a recession. As to the choice between funding this expenditure from borrowing versus printing, Keynes was on the face of it fairly indifferent between the two, while Lerner favoured printing (Musgrave, 2011, p. 5).
42. See Flassbeck, 1988, 2007, 2012; Flassbeck and Spiecker, 2005 and 2011; Goodley 1992; and among Polish authors: Łaski, 2011; Laski and Podkaminer, 2012; and Osiatyński, 2011.

References

Bhaduri, A., and S. Marglin (1990) 'Unemployment and the real wage: the economic basis for contesting political ideologies', *Cambridge Journal of Economics*, 14: 375–393.

Bhaduri, A. (2008) 'On the dynamics of profit-led and wage-led growth', *Cambridge Journal of Economics*, 32: 147–160.
Davidson, P. (2009) *The Keynes Solution: The Path to Global Economic Prosperity*, New York: Palgrave Macmillan.
Dunlop, J.T. (1938) 'The movement of real and money wage rates', *Economic Journal*, 48(3): 413–434.
Flassbeck, H. (1988) *Preise, Zins und Wechselkurs*, Mohr Siebeck: Tübingen.
Flassbeck, H. (2007) 'Wage divergencies in Euroland: explosive in the making' in J. Bilbow and A. Terzi (eds), *Euroland and the World Economy: Global Player or Global Drag*, London: Palgrave Macmillan.
Flassbeck, H. and F. Spiecker, (2005) Die deutsche Lohnpolitik sprengt die Europäische Währungsunion, WSI-Mitteilungen nr 12, http://www.boeckler.de/wsimit_2005_12_flassbeck.pdf .
Flassbeck, H. and F. Spiecker (2011) 'The Euro – a story of misunderstanding', *Intereconomics*, 4: http://shop.ceps.be/system/files/article/2011/07/Forum.pdf .
Hall, R.L. and C.J. Hitch (1939) 'Price theory and business behaviour', *Oxford Economic Papers*, 2: 12–45.
Kalecki, M. (1932a/1990) 'Reduction of wages during crisis', in Kalecki (1990).
Kalecki, M. (1932b/1990) 'Is "capitalist" overcoming of the crisis possible?' in Kalecki (1990).
Kalecki, M. (1933a/1990) *Essay on the Business Cycle Theory*, in Kalecki (1990).
Kalecki, M. (1933b/1990) 'On foreign trade and "domestic exports"' in Kalecki (1990).
Kalecki, M. (1935/1990) 'The essence of the business upswing' in Kalecki (1990).
Kalecki, M. (1939a/1990) 'Money and real wages' in Kalecki (1990).
Kalecki, M. (1939b) 'Money and real wages', in *Essays in the Theory of Economic Fluctuations*, Allen and Unwin, London.
Kalecki, M. (1939c/1991) 'Money and real wages' in Kalecki (1991).
Kalecki, M. (1944/1990) 'Three Ways to Full Employment' in Kalecki (1990).
Kalecki, M. (1954/1991) *Theory of Economic Dynamics: An Essay on Cyclical and Long-Run Changes in Capitalist Economy*, in Kalecki (1991).
Kalecki, M. (1990) *Collected Works of Michał Kalecki, Vol. I, Capitalism: Business Cycles and Full Employment*, edited by J. Osiatyński, Oxford: Oxford University Press.
Kalecki, M. (1991) *Collected Works of Michał Kalecki, Vol. II, Capitalism: Economic Dynamics*, edited by J. Osiatyński, Oxford: Oxford University Press.
Keynes, J.M. (1930/1972) 'The Great Slump of 1930' in *The Collected Writings of John Maynard Keynes*, Vol. IX, London: Macmillan.
Keynes, J.M. (1936) *The General Theory of Employment, Interest and Money*, London: Macmillan.
Keynes, J.M. (1939) 'Relative movements of real wages and output', *Economic Journal*, 49(1): 34–51.
Knakiewicz, Z. (1967) *Deflacja polska 1930–1935* (*Polish Deflation 1930–1935*), Warszawa: Państwowe Wydawnictwo Ekonomiczne.
Łaski, K. (2009) *Mity i rzeczywistość w polityce gospodarczej i w nauczaniu ekonomii*, (*Myths and Reality in Economic Policy Making and in Teaching Economics*), Warsaw: Institute of Economic Science of the Polish Academy of Science.
Łaski, K. (2011) *Strukturalne przyczyny kryzysu finansów publicznych w Unii Europejskiej oraz w Unii Gospodarczej i Walutowej*, (*Structural Causes of the Public*

Finance Crisis in the European Union and the Economic and Monetary Union), Institute of Economic Science of the Polish Academy of Science, *Economic Studies*, 1: 7–17.

Łaski, K. (2012) 'Consolidation of public finance and the Euro Zone crisis', minutes of the talk given at the National Bank of Poland, 13 June.

Łaski, K. and L. Podkaminer (2012) 'The basic paradigms of EU economic policy-making need to be changed', *Cambridge Journal of Economics*, 36(1): 253–270.

Lerner, A.P. (1943/1983) 'Functional finance and the federal debt' in D.C. Colander (ed.), *Selected Economic Writings of Abba Lerner*, New York: New York University Press.

Marglin, S. and A. Bhaduri (1988) *Profit Squeeze and Keynesian Theory*, WIDER Working Papers No. 39.

Mitchell, B. (2010) (billy blog) 'Barnaby, better to walk before we run', http://bilbo.economicoutlook.net/blog/?m=20100209 (access as of 23 July 2012).

Mitchell, B. (2012a) (billy blog) 'Introducing economic dynamics', http://bilbo.economicoutlook.net/blog/?p=20509 (access as of 7 September 2012).

Mitchell, B. (2012b) (billy blog) 'On strategy and compromise', http://bilbo.economicoutlook.net/blog/?m=20120703 (access as of 18 July 2012).

Musgrave, R.S. (2010) 'Government borrowing is nearly pointless where government issues its own currency', *Munich Personal Archive Paper*, nr 23785, http://mpra.ub.uni-muenchen.de/20057/1/GovtBorrow.docx.pdf (access as of 13 July 2012).

Musgrave, R.S. (2011) 'Monetary and fiscal policy should be merged, which in turn changes the role of central banks', *Munich Personal RePEc Archive*, http://mpra.ub.uni-muenchen.de/30521/, MPRA Paper No. 30521, posted 26. April 2011 (access as of 23 July 2012).

Osiatyński, in Kalecki 1990 – See n. 1, n. 10, n. 30.

Osiatyński, in Kalecki 1991, 518 – See n. 6., n. 21

Osiatyński, J. (2011) 'Warunki gotowości Polski do wejścia do strefy euro' (Preconditions of Poland's entry to the Euro area), *Ekonomista*, 5: 659–675.

Palley, T.P. (2009) *America's Exhausted Paradigm: Macroeconomic Causes of the Financial Crisis and Great Recession*, Washington, DC: New America Foundation.

Robinson, J.V.R. (1964) 'Kalecki and Keynes' in *Problems of Economic Dynamics and Planning: Essays in Honour of Michał Kalecki*, Warsaw: Państwowe Wydawnictwo Naukowe; reprinted in: Joan Robinson, *Collected Economic Papers*, Vol. III, Oxford: Basil Blackwell, 1965.

Sawyer, M.C. (2010) 'Progressive approaches to budget deficits', http://www.boeckler.de/pdf/v_2010_10_25_sawyer.pdf, (access as of 7 September 2012).

Święcicki, M. (1960) *Instytucje polskiego prawa pracy w latach 1918–1939* (*Institutions of Polish Work Law*), Warszawa: Państwowe Wydawnictwo Naukowe.

Tarshis, L. (1939) 'Changes in money and real wages' *Economic Journal*, 49(1): 535–550.

Terzi, A. (2010) *The 'Keynesian Moment' in Policymaking, the Perils Ahead, and a Flow-of-funds Interpretation of Fiscal Policy*, Working Paper no. 614, Levy Economics Institute of Bard College.

Wątecki, J. (1938) *Sztywne płace źródłem bezrobocia* (*Rigid Wages as a Cause of Unemployment*), Kraków: Towarzystwo Ekonomiczne.

3
Kalecki and Post-Keynesian Economics[1]

Marc Lavoie

Michał Kalecki is recognized by many observers as an important contributor and inspiration of post-Keynesian economics.[2] For instance, Joan Robinson, Geoff Harcourt and Malcolm Sawyer have constantly reasserted the importance and relevance of Kalecki's work, arguing, as Philip Arestis (1996, p. 11) did, that 'there is very little doubt that Kalecki's role in post-Keynesian economics is both extensive and paramount'. This, however, is not the opinion of all post-Keynesians. Undoubtedly, the most reluctant author to induct Kalecki within the post-Keynesian Hall of Fame is the long-time editor of the *Journal of Post Keynesian Economics*, Paul Davidson. As recalled by John King (1996, p. 151), Davidson's reluctance to pay homage to Kalecki is not something new; from the very beginning of his career in the early 1960s, Davidson found little of interest in Kalecki's writings. This, of course, can be contrasted with the views of another prominent American post-Keynesian, namely Hyman Minsky, who from 1977 on explicitly adopted Kalecki's macroeconomic theory of profits.

King (1996, p. 152) also points out that Davidson barely made any reference to Kalecki during the first 30 years of his academic career. When he did, it was to challenge Tom Asimakopulos's belief that 'the Kaleckian version of macroeconomics is superior to Keynes's analytical framework' and thus to argue that Kaleckians carry 'so much Classical baggage' in their mind that they are unable 'to catch the clues that Keynes is throwing to [them] in the analysis of finance, money and savings' (Davidson 1995, pp. 60–61). In a later work (Davidson 2000), he decided to have a first go at identifying the major differences between the employment theories of Kalecki and Keynes. This piece, which is mainly devoted to a reiteration of his views on Keynes, generated three comments: one from a former student of Kalecki, Julio López (2002), and two from other Kaleckian experts, Peter Kriesler (2002) and

Robert Dixon (2007), as well as a reply by Davidson (2002) himself. A few years later, aroused by the contents of King's (2002) *History of Post Keynesian Economics Since 1936*, Davidson (2003–2004) made another effort to express the differences between Kalecki's and Keynes's analyses in an attempt, in his own words, to set the record straight. This in turn generated three comments (King 2005; Lavoie 2005; Dow 2005) and once more a reply by Davidson (2005).

The fact that one of the main leaders of the post-Keynesian school of thought, and also the editor of its main journal, has little or no admiration for Kalecki's work is rather intriguing (although Davidson (2000, p. 3) did call Kalecki a genius). The purpose of this chapter is to review the reasons for which Davidson objects to integrating the contributions of Kalecki within post-Keynesian economics. I start by presenting and discussing the objections put forward by Davidson in his first article, showing that most of these objections are rather dubious. I then deal with his second article, where Davidson makes more general remarks on what belongs and does not belong to post-Keynesian economics. I conclude by recalling that some post-Keynesians believe that Kalecki, rather than Keynes, provides the best foundations for post-Keynesian theory.

3.1 Davidson's objections

We start with the arguments offered in Davidson (2000). There, Davidson seems to concede that Kalecki did put forward the idea of the income multiplier in the early 1930s, at the same time that Keynes did. He even goes so far as to recognize that 'the investment-consumption spending dichotomy and its multiplier implications for explanation of the determination of the level of output and employment are very similar in Keynes's and Kalecki's effective demand analysis' (Davidson, 2000, p. 9). However, in contrast to Patinkin who believes that the income multiplier is the revolutionary essence of the Keynesian revolution, Davidson does not consider that this is so: for Davidson, the income multiplier is not at the heart of the principle of effective demand; it is just an add-on. As a consequence, if Kalecki says anything really interesting, it is not tied to the income multiplier.[3]

A first distinctive feature of Keynes's theory, relative to that of Kalecki, still according to Davidson (2000, pp. 11–13), is that aggregate demand in Keynes is made up of two components. Davidson argues that this is an essential feature of Keynes's *General Theory*, as the division of expenditures into two demand classes allows Keynes to reject Say's Law, which itself is based on the assumption that all spending can be reduced to a single category. The two components of aggregate demand are defined by expenditures that depend on aggregate income and hence on the level of employment, and those that do not depend on income and employment (the autonomous expenditures), so that we have:

$$D = D_1 + D_2, \text{ with } D_1 = f(N) \text{ and } D_2 \neq f(N).$$

The second claim of Davidson (2000, p. 8), somewhat similar to the first one, is that 'for Kalecki, unlike Keynes, the rate of interest does *not* play an important role in the determination of aggregate demand'. By contrast, 'Keynes held that the three primary determinants of investment are (1) the rate of interest, (2) expectations regarding future quasi-rents in a world of uncertainty, and (3) the costs of newly produced capital goods (the supply price of capital)' (ibid.). In addition, Kalecki is said to give no attention to liquidity preference, that is, the decision that savers must make between holding liquid or illiquid assets, tied to precautionary or speculative motives within an environment of radical uncertainty.

Davidson's third claim is that Kalecki blames the existence of unemployment on an inadequate income distribution arising from the monopoly power of firms, with a more unequal (personal or functional) income distribution leading to higher unemployment, whereas Keynes would attribute unemployment to expectations about an uncertain future and to the behaviour of financial markets. Thus, according to Davidson, with pure or perfect competition, there would be no unemployment in the Kaleckian model. From this, Davidson (2000, p. 5) concludes that 'Kalecki's theory of effective demand, therefore, like the classical theories that preceded it and the New Keynesian theories of modern times, places the ultimate cause of unemployment on the absence of competition in product markets'. Davidson (2000, p. 11) further criticizes Kalecki's view by pointing out that, despite an especially unequal income distribution, 'the United States appears to be immune to the unemployment disease that has gripped the rest of the world's market economies'. This was published in 2000, just one year before the stock-market crash of 2001that accompanied a tough American recession, and of course just a few years before the Great Recession that many heterodox economists attribute precisely to a rising inequality in income distribution.

We can now deal with each of the three main claims made by Davidson. When it comes to the two components of aggregate demand, it would seem that Kalecki is very close to Keynes. With respect to D_1, Kalecki has workers' consumption assumed to be equal to the wage bill, so that surely we can say that this component depends on current income and employment, so that $D_1 = w.N$, where w is the nominal wage rate. Now what about, D_2, the component of aggregate demand that does not depend on current income? Davidson (2000, p. 8) believes that 'whatever portion of earned profits entrepreneurs do not spend on consumption is saved, but these savings are necessarily spent on buying newly produced capital goods'. From this Davidson can conclude that Kalecki does not have a second component D_2. From an accounting point of view, what Davidson says here is correct: it can be deduced from Kalecki's profit equation: $P = I + C_p$. Profits are equal to investment expenditures plus consumption out of profits, so that the profits that are not consumed are invested since there is no saving out of wages.[4] From this Davidson (1995, p. 63) concludes that 'the aggregate income-budget line is the ultimate constraint on current spending in Kalecki's model'. In other words, Davidson believes that within Kalecki's system there can be no money creation, so that in his words, money is neutral.

But this is certainly not how Kalecki must be interpreted. First, the D functions are related to *planned* expenditures, not the *ex post* relationships. Kalecki (1971, pp. 110–113) argues that realized investment expenditures occur several periods after the investment decisions have been taken. Second, the planned amount of investment depends on several factors, only one of which is retained earnings. Planned investment also depends on the increase in profits and on some constant, which itself depends on some long-run assessment of the rate of technical progress. Thus, as in Keynes, planned investment expenditures do not depend only on current income and employment. There is thus a D_2 component in Kalecki, just as there is in Keynes, which is independent of current income. As López (2002, p. 617) points out in his comment on Davidson's paper, 'actual investment may be equal, fall short, or exceed business prior savings'. Kalecki's and Keynes's analyses are similar on this issue. Kalecki himself made it very clear that expenditures of capitalists are not limited to their current profits, showing which way the causality goes: 'Now it is clear that capitalists may decide to consume and to invest more in a given period than in the preceding one, but they cannot decide to earn more. It is, therefore, their investment and consumption decisions which determine profits, and not vice versa' (Kalecki, 1971, pp. 78–79).

This leads us to three primary determinants of Keynesian investment according to Davidson. What I wish to argue is that, once more, the differences between Keynes and Kalecki are minimal. According to Davidson, Keynes's investment depends on the cost of newly produced investment goods (their supply price). It is also the case in Kalecki (1971, p. 111) when he says that the retained earnings of firms, as a determinant of future investment, 'have to be deflated by the index of the prices of investment goods'. He adds further that 'when the profitability of new investment projects is being weighted, expected profits are considered in relation to the value of new capital equipment. Thus, profits are taken in relation to the current prices of investment goods' (1971, p. 112). Things could not be any clearer. So this certainly takes care of part (c) of Davidson's second argument. What about part (b), which says that Keynes's investment depends on expected future profits? The previous sentence already incorporates the words 'expected profits'. The current change in profits – the rate of change in aggregate profits – acts as a proxy for expected future profits. They play the role of the marginal efficiency of capital, which is the expected profit component in Keynes's theory of investment. We cannot say that Kalecki ignores expected profits in his theory of investment. However, in contrast to Keynes, who gives us little clues as to what determines the marginal efficiency of capital, Kalecki tells us that the impact of expected profits on investment is likely to be a function of current increases in profits. As pointed out by López (2002, p. 613), Kalecki 'insisted that capitalists do not react solely on expectations, but rather make their decisions on the basis of realized profits, which provide both the finance and the stimuli for investing'.

Now, what about part (a) of Davidson's second argument, the claim that interest rates play no role in Kalecki's determination of investment? Here we could cautiously say that Davidson seems to have a point since the rate of interest does not enter explicitly into Kalecki's investment equation. Also Kalecki (1971, p. 113), on a number of occasions, maintains that 'the long-term rate of interest does not show marked cyclical fluctuations'. But this rate of interest, presumably, is the rate on government securities because Kalecki added immediately that 'it is true that the yields of business debentures sometimes increase appreciably during depressions because of crises of confidence'. Here we have a Minskyan Kalecki before Minsky! As the economy slows down or falls into a recession, interest rates on long-term private debt rise because of a lack of confidence, presumably because rentiers prefer to switch their portfolios towards government securities and short-term assets. Will this have any impact on business investment? Kalecki believed so. He argued that this will have the same effect as a fall in current profits, and thus can be represented in a recession regime by an increase in the parameter of the change in profits variable (as profits are falling, this will enhance the negative impact on investment). Thus, once more we can conclude that there is no substantial difference between the analyses of Keynes and Kalecki regarding the determination of investment.

We then move to Davidson's third claim, which says that Kalecki was some sort of imperfectionist, for whom labour unemployment is caused by the existence of monopolies on product markets. Here things are a bit more complicated because when Davidson makes this claim he also refers to a passage of Kalecki (1971, p. 97) on the behaviour of a socialist economy. Before dealing with the socialist system, let us deal with the case of the capitalist economy. My understanding of Kalecki's argument, as well as Kriesler's (2002) and Dixon's (2007) understanding, is that unemployment in capitalist economies is the result of insufficient aggregate demand, both in a competitive and in an oligopolistic economy. Kalecki argued that in a competitive economy a reduction in wages will lead to an equal reduction in prices, and hence will have no effect on employment, since real wages will remain roughly the same, whereas in an oligopolistic economy, the reduction in nominal wages will make things even worse as real wages will fall, thus reducing consumption demand, with no reason for investment demand to increase.

When dealing with the competitive economy, Kalecki's arguments are once more not that much different from those of Keynes. Kalecki (1969, p. 49) argued first that the lower prices that accompany the lower wages in the competitive case will reduce the demand for transaction balances and may induce a small decrease in short-term interest rates. However, Kalecki discarded the relevance of this effect because he believed that it is unlikely that the reduction in short-term interest rates will have any significant effect on long-term interest rates and hence on investment. This is no different from the well-known Keynes effect that can be found in chapter 19 of the *General Theory*, and about which Keynes (1936, p. 266) says 'there is indeed, nothing to hope in this direction'. Keynes (1936, p. 264) also contended that lower prices are likely to depress the enthusiasm of entrepreneurs because of 'their greater burden of debt'. It is well-known that Kalecki (1944) objected to the positive effects of lower prices and Pigou's real money balance effect by also invoking the debt effect. But he also made this argument in 1939, claiming that 'a general reduction in prices increases the burden of indebtedness, since money incomes diminish while the "old" debts do not. This causes difficulties in servicing the debts, ending frequently in failures. As a result confidence in the solvency of firms is undermined which may lead to an increase in the long-term rate of interest even though the short-term rate declines' (Kalecki, 1969, p. 49). Thus Keynes and Kalecki are on the same page with regards to the possible negative effects of falling wages and prices. And again we find in Kalecki the idea that interest rates on long-term private debt may rise in a recession, because of falling confidence, thus mixing real and financial phenomena.

López (2002, p. 611) is rather puzzled by Davidson's accusation that Kalecki is no different from New Keynesians when it comes to explain unemployment. López points out that in Kalecki, the downturn within an oligopolistic economy is likely to induce lower real wages, with reduced consumption and hence lower employment. But within the standard neoclassical framework, it is an *increase* in real wages, a real wage in excess of the equilibrium real wage, which will generate a fall in the demand for labour and a fall in employment, as employers decline to employ more workers. All this is rather confusing because the standard neoclassical story, based on standard demand and supply analysis in the labour market, is different from the New Consensus story entertained by New Keynesians in their dynamic stochastic general equilibrium (DSGE) models. In these latter models, some negative shock will reduce the real wage and lead to a reduction in employment because *workers* will decline to offer their services (Dullien, 2011). In the DSGE model, a lower real wage is associated with a lower employment level, but the mechanism is entirely different. Changes in economic activity are entirely supply-led, and there is no involuntary unemployment. It would thus be rather unfair to associate Kalecki with either the neoclassical or the New Keynesian mechanisms.

Things are slightly more complicated because, as evoked earlier, Kalecki has suggested that in a socialist economy, prices would be flexible and would guarantee full employment (which helps to explain why Davidson believes that Kalecki is an imperfectionist). If there was a fall in investment activity, 'the workers released from the production of investment goods would be employed in the consumption goods industries. The increased supply of these goods would be absorbed by means of a reduction in their prices' (Kalecki, 1971, p. 96). Real wages would rise and ensure that aggregate demand for consumption goods would absorb the additional production of consumption goods. In my view, Kalecki is overly optimistic here, and does not seem to be aware of the stability and sustainability problems that can occur during a full-employment traverse, as underlined by John Hicks (1965) and Adolph Lowe (1976), and as they have been graphically described by Henry and Lavoie (1997). On this, Dixon (2007, pp. 13–14) contends that the ultimate cause of unemployment for Keynes has to do with the existence and the use of money, whereas Kalecki would go one step further, arguing that class interests would stop the government from acting to achieve full employment. This would be the crucial difference between the two authors.

3.2 The advantages of Kalecki's analysis

Davidson's apparent annoyance with Kalecki was rekindled with the appearance of King's (2002) *History of Post Keynesian Economics Since 1936*. Having been at the vanguard of the American post-Keynesian movement, Davidson felt the need to set the record straight. While King identified the first post-Keynesians as being Robinson, Kaldor, Harrod and Kalecki, Davidson (2003–2004, pp. 247–248) objected to Kalecki being included in this group, going so far as to proclaim that 'Kalecki's monetary analysis is so different from Keynes's *General Theory* that Kalecki cannot be classified as a Post Keynesian'. In this paper Davidson reiterates the accusation that Kalecki is an imperfectionist, asking King why he would include Kalecki within the post-Keynesian camp when the latter's analysis of money and uncertainty is so weak. Kalecki, however, is not the only famous heterodox author to be excluded from the 'Post Keynesian' school as defined by Davidson (2003–2004): Sraffian authors are also excommunicated, as are contemporaries of Davidson, namely Alfred Eichner, Jan Kregel and Hyman Minsky, all of whom contributed from the start to the institutionalization and the organization of the post-Keynesian school.[5] Indeed only five authors seem to make the cut: Davidson himself; Sidney Weintraub, Davidson's supervisor; Basil Moore, a friend of Davidson; Tony Thirlwall, who looks and speaks like Keynes; and Kaldor, although ironically we will see that he was rather critical of Keynes. Somewhat surprisingly, King (2005, p. 379) only devoted six lines to defend Kalecki, counter-arguing that Kalecki was not an imperfectionist while Keynes was an obvious 'neoclassical synthesizer'!

I have published my comments (Lavoie, 2005) on Davidson's outrageous claims, so I will not repeat them here. Suffice it to say that this 'narrow-tent' approach is not congenial to the development of a strong heterodox community. In addition, as I have tried to show in the previous section, the attempt by Davidson to demonstrate that the economics of Keynes is quite different from the economics of Kalecki has failed. All the points made by Davidson can be contested. I think that it is more productive to go for a 'wide-tent' approach and recognize that there are several strands within post-Keynesian economics, and that each of these strands has its advantages and drawbacks. Thus one can argue that there are five post-Keynesian strands: the Fundamentalists (of which Davidson is part), the Sraffians, the Institutionalists, the Kaldorians, and of course the Kaleckians (Lavoie, 2011). Davidson (2005, p. 397) believes that the multiplication of the strands in the post-Keynesian school has produced 'an incoherent babble' without 'coherence and consistency'. This may be so, but it has also provided some vitality to this school of thought, despite difficult times, as participants felt free to pursue their own interests without being constrained to follow a single line of thought, as is the case with neoclassical macroeconomics and its DSGE model. In particular, it allowed Kaleckians to develop economic theories devoid of neoclassical content.

In his response to Davidson, López (2002) makes at least four claims regarding the advantages of relying on Kalecki's theories. First, except for a brief period, Kalecki dismissed neoclassical theory and relied on much different foundations. Kalecki rejected the neoclassical production function and its universal assumption of diminishing returns and increasing marginal costs.[6] Kaleckian economics is thus founded on constant marginal costs (up to full capacity). López also argues that Kalecki relied explicitly on the assumption of an endogenous supply of money – a key feature of modern post-Keynesian economics – whereas Keynes's *General Theory* relies instead on an exogenous supply of money. Thirdly, López underlines the importance of Kalecki's principle of increasing risk, which is the heart of Minsky's financial fragility hypothesis. Fourthly, related to this, Kalecki emphasized the importance of retained earnings in the financing of investment, a feature which has been corroborated time and again by empirical studies of investment. Finally, despite Keynes's (1973, xii, p. 831) belief that all this was 'esoteric abracadabra', Kalecki has stressed the importance of excess capacity, arguing that firms would not be operating at full capacity utilization, even in the long run. These are all important ideas now in use by modern Kaleckians.

In his own response to Davidson, Kriesler (2002, p. 629) sees at least four advantages in seeking inspiration from Kalecki: his non-neoclassical microfoundations, his oligopolistic environment, his assumption of endogenous money and the key role played by income distribution. These starting blocks provide an eminently useful apparatus to provide pedagogical and empirical tools. In addition, Kriesler (2002, p. 628) maintains, as we did here, that Keynes and Kalecki share several elements: they both argued that aggregate demand is the main determinant of employment; they both denied that falling wages will provide full employment and that there exist automatic mechanisms bringing back the economy to full employment; they both contended that investment determines saving rather than the converse; and they both rejected the dichotomy between the monetary and the real sectors.

If another example of convergence between Keynes and Kalecki may be given, let us recall a statement on the possibility of crowding out that these two authors made. When arguing in favour of an expansionary fiscal policy and public works in an attempt to reduce unemployment, Keynes (1936, p. 120) issued the following warning: 'With the confused psychology which often prevails, the government programme may, through its effect on "confidence", increase liquidity-preference or diminish the marginal efficiency of capital, which, again, may retard other investment unless measures are taken to offset it.' This comment could certainly be used as a good example of the attention that Keynes paid to the behaviour of both portfolio owners and entrepreneurs within a world of fundamental uncertainty. Similarly, in 1943, Kalecki (1971, p. 139) made the following remarks, which appear quite prescient in view of the current fiscal situation in Europe and in the United States: 'Under a *laissez-faire* system the level of employment depends on the so-called state of confidence.... This gives to the capitalists a powerful indirect control over Government policy: everything which may shake the state of confidence must be carefully avoided because it would cause an economic crisis.... The social function of the doctrine of "sound finance" is to make the level of employment dependent on the "state of confidence".' Thus, once more, we see the importance that Kalecki attached to the notion of confidence, just like Keynes did, although Kalecki did not deal explicitly with the concept of fundamental uncertainty.

The other weakness of Kalecki's analysis is alleged to be its lack of interest for financial and monetary matters, in contrast to Keynes's own obsession with these issues. Although there is certainly some truth in this claim, we have seen already that Kalecki paid much attention to the consequences of a recession on the ability of firms to borrow from banks or on capital markets since lenders would ask for higher rates of return on private debt and borrowers would be credit constrained by the lack of their own funds – an outcome of the *principle of increasing risk*. Kalecki also deals with financial matters, but in a way which is different from that of Keynes. As indicated by Kriesler (1997, p. 312), in Kalecki's works, 'the financial sector's role in the investment process was through the medium of the availability of credit. This represents a substantial difference to Keynes, who stressed the role of the cost of finance rather than its availability.'

Gary Dymski (1996) and Malcolm Sawyer (2001) have shown that quite a bit could be said about Kalecki's monetary writings. In particular, Kalecki had a good understanding that bank credit was crucial to the expansion of an economy, predicated on the expansion of balance sheets when firms engaged in the production process, followed by the reflux of bank advances as firms made their sales and paid back their loans. Sawyer (2001, p. 504) further points out that Kalecki was rather sceptical about the ability of the monetary authorities to regulate aggregate demand through monetary policy. This is certainly the post-Keynesian consensus today, especially in view of the recent events in the world economy, when even zero interest rates are unable to kick start the economy. Keynes himself entertained doubts about the potency of monetary policy in the *General Theory*.

Thus, we cannot but fully agree with López (2002, p. 620) when he concludes that what he finds amazing is not the differences between Kalecki and Keynes, 'but rather how close these two economists – with such different ideological, political and theoretical backgrounds, and with such dissimilar working experiences – were in their conclusions, and even in many details of their theories'. Still I believe that Kalecki has something to offer that Keynes does not have.

Davidson (2003–2004, p. 397) is surprised that Sraffians, Minskyans and Kaleckians reject the analytical usefulness of Keynes's aggregate demand and aggregate supply apparatus found in Keynes's *General Theory*, developed by Weintraub and later retrieved by Davidson himself. The reason, I submit, is that most post-Keynesians feel uncomfortable with this apparatus. Keynes's treatment of price theory is deemed by many to be too closely associated with neoclassical views to be kept within a post-Keynesian synthesis. Indeed, the endless debates about the appropriate representation of Keynes's aggregate supply function, or what has become the *Z* function, as well as the recursive and inconclusive debates about Keynes's classical postulates regarding the determination of employment, demonstrate that the adoption of neoclassical core assumptions within post-Keynesian economics only leads to sterile controversies, even if these assumptions are turned on their head.[7] Indeed, the confusion about Keynes's aggregate supply function has been so great over the years that the editors of the *Cambridge Journal of Economics* have felt it necessary to issue a statement to the effect that they wished 'to discourage further submissions of comments on the Z function' (Editors, 2011, p. 635).

A number of observers have complained that heterodox economists, including post-Keynesians, tend to avoid questioning founding contributors, acting as self-appointed Guardians of the Temple, who are defending the true faith and the holy scriptures of their favourite authors. If Keynes did not abandon, but only modified the Quantity Theory of Money in his *General Theory*, thus being overly monetarist for contemporary post-Keynesians, as noted both by Kaldor (1982, p. 21) and the recanted Hicks (1982, p. 264), this does not mean that we must try to rescue him by making fancy distinctions between a *constant* and a *given* supply of money. If Keynes assumed decreasing returns and a negative relationship between real wages and employment when discussing the unemployment problem in the *General Theory*, this does not mean that we have to follow him despite all the empirical evidence to the contrary. As recalled by Herbert Simon (1997, p. 14), the founder of the original behavioural economics and of the concept of bounded rationality, 'a large part of the book [the *General Theory*] is an exercise in neoclassical analysis', an opinion which is reminiscent of the one offered by King (2005) and noted earlier.

One difference between Keynes and Kalecki is that the *General Theory* was 'aimed at showing both the errors of the prevailing orthodoxy and Keynes's own theory', whereas Kalecki did not attempt 'to engage in polemic with other economists' and 'was not concerned with making his ideas intelligible to the prevailing orthodoxy' (Kriesler, 1997, pp. 313–314). Keynes may have had good strategic reasons for presenting his analysis the way he did. These reasons are no longer valid. 'Keynes's choices probably were adequate to carry out a more convincing criticism of the neoclassical dominant paradigm. However, in my opinion, they cannot be regarded as acceptable when the emphasis of the analysis is shifted toward the explanation of how actual economies work' (Sardoni, 2001, pp. 10–11). In any case, this strategy turned out to be a failure because, as pointed out by the French translator of Keynes, the adornment of Marshallian microfoundations with diminishing returns in the *General Theory* 'made it possible to invoke the authority of the latter in favor of opinions directly contrary to its essential teachings' (de Largentaye, 1979, p. 9).

The purpose of post-Keynesian economics is 'to understand reality as a central point of its research and theory development' (Jespersen, 2009, p. 15). We must thus start the analysis with assumptions that are grounded in empirically observed facts, that is, use assumptions that are realistic. This is not the case of the neoclassical production function and the assumption of decreasing returns, which Keynes accepted (certainly until 1939, when Dunlop and Kalecki presented their objections to Keynes). As pointed out by Johann Deprez (1996, p. 141), '[The] Davidsonian approach to the labour market is one true to Keynes's method of building with Marshallian tools and of giving the classicals as much as possible and still end up with unemployment conclusions. As such, it is not – nor is meant to be – a fully positive, descriptive approach to what actually happens in the labour market.' To understand the working of actual economies, these mainstream assumptions about the firm and production must be given up. Kaldor (1983, p. 10) issued a harsh warning when he wrote that 'so long as one sticks to neoclassical micro-economics, Keynesian macro-economics amounts to very little'.

3.3 Conclusion

The point I am trying to make here is that post-Keynesian economics is much more than a modernized version of the economics of a single contributor – Keynes. In some sense, post-Keynesian economics is a misnomer, because it encompasses several founding contributors besides Keynes, including, most importantly, Kalecki. Indeed, this is why post-Keynesian economics can be said to be made up of five distinct strands. Still, despite their idiosyncrasies, the leaders of these various strands carry a message that shows a substantial amount of overlap.

All strands have something important to contribute to the development of post-Keynesian economics. Some strands turn out to have a stronger background over some fields. Various historical events highlight the strength of different strands. The global financial crisis has demonstrated the particular relevance of Fundamentalist Keynesianism, notably with its emphasis on the fragility and instability of financial markets *à la* Minsky, as well as the need for liquid assets and the crucial role played by liquidity preference, a theme developed by Keynes, Davidson and several other authors in this tradition. But although we experienced a financial crisis, the economics of Kalecki remain fundamental to understand the evolution of the crisis, with Kalecki's emphasis on the importance of income distribution, his profit equations and the point that he made, almost as an aside, about the lack of confidence associated with a recession that would drive up the interest rates on private debt.

Despite all the qualms expressed by Davidson, a large number of post-Keynesians believe that the economics of Kalecki provide a preferable foundation for an alternative to orthodox theory, at least when dealing with problems tied to the concept of effective demand. This is because Kalecki is concerned with the real world as it is, and not with some hypothetical economy with perfect competition, which would either be the idealized optimum to be attained or the benchmark of the analysis. As Robinson (1977, p. 15) points out, 'Kalecki was free from the remnants of old-fashioned theory which Keynes had failed to throw off'. This was so because, as explained by Kriesler (1997, p. 314),

Kalecki 'never formally studied economics', or more precisely he did not formally study neoclassical economics, while 'his training was the result of early reading of Marxist economists in the under-consumption tradition, plus the knowledge of his father's business.[8] As a result, Keynes's Marshallian framework 'required indirect and rather convoluted arguments to make points which are crystal clear in Kalecki's exposition' (Harcourt, 2006, p. 14).

Most explicit is Gilles Dostaler (1988, p. 134), the famous historian of thought, who held that 'Kalecki can be considered to be the real founder of post-Keynesian theory'. Similarly, Bhaduri (1986, p. ix), believes that the radical content of Keynesianism must be learned from Kalecki, as he set out its central propositions 'with striking clarity'. Even those who contributed to the development of the Keynesian revolution at Cambridge have made similar judgments. Kaldor (1983, p. 15) has noted that 'Kalecki's original model of unemployment equilibrium which takes monopolistic competition as its starting point, is clearly superior to Keynes's'. It can be said that over time, both Kaldor and Robinson turned away from Keynes and tended towards Kalecki. Robinson (1977, pp. 14–15) has argued that because 'Kalecki was free from the remnants of old-fashioned theory which Keynes had failed to throw off', he was better able 'to weave the analysis of imperfect competition and of effective demand together and it was this that opened up the way for what goes under the name of post-Keynesian theory'. As to John Kenneth Galbraith (1981, p. 75), he paid the greatest compliment to Kalecki, by claiming that Kalecki was 'the most innovative figure in economics I have known, not excluding Keynes'.

Notes

1. I would like to thank Peter Kriesler for his useful comments and suggestions.
2. Some recent book-length introductions to post-Keynesian economics can be found in Harcourt (2006), Lavoie (2006) and Fontana (2009), as well as the books of readings edited by Hein and Stockhammer (2011) and King (2012).
3. Davidson (2000, p. 4) seems to be a bit confused regarding the Kaleckian multiplier and the determinants of GDP. He writes these as:

   $Y = I/(1-a)(1-q)$

   where q is the marginal propensity to consume out of profit and where a is said to be the 'marginal consumption propensity of workers'. As clearly indicated by Kalecki (1971, p. 96), a is the share of national income going to wages, not a propensity to consume, so that the denominator is the product of the profit share and the propensity to save out of profits, that is, the overall propensity to save, as in Keynes. The mistake was also picked up by Dixon (2007).

4. As Harcourt (2006, p. 14) points out, there are similarities between Kalecki's profit equation and Keynes's widow's cruse explanation of profits which can be found in his *Treatise on Money*.
5. Vela Velupillai (2013, p. 431) was stunned by Davidson's position, writing that 'I would be dishonest if I did not also confess that I was both mystified and saddened – from a purely intellectual point of view – by the review of King (2002) by Davidson (2003–2004)'.
6. Here again there is some similarity between Keynes and Kalecki. López (2002, p. 610) mentions that in one of his early papers Kalecki approved of increasing marginal costs on the grounds that more production would require the use of older and less productive machines. Similarly, in the *General Theory,* Keynes justified the assumption of rising marginal costs by claiming that higher economic activity would bring in a less trained and less efficient labour force.
7. Davidson argues that, in his scheme, a higher employment level causes a lower real wage rather than lower real wages being conducive to more employment.
8. This reminds me of my former co-author, the late Wynne Godley, who also had little formal training in economics, much of it being however with P.W.S. Andrews, the originator of normal cost pricing, who held non-orthodox views. Godley was a highly original and pragmatic thinker, who was unable to make any sense of the little that he knew of mainstream economics, because his practical knowledge of economics, acquired through his studies with Andrews and his work as a forecaster and adviser at the British Treasury, clashed with neoclassical assumptions and models. There is an advantage in not being brainwashed by neoclassical theory.

References

Arestis, P. (1996) 'Kalecki's role in Post Keynesian economics: an overview' in J.E. King (ed.), *An Alternative Macroeconomic Theory: The Kaleckian Model and Post-Keynesian Economics,* Boston and London: Dordrecht, 11–34.

Bhaduri, A. (1986) *The Dynamics of Commodity Production,* Armonk: M.E. Sharpe.

Davidson, P. (1995) 'The Asimakopulos view of Keynes's *General Theory*' in G. Harcourt, A. Roncaglia and R. Rowley (eds), *Income and Employment in Practice,* London: Macmillan, 40–66.

Davidson, P. (2000) 'There are major differences between Kalecki's theory of employment and Keynes's general theory of employment, interest and money', *Journal of Post Keynesian Economics,* 23(1), Fall: 3–26.

Davidson, P. (2002) 'Keynes versus Kalecki: responses to López and Kriesler', *Journal of Post Keynesian Economics,* 24(92), Summer: 631–642.

Davidson, P. (2003–2004) 'Setting the record straight on *A History of Post Keynesian Economics*', *Journal of Post Keynesian Economics,* 26(2): 245–272.

Davidson, P. (2005) 'Responses to Lavoie, King, and Dow on what Post Keynesianism is and who is a Post Keynesian', *Journal of Post Keynesian Economics,* 27(3), Spring: 393–409.

Deprez, J. (1996) 'Davidson on the labor market in a monetary production economy', in P. Arestis (ed.), *Keynes, Money and the Open Economy: Essays in Honour of Paul Davidson: Volume One,* Cheltenham: Edward Elgar, 123–143.

Dixon, R. (2007) 'Investment, profits and employment in Kalecki and Keynes', Research paper #990, Department of Economics, University of Melbourne, http://www.economics.unimelb.edu.au/downloads/wpapers-07/990.pdf
Dostaler, G. (1988) 'La théorie post-keynésienne, la Théorie Générale et Kalecki', *Cahiers d'Economie Politique*, 14–15: 123–142.
Dow, S.C. (2005) 'Axioms and Babylonian thought: a reply', *Journal of Post Keynesian Economics*, 27(3): 385–392.
Dullien, S. (2011) 'The new Consensus from a traditional Keynesian and Post-Keynesian perspective: a worthwhile foundation for research or just a waste of time?, *Économie appliqué*, 64(1): 173–200.
Dymski, G.A. (1996) 'Kalecki's monetary economics', in J.E. King (ed.), *An Alternative Macroeconomic Theory: The Kaleckian Model and Post-Keynesian Economics*, Boston and London: Dordrecht, 115–140.
Editors (2011) 'Editorial note', *Cambridge Journal of Economics*, 35(3), May: 635.
Fontana, G. (2009) *Money, Uncertainty and Time*, London: Routledge.
Galbraith, J.K. (1981) *A Life in Our Times: Memoirs*, Boston: Houghton Mifflin.
Harcourt, G.C. (2006) *The Structure of Post-Keynesian Economics: The Core Contributions of the Pioneers*, Cambridge: Cambridge University Press.
Henry, J. and M. Lavoie (1997) 'The Hicksian traverse as a process of reproportioning: some structural dynamics', *Structural Change and Economic Dynamics*, 8(2): 157–175.
Hein, E. and E. Stockhammer (eds) (2011) *A Modern Guide to Keynesian Macroeconomics and Economic Policies*, Cheltenham: Edward Elgar.
Hicks, J. (1965) *Capital and Growth*, Oxford: Oxford University Press.
Hicks, J. (1982) *Money, Interest and Wages*, Cambridge, MA: Harvard University Press.
Jespersen, J. (2009) *Macroeconomic methodology A Post-Keynesian perspective*: Cheltenham: Edward Elgar.
Kaldor, N. (1982) *The Scourge of Monetarism*, Oxford: Oxford University Press.
Kaldor, N. (1983) 'Keynesian economics after fifty years', in D. Worswick and J. Trevithick (eds), *Keynes and the Modern World*, Cambridge: Cambridge University Press, 1–28.
Kalecki, M. (1944) 'Professor Pigou on the classical stationary state: a comment', *Economic Journal*, 54, April: 131–132.
Kalecki, M. (1969) *Studies in the Theory of Business Cycles 1933–1939*, Oxford: Basil Blackwell.
Kalecki, M. (1971) *Selected Essays in the Dynamics of the Capitalist Economy*, Cambridge: Cambridge University Press.
Keynes, J.M. (1930) *Treatise on Money* – See n. 4.
Keynes, J.M. (1930/1973) *Treatise on Money Volume 1 The Pure Theory of Money* London: Macmillan, p. 125.
Keynes, J.M. (1936) *The General Theory of Employment, Interest and Money*, London: Macmillan.
Keynes, J.M. (1973) *The Collected Writings of John Maynard Keynes: Economic Articles and Correspondence: Investment and Editorial*, volume xii, London: Macmillan, St. Martin's Press and Cambridge University Press.
King, J.E. (1996) 'Kalecki and the Americans', in J.E. King (ed.), *An Alternative Macroeconomic Theory: The Kaleckian Model and Post-Keynesian Economics*, Boston and London: Dordrecht, 141–167.

King, J.E. (2002) *A History of Post Keynesian Economics Since 1936*, Cheltenham: Edward Elgar.
King, J.E. (2005) 'Unwarping the record: a reply to Paul Davidson', *Journal of Post Keynesian Economics*, 27(3), Spring: 377–384.
King, J.E. (ed.) (2012) *The Elgar Companion to Post Keynesian Economics, Second Edition*, Cheltenham: Edward Elgar.
Kriesler, P. (1997) 'Keynes, Kalecki and *The General Theory*', in G.C. Harcourt and P.A. Riach (eds), *A 'Second Edition' of The General Theory*, London: Routledge, 300–322.
Kriesler, P. (2002) 'Was Kalecki an "imperfectionist"? Davidson on Kalecki', *Journal of Post Keynesian Economics*, 24(4), Summer: 623–630.
de Largentaye, J. (1979) 'A note on the *General Theory of Employment, Interest and Money*' *Journal of Post Keynesian Economics*, 1(3), Spring: 6–15.
Lavoie, M. (2005) 'Changing definitions: a comment on Davidson's critique of King's history of Post Keynesianism', *Journal of Post Keynesian Economics*, 27(3), Spring: 371–376.
Lavoie, M. (2006) *Introduction to Post-Keynesian Economics*, Basingstoke: Palgrave Macmillan.
Lavoie, M. (2011) 'History and methods of post-Keynesian economics', in E. Hein and E. Stockhammer (eds), *A Modern Guide to Keynesian Macroeconomics and Economic Policies*, Cheltenham: Edward Elgar, 1–33.
López, J. (2002) 'Two versions of the principle of effective demand: Kalecki and Keynes', *Journal of Post Keynesian Economics*, 24(4), Summer: 609–622.
Lowe, A. (1976) *The Path of Economic Growth*, Cambridge: Cambridge University Press.
Robinson, J. (1977) 'Michal Kalecki on the economics of capitalism', *Oxford Bulletin of Economics and Statistics*, 39(1), February: 7–17.
Sardoni, C. (2001) 'On the microeconomic foundations of macroeconomics: A Keynesian perspective', in P. Arestis, M. Desai and S.C. Dow (eds) *Methodology, Microeconomics and Keynes Essays in honour of Victoria chick, Volume Two*. London: Routledge.
Sawyer, M.C. (2001) 'Kalecki on money and finance', *European Journal of the History of Economic Thought*, 8(4), Winter: 487–508.
Simon, H.A. (1997) *An Empirically Based Microeconomics*, Cambridge: Cambridge University Press.
Velupillai, V. (2013) 'Postkeynesian precepts for nonlinear, endogenous, nonstochastic, business cycle theories', in G.C. Harcourt and P. Kriesler (eds), *The Oxford Handbook of Post-Keynesian Economics, Volume 1: Theory and Origins*, Oxford: Oxford University Press, 415–442.

4
Effective Demand and Path Dependence in Short- and Long-Run Growth

Amit Bhaduri

4.1 The short run and the long run

It is a common practice in mainstream neoclassical economics to bypass awkward problems by assuming they are transient, basically temporary failure of the price mechanism in the 'short run' that gets resolved in the 'long run'. Depending on the context this might mean different things, for example, slow speed of adjustment to equilibrium like in some older theories of frictional unemployment or in some modern search theories of unemployment. It might mean deficient learning in the short run that gets remedied in the long run, that is, people are wiser in the long run (even if dead!). It was captured by Milton Friedman's famous quip against money illusion, 'you cannot fool all the people all the time'. This view became an obsession with later Chicago monetarists who argued that money is neutral in the long run as enough information becomes available; continuous market clearing 'rational expectations' is only a short step from it on the assumption that the market most efficiently processes all the available information implying that market generated prices provide the best guidance.

The distinction between the short and the long period is made not only in terms of the state of information. In economics, but also in engineering and physical sciences, time-dependent variables are classified in groups for analytical tractability. Known variously as adiabatic approximation, enslavement principle or fast and slow dynamics, the basic procedure is to set the variables with faster speed of adjustment at their equilibrium values, that is, the differential equations capturing the short-term dynamics are set at zero to solve for the equilibrium values to focus on the dynamic system of the slower moving variables (Haken, 1983, Chapter 7).

In his distinction between the short and the long period, Marshall made fruitful use of this procedure in economics by grouping variables on the supply side. Variables that adjust fastest, for example the supply of a given quantity, relate to the very short run. Adjustment to varying demand is possible only through price movements; gradual adjustment in the quantity supplied in response to price relate to the medium term and, finally, secular adjustment of all the relevant variables is the concern of the very long run.[1]

An important textbook example is capital stock, which is treated as given in the short run. Consequently, the supply of quantities produced by the capital stock can change through variation in capacity utilization in the short run within limits, for example, through more shifts and overtime. Marshall himself paid little attention to variation in capacity utilization. He was more concerned with adjustment in 'capital intensity' through technological choice which became a hallmark of neoclassical economics. However, the capital stock itself changes over time, but relatively slowly through net investment and technical progress, making it a variable suited for longer-term analysis. It was a Marshallian heritage to assume that capacity utilization and supply is given in the short run. This implies prices are the variables that adjust in the short run in response to discrepancies between demand and supply. Production capacity and output adjust only in the long run as the capital stock changes. As a theoretical simplification, this allowed price adjustment mostly in the short run and quantity adjustment in the long run.

This traditional ordering of price and quantity variables according to their speeds of adjustment was inverted by Keynes (Leijonhufvud, 1968, Chapter 2) and Kalecki in their independent formulations of the theories of output and profit determination, respectively. Both realized that in situations of depression characterized by excess capacity and unemployment output adjusts to higher demand faster in the short run with little impact on price. As a former student of Marshall, Keynes was more hesitant. His formulation in the *General Theory* allowed price to rise faster than money wage under money illusion of workers because standard neoclassical theory needed the real wage rate to fall to make it consistent with profit maximization. This became a vulnerable aspect of his theory, suspiciously close to the neoclassical theory which he was attacking. Friedman later exploited this to argue the case against the effectiveness of fiscal policy in the long run (Friedman, 1968).

However, Kalecki, without the excess baggage of traditional theory, was more direct and convincing. He made the distinction between cost-determined and demand-determined price, the former typical of manufacturing industry with relatively constant average variable cost until full capacity utilization. With price determined by a fixed percentage as 'mark-up' on average variable cost, output and total profit is determined by the quantity demanded and sold until full capacity. Micro-economically, mark-up pricing is consistent with both empirical observations and 'satisficing' rather than precise profit maximizing behaviour by firms under incomplete information (Simon, 1979). Macro-economically, Kalecki linked mark-up to the concept of 'degree of monopoly'. It is meant to capture the extent of deviation of the market structure form from perfect competition reflected in the difference of price from marginal cost. His colleague Steindl tried to measure it by the degree of concentration in an industry (Steindl, 1952). According to another view, the degree of monopoly is reflected roughly in the share of profit because, ideally 'excess profit' should tend to zero under perfect competition. The concept of the degree of monopoly provides some useful hints, but is fraught with the difficulty of distinguishing tautology from explanation in empirical work. Nevertheless, the model of simultaneous determination of price and output, where output is demand determined through variation in capacity utilization, and price is cost determined through a given mark-up in the short period, is the most consistent explanation available for reconciling micro with macro considerations. More than anyone else, we owe it to Kalecki's path-breaking work in this respect.

The problem of disentangling short- from long-run analysis gets far more complex when we try to deal with changing capital stock over time. Growth theory which assigns a central role to the evolving stock of long-lived capital goods cannot escape several difficult problems arising from how to combine short- with long-period analysis. Mainstream economists take recourse to unhelpful, over-simplified intellectual fudge typical of aggregate neoclassical growth models.[2] A single good world is assumed in which both capital and output are the stock and flow respectively of the same commodity with the technology depicted by a smooth production function with possibilities of instantaneous costless substitution between 'capital' and labour as the two factors of production. This implies that no mistake can ever be made in choosing the profit maximizing technology or factor proportions in relation to the ruling factor prices and perfect foresight with respect to technological choice is built in by the assumption of malleable capital.[3] This gives the market mechanism full play under perfect competition to equilibrate market imbalances through factor substitution while the associated marginal productivity theory avoids uncomfortable questions of conflicting class interests and economic power over the distribution of income by making factor prices determined entirely through relative factor scarcity. Even then, the problem of deficiency in effective demand remains unresolved. It is dodged in two steps. First, it is assumed that all resources are fully employed by the perfect working of the price mechanism. Second, it is presumed that full employment saving is always automatically invested.

This sort of models, despite their unrealism, has come to dominate neoclassical academic thinking about growth in post-war years. In its intellectual defence it was often claimed that growth theory deals with the 'long run' when the price mechanism has solved problems of effective demand as well as choice of optimal technology through costless and timeless adjustments in technology reflected in the capital output ratio. The awkward question as to whether there is any point in discussing such a mythical long-run state when everything has worked out satisfactorily, without considering the persistent problem of deficient demand in the short period is left unanswered. There are many problems which economic theory cannot yet analyse satisfactorily, but the effective demand problem is not one of them thanks to Kalecki and Keynes. Hence this omission is especially unacceptable.

This paper argues that the succession of short runs afflicted typically by problems of demand leave their marks on the economy to create a path-dependent growth process. In turn this defines the path to or away from long-run equilibrium. Indeed this should have been the primary focus of enquiry of any growth theory that tries to reckon with historical time seriously.[4]

However, post-Keynesian models of growth provided some relief in so far as they posed the problem of effective demand, integrating also the influence of class distribution of income into the analysis. And yet, the problems of optimal adjustment of technology or capital stock to the evolving wage rental ratio remains unresolved and requires restricting this class of Keynesian growth models to comparisons of properties of steady-state growth with fully adjusted capital stock.[5]

The problem concerned involves enormous complexity because the specifics of a particular historical path intervene to limit the generality attempted in formal modelling. While this tension between descriptive historical analyses, emphasizing the particular path, and formal modelling exercises focusing on the general features is unavoidable, it is important to recognize rather more precisely how this path dependence arises and impacts on formal analysis. Path dependence can be visualized as a process of growth that links successive short periods. Their cumulative influence on the growth path of an economy is reflected partly in the capital stock inherited in so far as the role of 'history' can be incorporated in formally tractable macro growth theory.

The present paper is a modest attempt taking a first step in this direction. It retains many standard and unrealistic assumptions to focus on a particular problem arising from path dependence of capital stock in relation to aggregate demand. We continue to operate in a one-commodity framework to avoid problems of adjustment of technology. We analyse instead how, even in a one-good model, variations in the level of aggregate demand impact on the time structure of capital stock to exhibit some properties of path dependence.

4.2 Path-dependence

Our formal analysis is greatly simplified by assuming that investment in the economy over the relevant past has been growing at some steady compound rate, g. This growth rate might even be thought of as the trend or average growth rate with year-to-year variations in the past. But incorporating this complication makes the algebra cumbersome without adding to our understanding. We assume investment to have a gestation lag of θ periods, with investment expenditure uniformly spread over θ periods. As a convention for reckoning with discrete time, we consider the value of variables at the end of each period, for example, investment of period $(t-1)$ is investment undertaken during the entire period $(t-1)$ which is the same as investment outstanding in the beginning of the next period. Thus investment maturing (i.e., net of increase in the stock of work in progress) is given as,

$$I^*(t) = (1/\theta)[\, I(t-1) + I(t-2) + \ldots\ldots + I(t-\theta)]$$
$$= (1/\theta)\mathrm{I}(t)[\{1/(1+g)\} + \{1/(1+g)^2\} + \ldots\ldots + \{1/(1+g)^\theta\}], \text{ or}$$

$$I^*(t)/I(t) = [1/g\theta].[\{(1+g)^\theta - 1\}/(1+g)^\theta] = \mathrm{M} \quad (4.1)$$

where M is the 'correcting coefficient' for gestation lag linking effective investment at the beginning of period t, that is, $I^*(\mathrm{t})$ to investment expenditure up to the end of period $I(t-1)$.

Linear approximation of (4.1) yields,

$$M \approx 1-(g\theta/2). \qquad (4.2)$$

It would be a reasonable approximation if $g\theta$ is sufficiently small.[6] The term $(\theta/2)$ would be recognized as the Austrian 'average period of production' or the first moment of the time distribution of investment resources locked in gestation. However, when higher moments are powerful enough this approximation becomes misleading. That it plays havoc with many received wisdoms by opening up possibilities of re-switching of techniques of production, and making logical nonsense of the idea of the rate of profit or interest as the 'reward for waiting' should be well known by now.[7,8]

When this linear approximation in (4.2) is reasonable for parameter values, a further approximation may be useful to correct for non-uniform time distribution of investment cost over the lifetime of a project as,

$$M \approx 1-(zg\theta/2) \qquad (4.3)$$

with $z = 2$, implying all costs concentrated in the first period of production; $2 > z > 1$ implies costs are more concentrated in the earlier periods of production; $z = 1$ corresponds to the case of uniformly distributed investment costs, while $1 > z > 0$ implies costs concentrated towards the later periods of production.

If we assume the average working life of capital goods to be n, then the capital stock effective for production at the beginning of period t is given as the sum of effective investments of the previous n periods, that is,

$$K^*(t) = \Sigma I^*(t-j),\ j=1,\dots,n.$$

It is summed up to yield a relation between the effective stock of capital and the flow of investment at the beginning of period t as

$$K^*(t) = M.\ [\{(1+g)n-1\}/g(1+g)n].I(t) = M.N.I(t),\ N = [\{(1+g)n-1\}/g(1+g)n]. \qquad (4.4)$$

For instance, if the uniform gestation period $\theta = 3$ years, $n = 12$ years and $g = 0.15$, from Equation (4.4), $K^*(t)$ is about 4.12 times $I(t)$. Given the same values of the other parameters, for $g = 0.10$, $K^*(t)$ increases to 5.66 times $I(t)$, and 8.06 times for $g = 0.05$.

To establish a relation between the time profile of past investments and output capacity, we may assume that the increase in output capacity per unit of investment, or the incremental output-to-capital ratio, is given as $x(t)$ for each period t. Assuming x to be constant, the potential GDP or output from the supply side is given as Y_s where

$$Y_s = x\Sigma I(t\text{–}j),\ j = 1, \ldots .n, \quad \text{which yields from (4.4),}$$

$$Y_s = x.\ K^*(t) = \text{x.} = \text{x. M. N. } I(t). \tag{4.5}$$

If technical progress occurs steadily through time, each period's investment on fresh projects only would embody technical progress. Thus, looking back at Equation (4.1), only $I(t\text{–}1)$ embodies technical knowledge $x(t\text{–}1)$ of that period, whereas the remaining investments $I(t\text{–}2)$. $I(t\text{–}\mathrm{n})$ are investments committed on projects of various earlier periods. Therefore, investment maturing at time t, $I^*(t)$ involves incremental output capital ratios of various periods in the presence of continuous technical progress. These complications are short circuited by the assumption of a constant incremental capital output ratio x throughout in line with the Harrodian notion of 'neutral' technical progress (Harrod, 1942). It serves our present purpose in so far as it provides a measure of potential GDP from the supply side, Y_S. Thus, for uniform gestation period $\theta = 3$ years, $n = 12$ years and $x = 0.40$, at $g = 0.05$ $Y_s(t) = 3.24I(t)$.

The simple computation allows us to link the level of aggregate demand to the supply potential of the economy through a path-dependent time structure of the capital stock. Suppose that a stable value of the multiplier determined by saving propensity operates on the level of investment is m, such that $Y_d(t) = m\, I(t)$. Consequently, full capacity utilization requires,

$$Y_d(t) = m.\ I(t) = Y_s(t) = \text{x.MN}I(t) \tag{4.6}$$

Continuing with the preceding arithmetical example, the particular value of the multiplier required to maintain full capacity utilization is, $m = 3.24$. This means given autonomous level of investment saving propensities must be such as to satisfy this particular value of m maintaining full utilization of capacity. This exercise highlights the Keynes-Kalecki view of how short-term demand problems affect long-run potential full capacity growth path. This means the degree of capacity utilization at time t measured as $z(t) = [Y_d\,(t)/Y_s(t)] = m/x\mathrm{MN}$ which is equal to unity if,

$$m = x\mathrm{MN} \tag{4.7}$$

If saving propensities and class distribution, together determining the multiplier value *m*, fail to satisfy in (4.7) the 'technological' parameters determining the supply side of full capacity output capital ratio *x*, and the time structure of capital stock determined jointly by gestation period (M) and lifetime of capital goods (N), full capacity growth will be disturbed. This would require further consideration as to what sort of adjustments would be set in motion.

Indeterminacy of the path arising from the specific nature of the disturbance in parameter values, that is, arbitrary changes in *m*, *x*, M or N in any particular short period, force us to focus on subsequent short period adjustments without merely elaborating the properties of the long period pre-determined path of full capacity utilization. Indeed, it will be realized that there is no unique adjustment path: a particular sort of adjustment has to be picked to elaborate on a particular path. This is indeed how historical events intervene and indeterminacy sets in making any pre-determined long-run path irrelevant.

The point may be elaborated with examples. For instance, it remains a matter of speculation how the inherited capacity would adjust in response to a sudden change in either the level of investment or the multiplier that changes the level of demand Y_d in relation to the level of supply Y_s inherited from a given trajectory of past investments. If excess capacity does not exist at that point, adjustment might be postulated to take place through the rate of obsolescence determined by the depreciation and replacement policies of firms that would affect gradually the average lifetime of capital goods. However, such a change affects significantly the average lifetime of capital stock only if continued over several periods. And for this to continue, the level of demand has to persist at the particular level for a sufficiently long time so that expectations about how the new level of demand affects such depreciation and replacement policy over time also settle down. This example points to the difference in the impact of transient and persistent expectation as a typical feature of path-dependent growth. Since a long-lasting change in expectation can have quite a different effect from a transient change in expectations, it has some interesting implications. This is not a matter of complete information being available in the long run, but the degree of confidence with which expectations are held in an uncertain world. At another level it also makes clear why practical policies have to operate mostly on the demand side by stimulating public investment which is not predicated on persistent change in expectations. In contrast, stimulation of long-term private investment depends on the 'investment climate' which requires precisely such changes in policy persisting over time.

For similar reasons the role of the price mechanism in correcting imbalances through supply-side incentives looks problematic once path dependence is taken into account through the time structure of the capital stock. Unless a change in factor price, for example a lower real wage, is expected to be persistent over several short periods, it would not induce factor substitution. Moreover, factor substitution in this model is not at the intensive but at the extensive margin. It would appear as the Ricardian closure rule according to which the marginal machine (land) satisfies the zero profit (rent) condition to determine the lifetime of the machines (n) in use which in turn affects the time structure of capital. As in the so-called vintage models, at a lower real wage rate the margin would be extended to lengthen the average life of the capital stock, which would increase the productive capacity from the supply side. This might generate more excess capacity and unemployment if the lower wage results in lower effective demand in a regime of wage-led growth, and the profit maximizing solution of extending the margin would exacerbate instead of correcting the economic imbalances through factor substitution.[9] Indeed, the market mechanism might fail even more dramatically over time, as the mismatch between aggregate demand and inherited capacity widens, if the investment climate deteriorates on account of persistent and high excess capacity (Harrod, 1939). Similarly, a lower real wage would tend to reduce immediate consumption demand, but might increase investment demand through higher profitability not only if the lower real wage is expected to be a persistent change, but investment is instantaneously stimulated sufficiently to overcome the shortfall in demand. It is a logical possibility but implausible in so far as investment climate improves slowly (Bhaduri and Marglin, 1990).

From these examples it should be clear that path-dependent growth would allow for many possibilities contrary to conventional policy prescriptions, due to a shortfall in aggregate demand in a particular short period. Oversimplified production-function-based analysis as an expository model becomes not merely a limited but a misleadingly dangerous device because it prevents us from asking these questions. Assumptions like smooth capital labour substitution and full utilization of all resources and no serious attempt to incorporate path dependence through at least the time structure of capital allow simple manipulation while creating the illusion of predictability through simple formal manipulations. At the logical level, it refuses to recognize the logical inconsistencies of neoclassical capital and distribution theory (Sraffa, 1960; Harcourt, 1969). At the political level it misleadingly exaggerates both the predictability and the efficacy of the market mechanism and serves mostly as a convenient ideological device, banishing inconvenient questions about the functioning of market capitalism.

Notes

1. This is not exactly the classification Marshall used, but corresponds to the main outline of his argument.
2. The framework for neoclassical growth models was set by Solow (1956) and Swan (1956), and continues with more recent models of intertemporal optimization models of growth (e.g., Cass, 1965; Koopmans,1965) and endogenous growth (e.g., Barro and Sala-i-Martin, 1995).
3. Robinson (1956) in particular faced these problems as soon as she tried to formulate her ideas on growth, emphasizing both the non-malleable structure of capital and the role of expectations. Hicks (1973) tried an Austrian capital theoretic alternative route for approaching the same problem.
4. See Bhaduri (1985) for a simple exposition of some of these ideas. Irreversibility of time and the cumulative influence of 'small probability events' through strong positive feedbacks over time results in path dependence and increasing returns (e.g., Arthur, 1994; Kaldor, 1978). This paper is concerned only with path dependence arising from the time structure of the capital stock, which is analytically more tractable.
5. Robinson (1956) and Pasinetti (1962), for instance, based their analyses on comparisons of steady-state growth paths.
6. Reddaway (1962) uses this formula to estimate the increment in construction in progress as a proportion of investment. This way of dealing with the problem of the time structure of capital stock without a subjective time rate of discount is due to Kalecki and Rakowski (1964), developed further by Bhaduri (1968; 1972).
7. Samuelson (1966). Bhaduri (1970) uses increment in construction in progress associated with different gestation lags for interpreting physically the problem of reswitching of techniques of production.
8. This is a restatement of Harrod's (1939) original growth equations, as can be seen by dividing both sides by the capital stock, but taking explicitly in account in this formulation the time structure of the capital stock.
9. Implied in Malinvaud's (1977) distinction between profit maximizing 'classical unemployment' and demand constrained 'Keynesian unemployment' which was analysed with a neoclassical aggregate production function. It was reformulated as a vintage model and criticized for its unwarranted conclusions in Bhaduri (1983).

References

*This is a thoroughly revised and extended version of 'A simple model of path dependent growth and effective demand', in N. Salvadori, C. Gehrke (eds), *Keynes, Sraffa and the Criticism of Neoclassical Theory*, New York and London: Routledge, 2011. The paper is also extended to bring into focus Kalecki's path-breaking contributions to the range of issues discussed here.

Arthur, W.B. (1994) *Increasing Returns and Path Dependence in the Economy*, Ann Arbor: Michigan University Press.
Barro, R. and X. Sala-i-Martin (1995) *Economic Growth*, New York: McGraw-Hill.
Bhaduri, A. (1968) 'An aspect of project selection: durability vs. construction period', *Economic Journal*, 78: 344–348.
Bhaduri, A. (1970) 'A physical analogue of the reswitching problem', *Oxford Economic Papers*, 22(2): 148–155.
Bhaduri, A. (1972) 'Unwanted amortization funds: a mathematical treatment', *Economic Journal*, 80: 674–677.
Bhaduri, A. (1983) 'Real Wages and Unemployment with Effective and Notional Demand for Labour', *Review of Radical Political Economics*, 35(2):166–182.
Bhaduri, A. (1985) 'Capitalist accumulation in logical and historical time', *Economic and Political Weekly*, Special Number, 1903–1907. (Originally published in *Economie Appliquee*, 1985, no. 2. Special volume in memory of Joan Robinson.)
Bhaduri, A. and S. Marglin (1990) 'Unemployment and the real wage: the economic basis for contesting political ideologies', *Cambridge Journal of Economics*, 14: 375–393.
Cass, D. (1965) 'Optimal growth in an aggregate model of Capital Accumulation', *Review of Economic Studies*, 32: 233–240.
Friedman, M. (1968) 'The role of monetary policy', *American Economic Review*, 58: 1–17.
Haken, H. (1983) *Synergetics*, Berlin: Springer.
Harcourt, G.C. (1969) *Cambridge Controversies in the Theory of Capital*, Cambridge: Cambridge University Press.
Harrod, R. (1939) 'An essay in dynamic theory', *Economic Journal*, 49: 14–33.
Harrod, R. (1942) *Towards Dynamic Economics*, London: Macmillan.
Hicks, J.R. (1973) *Capital and Time*, Oxford: Clarendon Press.
Kaldor, N. (1978) 'The irrelevance of equilibrium economics', *Economic Journal*, 1972, reprinted in his *Further Essays on Economic Theory*, London: Duckworth.
Kalecki, M. and M. Rakowski (1964) 'Generalized formula for the efficiency of investment' in A. Nove and A. Zauberman (eds) *Studies in the Theory of Reproduction and Prices*, Warsaw: Polish Scientific Publishers.
Koopmans, T.C. (1965) 'On the concept of optimal economic growth', in *The Econometric Approach to Development Planning*, Amsterdam: North Holland (for Pontifica Academy).
Leijonhufvud (1968) – See p. 3
Malinvaud, E. (1977) *The Theory of Unemployment Reconsidered*, New York: John Wiley and Sons.
Pasinetti, L. (1962) 'Rate of profit and income distribution in relation to the rate of economic growth', *Review of Economic Studies*, 29: 267–279.
Reddaway, W.B. (1962) *The Development of the Indian Economy*, London: Allen and Unwin.
Robinson, J. (1956) *The Accumulation of Capital*, London: Macmillan.
Samuelson, P. (1966) 'A summing up', *Quarterly Journal of Economics*, 80: 568–583.
Simon (1979) – See p. 3.

Solow, R. (1956) 'A contribution to the theory of economic growth', *Quarterly Journal of Economics*, 70: 65–94.
Sraffa, P. (1960) *Production of Commodities by Means of Commodities: Prelude to a Critique of Economic Theory*. Cambridge: Cambridge University Press.
Steindl, J. (1952) *Maturity and Stagnation of American Capitalism*, New York: Monthly Review Press (reprint).
Swan, T. (1956) 'Economic growth and capital accumulation', *Economic Record*, 32: 343–361.

5
Kaleckian Traverse, Socialist Planning and Hayekian Objections

Roni Demirbag and Joseph Halevi

This chapter will discuss the relations between Kalecki's macrodynamics and the method of the Traverse. It will be argued that outside the case of a deep depression all short- and long-term macroeconomic adjustments should be thought of in a Kalecki-Kaldor-Lowe type Traverse context. Indeed it was Nicholas Kaldor who developed in 1938 a fully fledged Traverse approach well before the coinage of the term by John Hicks in 1965 (Kaldor, 1938). We will argue that the only meaningful institutional, hence policy, framework of the Traverse approach is socialist planning as conceived by Kalecki himself (Kalecki, 1962, 1986). Hayek's views are similar to the conclusions that we draw from the traverse analysis. However, Hayek rejects the proposals for economic planning and instead insists on the ability of the market mechanism to achieve the necessary structural adjustment in order to achieve sectoral balance. The essay will discuss the Hayekian objections to socialist planning and will conclude that some form of socialist planning remains the only viable option.

5.1 The Traverse explained

The Traverse method deals with the structural changes to which an economy is subjected with or without technical transformations. The central feature of the method is the heterogeneity of production between capital and consumption goods (Kaldor, 1938; Hicks, 1965). The more advanced case, put forward by Adolph Lowe (1952, 1955, 1976), is based on a heterogeneity in the capital goods sector itself. The capital goods sector is divided between a machine tools sector producing capital goods for itself as well as an intermediate branch which produces equipment exclusively for the consumption goods sector. Under these circumstances, if the economy is assumed to be in equilibrium or at a stationary/steady state, any significant change, whether caused by demographics or by technological mutations, will entail complex processes whose directions and outcomes cannot be determined beforehand. Hence the Traverse method breaks up the determinacy which has characterized most economic theorizing of either classical or neoclassical orientation. Furthermore, in the discontinuous context in which the Traverse method is set, the identification of possible outcomes can be obtained only by imposing upon the system behaviour that Adolph Lowe called 'goal oriented'.

A clear example is Lowe's treatment of a sudden increase in population or of a once-over labour-saving technical change in an otherwise fully employed stationary economy. For the system to absorb the sudden increase in the effective supply of labour (or an increase in population) available for work it is necessary that new productive capacity be created. The same is true as far as the employees displaced by labour-saving innovations are concerned. Where will the new capacity come from? Physically it should originate from decisions to withhold replacement capital goods to the intermediate investment sector in order to expand the primary equipment sector up to the level required to produce directly, and indirectly via the intermediate sector, the capital stock required to absorb the increased labour force (whether in the wake of a once-over increase in population or following labour-savings innovations). Thus, initially, through the reduction of gross investment flows to the intermediate sector, less capital goods will be made available to the consumption goods sector. Indeed, the transitional phase ought to start with workers being shifted from the intermediate to the primary equipment sector. Meanwhile, as in the next stage the consumption goods sector will receive less machinery from the intermediate sector, the supply of consumption goods will shrink and some of the employees working in that sector will be shifted to the primary equipment sector as it expands its own capacity. Here a guided, planned process is assumed. In the build phase, needed to absorb the increment in the labour force, real wages will decline since prices of consumption goods will have to rise in the light of a reduced supply.

But let us drop the guided process and consider a natural market reaction to the expansion of available labour separating, for the time being, the increase in population from the labour displacement caused by technical change. We should be able to find a trajectory where capacity liberation and the ensuing sectoral shifts should start from below as a consequence of price-driven phenomena. It may be assumed that the appearance of surplus labour will negatively impact existing money wages. If, however, competition leads to a proportional fall in consumption goods prices, nothing will change as already pointed out by Kalecki before the Second World War (Kalecki, 1939). Hence, in order to free up capacity by means of a decentralized mechanism, it is necessary that real wages fall, thereby causing a fall in effective demand for consumption goods with the emergence of unused capacity in that same sector. In a market-based economy, the fall in real wages is possible if oligopolistic conditions prevail so that prices are 'rigid'. Yet the unused capacity arising from such 'rigidity' is a passive phenomenon and does not connote any firm's strategy to move in the direction required to shift capacity and accumulation to the primary equipment sector. The most likely outcome is that unused capacity – arising in the consumption goods sector from either additional supply of labour (impacting on real wages) or from technical labour displacement – will be propagated through the system via the fall in effective demand, first for consumption goods and then for investment goods. Interestingly, whichever way prices behave they are bound to generate wrong signals since what is needed is the expansion of investment activity in the primary equipment sector independently of current demand.

This is, in essence, what the Traverse is all about. In the heydays of neoclassical growth theories, mainstream economists did try to come to terms with the issue and a whole literature on shiftable and non-shiftable capital sprang up. One of the most comprehensive endeavours undertaken by neoclassical economics in that direction was a symposium on growth theory hosted by the *Journal of Political Economy* in 1969. Virtually all the papers attempted unsuccessfully to fit standard neoclassical production functions in non-malleable capital models.

While traverse conditions exist in different social systems and stages of development, the method outlined above is best set in a context where the 'economy possesses a capital equipment which more or less matches the existing labor force, and therefore it generates a rather high income per capita provided that its resources are fully utilised' (Kalecki, 1976, p. 20). It will now be shown that there are two kinds of transition. One pertains to the movement towards full employment and another belongs to the longer run. Kaldor's 1938 paper connects the two phases, but its best insights relate to the first type of transition. The evaluation of the longer-run approach will be combined with Kalecki's views about the working of the capitalist system.

5.2 The short-run Kaldorian Traverse

The 1938 paper by Kaldor is remarkable in that one can find Marxian, Wicksellian, Austrian and also Keynesian influences. Furthermore, it anticipates both Harrod's type dynamics and the Hicksian method of 1965. However, its focus is practical. Given the Depression ruling at the time, the paper asks what is entailed in attempting to bring the economy to full employment and whether or not such a state is likely to be stable. The economy is formed by two Marxian sectors of production: capital and consumption goods. Machinery is not transferable between either of the two sectors. The short period is defined along Marshall's and Keynes's lines where the stock of capital is given. Unused capacities prevail in both sectors but, crucially, not in the same degree. Kaldor also assumed that, at full capacity, the stock of capital would more or less match the existing labour force. Yet in the light of different rates of capacity utilization, full employment cannot be defined only in terms of the aggregate level of real income. Instead, full employment requires a certain division of real income between capital and consumption goods. We can now explore the dynamics of the short period in a more straightforward way than Kaldor's examination. It suffices to assume fixed coefficients for each sector and two different rates of capacity utilization. We keep Kaldor's assumption that government investment policies towards full employment are in place.

With different rates of unused capacity, the likelihood that both sectors will jointly reach full employment is next to nil. Thus, if full capacity in the capital goods sector is attained first, the remaining unused capacity in the consumption goods sector signals: (a) that unemployment is still prevailing, (b) that additional investment demand will be weak since the consumption goods sector would have little interest in placing new investment orders with the capital goods industries. Under these conditions investment plans in the capital goods sector will also be negatively affected.

Two possible ways out exist which are not considered by Kaldor in that paper but may be gathered from the post-1945 writings of Kalecki. The first consists in that it is economically and technically possible to bring the consumption goods sector to full capacity and full employment by reducing the prices of consumption goods. However, there is no internal mechanism for this to happen. The aggregate level of profit is determined by the value of output of capital goods which, in this model, is equal to the value of investment and by capitalists' consumption that, for our purposes, can be considered negligible as a proportion of profits. The sectoral levels of profits are therefore mainly determined by that part of the value of aggregate investment output accruing to the capital goods sector and by the part accruing to the consumption goods sector. From Kalecki's use of Marx's schemes of reproduction, we know that the wage bill in the capital goods sector is, if fully spent, equal to the profits in the consumption goods sector. It follows that the value of the part of investment output accruing to the consumption goods sector is equal to the sector's profits and to the value of the wage bill in the capital goods sector. Thus a fall in consumption goods prices will not increase by one cent the sector's profit. It will not therefore induce firms in that sector to undertake new investment plans. Quite the opposite is more likely.

The second way out would be to push for an increase in unit wages, thereby expanding the wage bill in the capital goods sector, leading to the rise of monetary profits in the consumption goods sector. This can just be a sort of profit illusion because investment has already been decided so that the part accruing to the consumption goods sector is given. Hence the increase in unit wages will entail an increase in prices of capital goods. But this profit inflation can be conducive to expand plans in capital goods production since it is accompanied by the attainment of full capacity output in both sectors. A third solution lies in government expenditure targeting the consumption goods sector by expanding employment and the wage bill of the public sector.

Alternatively, if full capacity is reached first in the consumption goods sector, any further increase in real output and employment will have to take place in the capital goods sector while consumption goods prices will rise on account of the expansion in employment, and hence in the wage bill, of the capital goods sector.

5.3 The longer run

Kaldor's wording of the dynamic process is somewhat confused terminologically, but the way in which he set up the problem of stability and full employment by dividing between the short run – where changes occur through the differential variations in the respective sectoral rates of capacity utilization – and the longer run – where changes depend on sectoral rates of capital accumulation – allows us to grasp the essential macroeconomic features of capitalist dynamics. In this context the longer run is defined as the phase in which capital accumulation comes into being so that the stock of capital is itself expanding. From this perspective, an economy where normal capacity utilization is reached first in the capital goods sector is essentially an economy with a limited ability to accumulate. The opposite is the case whenever full capacity in the consumption goods sector is reached first. To gauge whether or not the economy is in a weak or strong position regarding potential real capital accumulation, it is necessary to evaluate the position of full employment attained in the short run with (a) the existence of labour reserves in other branches of the economy and (b) the growth rate of population. In advanced economic systems hidden labour reserves are limited, although in the last decades they have been rising because of the forced shift to part-time employment. Population growth is null in Europe and negative in Japan, while hovering around 1 per cent per annum in North America, mostly the result of immigration.

In the circumstances outlined above, an economy which, in the short run, reaches full capacity only in the capital goods sectors is in fact poised to adjust more easily to long-run full employment conditions. Yet this would mean that the level of investment will move at a much slower pace than during the short run when investment acts as a spending multiplier and helped bring the capital goods sectors to full capacity. From Kalecki's macroeconomics we know that profits stem from investment; indeed under no savings out of wages and no consumption out of profits, investment generates the whole amount of business's profits. It follows that a quasi-static investment dynamics implies static profits and negative future expectations. Furthermore it implies, this time as in Kaldor's 1956 adjustment process, a systematic fall in the share of profits in national income which, under the prevailing oligopolistic conditions, is unlikely to materialize. The economy will relapse again into a state of unused capacity and unemployment. Thus adapting the productive system to long-term full employment is possible mainly under socialist planning as it will be argued in the next section.

Let us now discuss the case where the consumption goods sector reaches full capacity while the capital goods one still exhibits unused capacity. As in the previous example, it is assumed that short-run full employment has been attained and that population growth is negligible. Under these conditions, the persistence of unused capacity in the capital goods sector will entail a structural impasse in the capital goods sector. The failure to achieve full capacity while the economy is at full employment will bring about a fall in the sector's internal investment with the consequent rise in unemployment. This will also reduce demand and capacity utilization in the consumption goods sector.

5.4 The socialist context of the advanced Traverse process

The contemporary capitalist economy has the technical capacity to attain full employment in the short run. Such an advantage becomes, however, problematic when we move from the short-run utilization of equipment to the longer run, since this would most likely entail a transition to a lower rate of accumulation and profits (were full employment to be maintained). Interestingly, both Michał Kalecki (1954, 1958, 1962, 1971, 1986) and Paul Sweezy (1968) saw the validity of socialist planning in the fact that in a socialist system the economy is not wedded to particular monopolistic formations and profit rates, being thereby capable of undertaking the process of transition to a lower rate of growth and accumulation. The Kalecki-Sweezy views are relevant because in past decades the contest between existing capitalism and the then-existing socialist countries was, generally, seen in terms of which camp would achieve the highest growth rates, produce more steel, chemicals and so on. This superficial attitude simply reflected the fact that the countries where Communist parties rose to power – from the USSR to China, with the sole exception of what today is the Czech Republic – were, in different degrees, largely agrarian and, in almost all cases, underdeveloped economies. Kalecki and Sweezy evaluated the social viability of the capitalist economy in its own context related not to its ascent phase but to the mature stage characterized by the level attained by the stock of capital due to past accumulation.

In Kalecki's work the multiplier works through the relation between investment and profits. The level of output is, in turn, related to profits via the share of profits in output. This share contains and is determined by the oligopolistic elements entering into the cost-wage relations. Thus a fall in investment triggers a fall in profits and in national income, impacting negatively on employment. In this context Kalecki (1971, p. 97) wrote:

> In order to bring into focus the nature of this process in a capitalist economy, it is useful to consider what the effect of a reduction of investment in a socialist system would be. The workers released from the production of investment goods would be employed in consumption goods industries – The increased supply of these goods would be absorbed by means of a reduction in their prices. Since profits of the socialist industries would be equal to investment, prices would have to be reduced to the point where the decline in profits would be equal to the fall in the value of investment. In other words, full employment would be maintained through the reduction of prices in relations to costs. In the capitalist system, however, the price cost relationship (...) is maintained and profits fall by the same amount as investment plus capitalists' consumption through a reduction in output and employment.

The Kalecki-Sweezy analysis of the structural conditions of economic maturity, analysed from Marx's schemes of reproduction in the context of the oligopolistic stage of capitalism, brings out the fact that in such a system changes in national income and employment are tied to investment, whereas in an advanced economy they ought to follow changes in productive capacity. It is worth quoting Kalecki again (1962, p. 40):

> If investment remained constant while the stock of fixed capital expanded prices would be reduced or wages raised. In this way the demand for consumption goods would increase in accordance with the expansion of the stock or capital.

It is important to observe that the difference in the way employment is determined defines the economic difference between capitalism and socialism when the productive forces are fully developed.

Contrary to the approach taken by more recent writers (Lavoie and Ramírez-Gastón, 1997), the full employment Traverse in Lowe, Kalecki and Sweezy is the only meaningful way to identify the conditions for transition to a new growth regime. Discarding the full-employment assumption leaves traverse analysis devoid of any determinate conclusions. The full-employment Traverse is conceivable in turn mainly in a socialist, centrally planned system. In this way Kalecki and Sweezy, while connecting employment to investment and its impact on effective demand in a capitalist economy, separate long-term full employment from aggregate demand policies.

Both Kalecki and Sweezy only outlined the transition to the new state of full employment following a fall in investment in the case of Kalecki and upon reaching a state of maturity in the case of Sweezy. When we look at the step-by-step conditions necessary to complete successfully the full-employment traverse and place those conditions in the context of an economy with heterogeneous capital goods, we must rely, at least, on the approach taken by Adolph Lowe. When the structure of production is characterized by several layers of capital goods, most of them either non-shiftable or movable only within their own areas of production, the transition to a lower growth rate will most likely entail the formation of unused capacities. As an example let us take Lowe's model where the output of the primary equipment sector is used to feed both self reinvestment and to provide machinery to the secondary equipment sector, whose output is the equipment producing consumption goods. Hence the output of the secondary equipment sector becomes the investment good for the consumption goods sector. If, in this context, the adjustment to the new, lower full-employment growth rate requires a significant shift in the composition of total production of capital goods (equal to total investment) towards the secondary equipment sector, the economy may well experience an expansion in the output of capital goods for the consumption goods sector in excess of the full employment level of demand (Halevi, 1998).

The more complex and heterogeneous is the structure of production, especially at the level of technologies and capital goods with the production of the latter cascading on further sectors thereby swelling their output capacity, the more likely will be the formation of unused capacity for structural reasons. Under these circumstances, keeping full employment during the transition period and the convergence to the new full-employment growth becomes a multidimensional exercise in planning not just the distribution of investment between the different sectors but also the distribution and mothballing of unused capacity. There are no fixed criteria for such policies. This should be enough for the Hayekian economist to be horrified and urging policy makers to let 'the market' decide precisely because the economy is too complex to be steered successfully.

5.5 Hayek's objections to planning

We have argued that socialist planning is the only meaningful policy framework that stems from traverse analysis. Achieving full employment is relatively simple. Maintaining it in a capitalist institutional setting is difficult and is inherently unstable. A similar conclusion, as far as the stability of full employment is concerned, was reached by Hayek. Even though Hayek did not deal with the issue of traverse in any detail (Garrison, 1994, p. 113), his approach to production as a process can be viewed as an alternative way of conceptualizing the structural change resulting from the traverse. Hayek treats production as a process that involves land and labour, which are in turn combined together to produce consumption goods (Hayek, 1935/1967). The different sectors in Kalecki and Lowe's framework correspond to the different stages of production in Hayek's approach. Capital goods will be the first stage of the production process, whereas consumption goods will be the final stage, and the various stages in between constitute the intermediate goods sector. Hayek's main concern was to do with the structural adjustment of the economy resulting from changes in the interest rate (ibid.). The adjustment of the economy would, according to Hayek, fundamentally depend on the reasons for the change in the interest rate. If the interest rate shifts due to changes in inter-temporal preferences of individuals, then Hayek argues the economy will continue in the path of growth and full employment. If the interest rate is deliberately kept below the equilibrium rate by the monetary authorities, the eventual outcome will be increased unemployment. For example, Hayek stated:

> The true, though untestable, explanation for extensive unemployment ascribes it to a discrepancy between the distribution of labour (and the other factors of production) among industries... and the distribution of demand among their products. This discrepancy is caused by a distortion of the system of relative prices and wages.... The cause of unemployment, in other words, is a deviation from the equilibrium prices and wages that would establish themselves given a free market and stable money. But we can never know beforehand at what structure of relative prices and wages such an equilibrium would establish itself. (Hayek, 1979, p. 8)

As the above quotation makes it clear, Hayek was aware of the structural adjustments that are needed for the maintenance of full employment in the capitalist economy. Furthermore, Hayek has explicitly stated that he does not dispute the claims that increasing employment via government policy is possible (O'Driscoll, 1977, p. 114). What is disputed by Hayek is the instability of such levels of employment because of the structural imbalances in the economy, which is in direct agreement with our analysis of the traverse. However, his optimistic view of the market's ability to adjust is untenable and must be rejected. As Dow has pointed out, 'neo-Austrian theory does not provide a logical basis for an economist to advocate anything. It is only the quite separate confidence in market forces which justifies their policy statements' (1985, p. 240).

Hayek's defence of the market as a mechanism to achieve the structural adjustments necessary for sectoral balances fundamentally relies on his attack against the limitations of planning as an alternative framework to maintain sectoral balance. Two main arguments against planning can be identified from Hayek's work, one pertaining to the dispersed knowledge in a complex economic system and the other based on the principle of non-coercion in economic exchange. Effective economic planning is neither possible because of the nature of dispersed knowledge, nor is it desirable because it necessarily involves coercion of individuals. We argue that Hayek's claim that decentralized markets deal with dispersed knowledge more efficiently than planned economies is untenable. Hayek's concept of spontaneous order that is used to support the superiority of decentralized markets is indeterminate. Furthermore, Hayek's knowledge argument (or epistemic argument as it has been commonly labelled) is only valid for certain kinds of knowledge and cannot be generalized to all forms of knowledge. This is particularly important in relation to structural analysis as certain types of knowledge, namely the balance between different sectors of the economy, is more suitable for centralization than other types of knowledge. The non-coercion or what we may call the liberty argument is equally problematic for Hayek and his followers. We argue that some level of coercion is unavoidable both in the market and planning systems. Hence Hayek's attempt to juxtapose capitalist markets with liberty and socialist planning with coercion is misleading.

5.6 Epistemic argument

According to Hayek (1945/1948), the existence of inarticulate tacit knowledge that cannot be codified and centralized poses an insurmountable obstacle to any attempts to plan centrally an economic system. Furthermore, the spontaneous order arising from the market enables the most effective use of the tacit knowledge that cannot be made available to any single individual (ibid.). Hayek's epistemic argument has been so convincing that most commentators have conceded the importance of the market mechanism (Kley, 1994; Hodgson, 1999).

Hayek argued that, unlike a centrally planned economy, in a market economy prices perform the role of disseminating information to individual economic agents. Hayek went further and argued that the main problem with economics concerned the dispersion of information that is never completely given to any one individual. Hayek argues:

> The peculiar character of the problem of a rational economic order is determined precisely by the fact that the knowledge of the circumstances of which we must make use never exists in concentrated or integrated form but solely as the dispersed bits of incomplete and frequently contradictory knowledge which all the separate individuals possess. The economic problem of society is thus not merely a problem of how to allocate 'given' resources – if 'given' is taken to mean given to a single mind which deliberately solves the problem set by these 'data.' It is rather a problem of how to secure the best use of resources known to any of the members of society, for ends whose relative importance only these individuals know. Or, to put it briefly,

it is a problem of the utilization of knowledge which is not given to anyone in its totality. (1945/1948, pp. 77–78)

This reinterpretation of the economic problem marks the beginning of Hayek's famous epistemic attack on the possibility of central planning. As many authors have pointed out, the argument is strong even if it was initially not given the credit it deserved (O'Neill, 1998, p. 132). Given the importance of dispersed knowledge, Hayek differentiates between three types of systems that are different on the basis of who decides on the plans. The first are the centrally planned economies. The second Hayek labelled as 'competition' that 'means de-centralised planning by many separate persons' (1945/1948, p. 79). The third, Hayek rather dismissingly labels as the 'halfway house between the two ... the delegation of planning to organized industries, or, in other words, monopolies' (ibid.). The most efficient of these systems, according to Hayek, will be the one that takes full advantage of the dispersed knowledge. Hence, Hayek's criterion of efficiency is explicitly related to the full use of the dispersed information that cannot be codified and centralized in any individual or institution (see below). This form of knowledge that cannot be codified is the concept of tacit knowledge put forward by Michael Polanyi (1958/1962).

Tacit knowledge is such knowledge that cannot be codified and generalized. In essence, tacit knowledge highlights the localized aspects of knowledge that do not lend themselves to easy transmission via codification (Polanyi 1958/1962). In other words, it is the kind of knowledge that individuals cannot pass on readily. It is because of this tacit knowledge that Polanyi pointed out 'we can know more than we can tell' (1967, p. 4). The implications of this kind of knowledge to economic planning signify that it is not possible for a central authority to collect this type of information even if we assume away all the rigidities of such a centrally planned economy. Hence, even if individual agents are willing and active participants in the planning process, by the very nature of tacit knowledge they are unable to assist the central planner in informing them of locally unique knowledge. It is because of the existence of tacit knowledge, according to Hayek, that we need a decentralized mechanism that will allow us to take full advantage of the 'knowledge of the particular circumstances of time and place'.

Hayek argued that the price mechanism of the market effectively resolves this dispersed knowledge problem by transmitting information to individuals so that they may adjust their actions accordingly.

The informational role of prices is of crucial importance for the market mechanism. Indeed, Hayek referred to the price system as a 'telecommunication' system. According to Hayek:

> The most significant fact about this system is the economy of knowledge with which it operates, or how little the individual participants need to know in order to be able to take the right action. In abbreviated form, by a kind of symbol, only the most essential information is passed on and passed on only to those concerned. It is more than a metaphor to describe the price system as a kind of machinery for registering change, or a system of telecommunications which enables individual producers to watch merely the movement of a few pointers, as an engineer might watch the hands of a few dials, in order to adjust their activities to changes of which they may never know more than is reflected in the price movement. (1940/1948, pp.186–187)

In order to prove the superiority of decentralized markets in effectively dealing with the knowledge problem, Hayek introduced the concept of 'order' as an alternative to the concept of equilibrium in economics. According to Hayek:

> Economists usually ascribe the order which competition produces as an equilibrium – a somewhat unfortunate term, because such an equilibrium presupposes that the facts have already all been discovered and competition therefore has ceased. The concept of an 'order' which, at least for the discussion of problems of economic policy, I prefer to that of equilibrium has the advantage that we can meaningfully speak about an order being approached to various degrees, and that order can be preserved throughout a process of change. While an economic equilibrium never really exists, there is some justification for asserting that the kind of order of which our theory describes an ideal type, is approached in a high degree' (1978, p. 184).

Employing the concept of order, Hayek argued that spontaneous orders are more productive and hence superior to deliberately designed orders, which he calls 'organizations'. Moving away from equilibrium to a concept of order does not necessarily provide a solid framework for Hayek. There is a major problem with Hayek's theory of spontaneous order. The spontaneous order that is supposed to materialize from decentralized decisions of individuals within the economy is indeterminate (Demirbag, 2011, Chapter 3). As many observers of Hayek have observed, the concept of spontaneous order on which Hayek relies fails to provide a method of demarcating between order and disorder. For example, as pointed out by Kley '[e]ven a depressed market economy is, on Hayek's account, still a spontaneous order' (1994, pp. 68–69). In order to avoid being charged with a natural fallacy, Hayek justified capitalist economic systems according to the positive 'effects on the discovery, preservation, transmission and coordination of knowledge, and for preserving liberty' (Caldwell and Reiss, 2006, p. 364). However, because he failed to provide a framework for identifying order and disorder, it is not possible to gauge the performance of the economy given that he openly acknowledged that spontaneous economic outcomes are not necessarily positive (Hayek, 1979/1982, p. 62). This is also primarily the reason why we stated above that the only meaningful condition in traverse analysis is the full employment one, contrary to Lavoie and Ramírez-Gastón.

In order to avoid the issues arising from indeterminacy, Hayek appealed to empirical verification as a way of demonstrating the superiority of spontaneous orders over deliberately designed orders. However, the empirical verifiability of this claim can only be applicable if we remain strictly within Hayek's proposed dichotomy between a completely centralized economy and spontaneous market processes (Kley, 1994, pp. 202–203). Once we recognize the existence of a variety of combinations of what Hayek calls 'organizations' and 'spontaneous orders', the problem shifts from being centred around the options between the two opposing systems, and the question becomes: by using the dispersed and inarticulate information more efficiently, what forms of combinations between 'organizations' and 'spontaneous orders' lead to higher output? Hayek's framework is inadequate to answer such a question. The strength of Hayek's argument against central planning, 'depends in part on the implausibility of assuming that all knowledge could be centralised upon some particular planning agency' (O'Neill, 1998, p. 132). The strength of Hayek's argument against central planning does not imply that it is also an equally strong argument in favour of decentralized markets.

Furthermore, Hayek conflates tacit knowledge with all other forms of knowledge, which if true would make any kind of planning impossible. There are different types of knowledge, of which tacit knowledge is only one part (O'Neill, 1998). The issue is identifying the types of knowledge that are easily decoded and centralized. The information pertaining to sectoral balance in the traverse analysis represents the type of knowledge that is conducive for centralization. The key point to emphasize is that only the minimum information required for the balance between different sectors needs to be centralized.

There are various proposed models of decentralized socialist economies, which attempt to address Hayek's criticism. For example, Adaman and Devine (1994, 1996) recognize the importance of tacit knowledge as an obstacle for central planning. Their proposal for participatory planning is an attempt to address the issues arising from the existence of tacit knowledge (ibid.). O'Neill also recognizes the strength of Hayek's epistemic argument against central planning (1998, Chapter 10). However, O'Neill argues that Hayek's epistemic argument does not apply to decentralized workers-owned cooperative economies (ibid.). Irrespective of the differences of the various models, the problem of coordination is resolved by a centralized mechanism that emphasizes cooperation rather than decentralized competition, which essentially is the result arising from traverse analysis. In the final section we will discuss the problems of coercion that is frequently raised by Hayek and his followers.

5.7 Freedom from coercion

The Austrian defence of decentralized markets does not just rely on the information transmission function. Hayek and other Austrians insist on the importance of non-coercive transactions between economic agents. Restricting price movements entails a coercion that is deemed unacceptable by libertarians (Rothbard, 1982). However, if non-coercive exchange is going to be defended, then what constitutes coercion needs to be properly defined. Hayek's notion of coercion is fundamentally ambiguous (Kukathas, 1989, pp. 149–153). For example, according to Hayek the owner of a spring in the desert who refuses to sell his water or demands an exceedingly high price because of his monopolistic control over 'indispensable supply' is involved in coercion (1960, p. 133). As pointed out by Hamowy, this appears to pose an 'insurmountable problem—what constitutes a "reasonable" price? By "reasonable" Hayek might mean "competitive". But how is it possible to determine what the competitive price is in the absence of competition?' Most importantly, 'at what price does the contract alter its nature and become an instance of "coercion"?' (1971/2005, p. 209).

The key method of dealing with issues of power is to resort to the competitive nature of markets. For example, Hayek argued that

> to believe that power which is thus conferred on the state is merely transferred to it from others is erroneous. It is a power which is newly created and which in a competitive society nobody possesses. So long as property is divided among many owners, none of them

> acting independently has exclusive power to determine the income and position of particular people – nobody is tied to him except by the fact that he may offer better terms than anybody else. (Hayek, 1944/2007, pp. 135–136)

As pointed out above, Hayek recognizes the problem that monopoly might create for the individuals within the market. Accordingly, he incorporated the behaviour of monopoly as coercion under certain conditions. Hayek argued:

> A monopolist could exercise true coercion, however, if he were, say, the owner of a spring in an oasis. Let us say that other persons settled there on the assumption that water would always be available at a reasonable price and then found, perhaps because a second spring dried up, that they had no choice but to do whatever the owner of the spring demanded of them if they were to survive: here would be a clear case of coercion. One could conceive of a few other instances where a monopolist might control an essential commodity on which people were completely dependent. But unless a monopolist is in a position to withhold an indispensable supply, he cannot exercise coercion, however unpleasant his demands may be for those who rely on his services. (1960, p. 136)

This raises an important question regarding what constitutes indispensable supply. Burczak discusses the problem of coercion in relation to the asymmetric relationship between capitalists and workers. According to Burczak (1995), in order to avoid coercion in the labour market, Hayek must assume full employment. However, absence of full employment implies that capitalists can deprive workers of an 'indispensable supply'; the means of production (Burczak, 1995, p. 175). There is no coherent answer to this problem from within the existing Austrian framework because the problem remains unrecognized. Power relations and their influence on economic outcomes is one of the weakest points of the Austrian perspective (Palermo, 2007).

Caldwell challenges Burczak's claims that Hayek assumes full employment. Caldwell declares, 'I do not believe that Hayek ever tried to demonstrate (or even to claim) that the market process leads to full employment. His claim is the much weaker one that an unrestricted market process holds the best chance that agents' plans will be coordinated, because freely adjusting relative prices provide information to agents about changing relative scarcities' (1994, p. 312). As pointed out by Burczak

(1994, p. 317), this argument contradicts Caldwell's earlier statements. For example, Caldwell had earlier stated that 'Hayek over his long career has never questioned the "empirical fact" that a tendency toward equilibrium exists; he has never wavered in his belief that the competitive market process tends to bring agents' plans into coordination' (1988, p. 530). Furthermore, Hayek's own statements are rather clear about his position as can be seen in the quotation in the previous section. If these comments were made by some casual observer of Hayek, one could understand. But coming from someone that claims to be an expert on Hayek, it once again demonstrates the unresolved contradictions in Hayek.

If we discard the assumption of full employment, then we are faced with a situation in which workers are coerced because they do not own the means of production. In order to avoid the coercion of workers, the structural adjustment needed during the traverse will necessarily have to take place at full employment, which as we have argued in the first section of this paper is untenable. So the choice ceases to be one of planned economy that involves a substantial level of coercion versus non-coercive decentralized markets. The inability of the market mechanism to maintain full employment that arises from the traverse analysis implies that coercion as defined by Hayek is an integral part of the very same mechanism. Hence, some level of coercion is unavoidable. The question becomes one of designing an economic system that minimizes coercion for most of the population, which implies a socialist planned economy.

5.8 Conclusion

This essay looked into the connection between the traverse analysis and Kalecki's macrodynamics. The achievement of full employment may be relatively straightforward in the short run, but maintaining full employment over longer periods of time requires structural adjustments that the decentralized pricing system of capitalist markets is unable to achieve. We argued that the sectoral adjustments required during the traverse can only be reasonably achieved by socialist planning as envisioned by Kalecki himself, if full employment is to be maintained. A leading critic of planning, Hayek, appears to agree with our conclusions on the instability of full employment policies. However, Hayek maintained a belief in the self-adjusting mechanism of the market process. We argued that Hayek's main objection to planning is untenable and a form of socialist planning continues to be the only viable option in maintaining full employment.

References

Adaman, F. and P. Devine (1994) 'Socialist renewal: lessons from the "calculation" debate', *Studies in Political Economy*, 43: 63–77.

Adaman, F. and P. Devine (1996) 'The economic calculation: lessons for socialists', *Cambridge Journal of Economics*, 20: 523–537.

Burczak, T.A. (1994) 'Reply to Bruce Caldwell: can subjectivism be non-hermeneutic?' *Economics and Philosophy*, 10: 315–317.

Burczak, T. (1995) 'Subjectivism and democratic firms: a response to Hayek's critique of socialism', in A. Callari, S. Cullenberg and C. Biewener (eds) *Marxism in the Postmodern Age: Confronting the New World Order*, New York: The Guilford Press, pp. 169–177.

Caldwell, B.J. (1988) 'Hayek's transformation', *History of Political Economy*, 20(4): 513–541.

Caldwell, B.J. (1994) 'Hayek's scientific subjectivism', *Economics and Philosophy*, 10: 305–313.

Caldwell, B.J. and Reiss, J. (2006) 'Hayek, logic, and the naturalistic fallacy', *Journal of the History of Economic Thought*, 28(3): 359–370.

Demirbag, R. (2011) *The Capitalist Calculation Problem: An Analysis of Economic Calculation in Capitalist Economies*, Unpublished PhD Thesis, Faculty of Economics and Business, The University of Sydney.

Dow, S.C. (1985) *Macroeconomic Thought: A Methodological Approach*. New York: Basil Blackwell.

Garrison, R.W. (1994) 'Hayekian Triangles and Beyond', in J. Birner and R. van Zijp (eds) *Hayek, Co-ordination and Evolution: His Legacy in Philosophy, Politics, Economics and the History of Ideas*, New York: Routledge, pp. 109–125.

Halevi, J. (1998) 'Structural analysis of development and underdevelopment', in H. Hagemann and H.D. Kurz (eds) *Political Economics in Retrospect: Essays in Memory of Adolph Lowe*, Cheltenham: Edward Elgar, pp. 164–194.

Hamowy, R. (1971/2005) *The Political Sociology of Freedom*, Cheltenham: Edward Elgar.

Hayek, F.A. (1935/1967) *Prices and Production*, New York: Augustus M. Kelly.

Hayek, F.A. (1940/1948) 'Socialist calculation III: the competitive "solution"', *Economica*, 7(26), reprinted in F.A. Hayek (1948) *Individualism and Economic Order*, Chicago: The University of Chicago Press, pp. 181–208.

Hayek, F.A. (1944/2007) *The Road to Serfdom: Text and Documents, The Definitive Edition*, in B. Caldwell (ed.), *The Collected Works of F.A. Hayek, Vol. II*, Chicago: The University of Chicago Press.

Hayek, F.A. (1945/1948) 'The use of knowledge in society', *American Economic Review*, 35(4): 519–530, reprinted in F.A. Hayek (1948) *Individualism and Economic Order*, Chicago: The University of Chicago Press, pp. 77–92.

Hayek, F.A. (1960) *The Constitution of Liberty*, Chicago: The University of Chicago Press.

Hayek, F.A. (1978) *New Studies in Philosophy, Politics, Economics and the History of Ideas*, London: Routledge.

Hayek, F.A. (1979) 'Unemployment and monetary policy: government as generator of the "business cycle"', CATO Paper No. 3, San Francisco: Cato Institute.

Hayek, F.A. (1979/1982) *Law, Legislation and Liberty: A New Statement of the Liberal Principles of Justice and Political Economy, Volume 1, The Political Order of a Free People*, London: Routledge.

Hicks, J. (1965) *Capital and Growth*, Oxford: Clarendon Press.
Hodgson, G.M. (1999) *Economics and Utopia: Why the Learning Economy Is Not the End of History*, London: Routledge.
Kaldor, N. (1938) 'Stability and full employment', *The Economic Journal*, 48(192): 642–657.
Kaldor, N. (1955) 'Alternative theories of distribution' *Review of Economic Studies*, 23, 83–100.
Kalecki, M. (1939) *Essays in the Theory of Economic Fluctuations*, London: George Allen and Unwin.
Kalecki, M. (1954) *Theory of Economic Dynamics*, London: George Allen and Unwin.
Kalecki, M. (1958) 'Central price determination as an essential feature of a socialist economy', reprinted in Kalecki (1986).
Kalecki, M. (1962) 'Observations on the theory of growth', *Economic Journal*, 72(285): 134–153.
Kalecki, M. (1971) *Selected Essays on the Dynamics of the Capitalist Economy*, Cambridge: Cambridge University Press.
Kalecki, M. (1976) *Essays on Developing Economies*, Hassocks: Harvester Press.
Kalecki, M. (1986) *Selected Essays on Economic Planning* (ed. by J. Toporowski), Cambridge: Cambridge University Press.
Kley, R. (1994) *Hayek's Social and Political Thought*, Oxford: Oxford University Press.
Kukathas, C. (1989) *Hayek and Modern Liberalism*, Oxford: Clarendon Press.
Lavoie, M. and P. Ramírez-Gastón (1997) 'Traverse in a two-sector Kaleckian model of growth with target-return pricing', *The Manchester School*, 65(2): 145–169.
Leijonhufvud, A. (1968) *On Keynesian Economics and the Economics of Keynes: A Study in Monetary Theory*. New York: Oxford University Press.
Lowe, A. (1952) 'A structural model of production', in *Social Research*, 19: 135–176.
Lowe, A. (1955) 'Structural analysis of real capital formation', in M. Abramovitz (ed.) *Capital Formation and Economic Growth*, Princeton: Princeton University Press, pp. 60–106.
Lowe, A. (1976) *The Path of Economic Growth*, Cambridge: Cambridge University Press.
McNally, D. (1993) *Against the Market: Political Economy, Market Socialism and the Marxist Critique*, London: Verso.
O'Driscoll, G.P. Jr. (1977) *Economics as a Coordination Problem: The Contributions of Friedrich A. Hayek*, Kansas City: Sheed Andrews and McMeel.
O'Neill, J. (1998) *The Market: Ethics, Knowledge and Politics*. London: Routledge.
Palermo G. (2007) 'The ontology of economic power in capitalism: mainstream economics and Marx', *Cambridge Journal of Economics*, 31(4), July: 539–561.
Polanyi, M. (1958/1962) *Personal Knowledge: Towards a Post-Critical Philosophy*, Chicago: University of Chicago Press.
Polanyi, M. (1967) *The Tacit Dimension*, New York: Anchor Books.
Rothbard, M.N. (1982) 'F.A. Hayek and the concept of coercion', in M.N. Rothbard (1998) *The Ethics of Liberty*, New York: New York University Press, pp. 219–229.
Simon, H.A. (1979) 'Rational decision-making in business organisations', *American Economic Review*, 69(4): 493–513, September.
Sweezy, P.M. (1968) 'A crucial difference between capitalism and socialism', in D. Horowitz (ed.), *Marx and Modern Economics*, New York: Monthly Review Press, pp. 315–325.

6

The Impact of Innovations on Investments and Economic Growth in the Thought of Kalecki

Łukasz Mamica

6.1 Introduction

Kalecki treats investment as a key point in a business cycle that is connected with the effect of that investment on demand and output. This is in contradiction to mainstream economics which treats external factors as major determinants of business cycles. The problem of innovation activity (which Kalecki often called technical progress) and its impact on economic development, mainly by the necessity for new investments, was analysed by Kalecki in many of his publications. Typically he analysed innovation not from a long-term perspective but as a chain of short-term decisions of entrepreneurs concerning their innovative activities. In his opinion (1968) the long-run trend is a chain of short-period situations. Innovation activity supported by profits which are achieved by it have, for Kalecki, a crucial impact on growth in the business cycle.

6.2 The literature on the impact of technical progress and innovation upon investments

Schumpeter treated innovation as the key dimension of economic change. According to him (1939), investment is determined by waves of optimism and pessimism which create clusters of innovation. In this way localized investments are created. However, Courvisanos (2012) points out differences between Schumpeter's and Kalecki's views of innovation. Schumpeter in his *Business Cycles*, published in 1939, treated technological change as one driver of such cycles. Kalecki, in Courvisanos's opinion, accepted the role of technological change in creating long-term trends in the economy but was more sceptical about systemic connections between new inventions, investment and growth. Whereas Schumpeter stressed the role of individual entrepreneurship in innovative technology development, Kalecki, having in mind the collapse of his father's business, was more sceptical about the effectiveness of the market to finance entrepreneurs' innovative projects. The ability to deliver a stable flow of money for innovation was, according to Kalecki, rather more possible in a socialism system than in capitalism, where firms' profits dominate.

Harrod, in his theory of growth (1948) and works connected with trade cycle (1936), pointed out that net investments in fixed capital are the results of the prospective increase of demand which cannot be satisfied by existing equipment. Technological inventions in his model have an impact on the amount of capital which is needed to produce the expected amount of goods. In this way technological change can alter the amount of additional capital necessary to equate the supply of goods to demand.

The problem of the role of innovation in economic growth was also present in the works of Kalecki's friend Steindl. He stressed the role of technological progress as a factor stimulating investments, which allows the transformation of the know-how into innovation. Innovations were, according to Steindl, one of three main factors (among internal accumulation and capacity utilization), which impact on investments (1981/1990). He compared the role of innovations to random, but always positive, shocks in business cycles. Steindl stressed the role of education in economic growth, especially the training of engineers. The weakness of educational systems was treated by him as an important barrier to technological development (Steindl, 1968).

Solow, in his neoclassical theory of economic growth (1956) noted the role of technological change in stimulating growth. According to him, an especially easy kind of technological change is connected with simply multiplying the production function by an increasing scale factor. Growth, which was not explained by variables in Solow's model, was treated as a result of exogenous technological change. Solow used his own model of economic growth for calculating the impact of technical progress on the US economy, which was estimated as being responsible for four-fifths growth in output per worker. Kaldor (1957) in turn treated technology as an endogenous factor in his model of economic growth based on the 'dynamic' approach originally developed by Harrod. He assumed a linear relation between the growth of capital per employee and growth of labour productivity. Kaldor regarded readiness to absorb technical change together with willingness to invest capital in business ventures as an important factor in economic growth. He stressed also the role of unexploited new inventions in economic recovery. In a neoclassical model the output-capital ratio is an endogenous variable. Analysing this model, Solow emphasized that the role as well as the increase and decrease in the rate of technological progress has no explanation in it. This statement is the basis for criticism of the neoclassical model that it leaves the role of technological progress unexplained.

Analysing the relationship between technical progress and investment, Kennedy (1961) pointed out that neutral technical progress speeds up the rate of replacements of machines as a consequence of more rapid obsolescence. But proper technical progress in the investment sector has an impact on the reduction of costs of machines and in this way has a capital saving effect on the economy treated as whole. The balance of savings due to capital-using technical progress in the consumption sector will require some new investment. Therefore, neutral technical progress for whole the economy will require net investments. Kennedy made a distinction between neutral technical progress (referring to the economy as a whole) and a neutral invention (referring to a particular line of production). According to him, a neutral invention does not require net investment for its implementation while neutral technical progress does require some net investments.

The growth model proposed by Nelson and Winter (1982) was based on an evolutionary approach. When firms' rate of return was lower than expected, firms started to imitate (use technologies already used in other companies) or look for new techniques (this kind of looking was named a local search). Firms in their model were looking for new combinations of labour and capital coefficient. One of the main selection factors in Nelson and Winter's model was return on techniques. This model was followed by other evolutionary models. In one of them, developed by Silverberg and Verspagen (1998), an important role is played by different investment routines in R&D.

The role of knowledge in long-run growth was included in a model presented by Romer (1986). In his model, knowledge was an input in production that has increasing marginal productivity. It was a competitive equilibrium model with endogenous technological change. Analysing endogenous technological change, Romer (1990) treated the index of the level of technology as one of four basic inputs in his model (among capital, labour and human capital). Because research projects exchange present costs for benefits in the future, Romer treated the rate of technological change as sensitive to the rate of interest. He saw the danger that subsidies to physical capital accumulation are very poor compared to subsidies directed to undertaking research.

Freeman and Perez (1988), analysing the relations between economy and innovation, noticed the problem of the mismatch of current investment to new available technology. They stress variations in the climate of confidence related to the kind of innovation which is responsible for this mismatch and in effect increases investment instability.

There are also critical opinions about the possible use of innovation to stimulate economic growth permanently. According to Gordon (2012), an innovative process should be understood as a series of discrete inventions followed by incremental improvements which allow the achievement of the full potential of the initial invention. Gordon stressed that the impact on economic development of the main sources of innovation within three industrial revolutions[1] is slowly decreasing. As a confirmation of such a tendency, he described the increase of economic growth from 1750 to the middle of the 20th century and a later slowdown (each of the successive periods in USA after 1950 is characterized by a downward step in per-capita real GDP growth and similarly in UK).

6.3 Innovations as a factor of increasing the long-run level of investment, supporting long-run upward trends in Kalecki's analysis

In his book *Theory of Economic Dynamics*, published in 1954, Kalecki analysed factors of development. He argued that innovations tend to increase the long-run level of investment and in this way support long-run upward trends. Inventions that increase aggregate profits make new investment projects more attractive. Although innovations were identified in the model with developments in technology, Kalecki argued that it could be applied to other phenomena like, for example, introduction of new products requiring new equipment for their manufacture. In his opinion, the slowing down of capitalist economies is probably accounted in some part with a decline in the intensity of innovations. It was the result of the diminishing importance of new sources of raw materials, hampering the application of new inventions, and connected with the increasing monopolistic character of capitalism. The last factor in the decline of the intensity of innovations given by Kalecki was the fact that the importance of 'assembly industries' is growing and there technological progress is largely concentrated on a 'scientific organization' of the assembly process that is not connected with heavy investment. He contrasted the positive effect of innovation with rentiers' savings, which have a negative impact on long-run development. In the same book Kalecki treated innovations as a part of 'development factors' which prevent the system from settling into a static position and have a positive impact on long-run upward trends. According to him, a reduction in the intensity of innovations will cause a disturbance in the cyclical fluctuation and in effect lower the long-run trend of investment (Kalecki, 1954/1991, pp. 327–328, 334–335). This way of thinking is close to Schumpeter's 'clustering' effect. Kalecki treated the impact of innovation upon investment among the effects which can break the impasse of cyclical fluctuations around a static position. According to him, only in such cases do cyclical fluctuations occur around an ascending trend line (Kalecki, 1962, p. 134).

There is a temptation to analyse the technical progress from long-run equilibrium as one would analyse other long-period problems. Kalecki admitted that such an approach is unrealistic in the case of technical progress. In the article 'A Theorem on Technical Progress', published in 1941, Kalecki considered some problems of technical progress without assuming long-run equilibrium but analysing a long-period dynamic process (1941/1991). He described the most important effects of technical progress upon economic development as follows. The first impact of technical progress was its influence in increasing the productivity of labour. Technical progress also changes the ratio of the maximum capacity of a plant to the amount of capital it contains and, by promoting concentration of industry, increases the degree of oligopoly. Kalecki also treated technical progress as a factor which lowers the general level of prices (despite the impact of the rise of the degree of oligopoly). The last effect of technical progress upon economic development was, in his opinion, the fact that it keeps the inducement to invest higher than it would be otherwise. It was explained by the increase in the prospective rate of profit due to new inventions. To examine the impact of technical progress on economic development in a system in which only pure changes in the technique of production take place (that is, only increases in labour productivity and changes in the relation of productive capacity to capital), Kalecki proposed an analysis based on the creation of a simplified economic system and a 'reference system'. In effect of these considerations, he formulated a rule[2] according to which the effect of technical progress is not to increase output but to save labour.

In a letter to Joan Robinson in 1936, Kalecki discussed the problem of invention, categorized it into 'neutral' and 'labour saving' (Osiatyński, 1990, pp. 504–505). He noticed that the 'neutral invention' will cause the price of output to fall in the same proportion as the rise in marginal productivity. In effect the new equilibrium is characterized by the same proportion of capital and labour. The 'labour saving' invention causes a higher decrease in price than the marginal productivity of capital and less than the increase in the marginal productivity of labour. Kalecki described the difference between initial invention and technical progress, stressing that invention in an investment goods industry causes a change in methods which are used in the industries oriented to buy its product. He noticed that technical progress saves labour also in the case of non-labour saving inventions, but only if those inventions increase the marginal productivity of capital. In Robinson's (1936) opinion, the impact of inventions upon the equilibrium level of output depends upon the effect of those inventions on the distribution of income. When this invention reduces the share of labour in a given income, in effect the equilibrium level of output is reduced. In a case when invention increases the share of labour, we can observe an increase of equilibrium output.

Kalecki also described innovation in his *Studies in Economic Dynamics*, published in 1943, as probably one of the main forces behind long-run economic development. The impact of innovation on investment was, according to him, connected with making some types of investments more profitable than others (Kalecki, 1943/1991, pp. 187–190). The process of replacing old equipment is a factor which has a negative impact upon investment decisions. Innovations automatically cause lower profitability of older inventions. Kalecki even used the term 'liquidating' old inventions. According to him, the effects of new inventions on investment were exactly offset by the 'liquidation' of old ones, but only in an economy of a given size. The larger the economy, the higher is the positive impact upon new investments. The higher rate of technical progress causes higher current long-run investment. The factors which can negatively affect technical progress are the formation of industrial monopolies, which minimize the application of new inventions, or result in concentrating technical progress on the 'scientific organization' of labour. The role of investment in stimulating economic growth was connected by Kalecki with the marginal efficiency of capital. Planned investments by firms will generate higher demand and as a consequence bigger profits. Therefore, firms will make new investment decisions, and this process has a cumulative character (Sawyer, 1985).

The problem of technical progress was also included in Kalecki's book *Theory of Growth in a Socialist Economy*, published in Polish in 1963. Here Kalecki introduced a curve of production based on the body of technical knowledge which was created by previous technical progress (Kalecki, 1963/1993, pp. 53–56). Its impact on economic growth was closely connected with its accumulative character. Kalecki had divided the impact of technical growth on productivity into three categories. He named the first neutral, when technical progress shifts towards higher capital intensity, increasing productivity but without raising the rate of increase of productivity. The second he named 'encouraging capital intensity', when the rate of increase in productivity implies an increase in capital intensity, and the third he called 'discouraging capital intensity' when the rise in capital intensity will bring about an increase in the productivity and simultaneously reduce the rate of decrease in labour productivity. Courvisanos (2012, pp. 5–6) points out that Kalecki identified innovation as a direct motivation for three main forms of investments from the perspective of the impact on economy and society, analysed in various schools of economic thought. The first is connected with capital accumulation in firms (tangible investment), the second with codified and tacit knowledge within firms (intangible investment). The last one concerns public investment in knowledge based-infrastructure accompanied by the creation of innovation capacity.

6.4 Obstacles in measuring the impact of technological progress and innovation on economic growth

The results of an innovative project are by nature difficult to predict. The impacts of the same amount of funds invested in innovation are differentiated not only because of differences in organizational capacities, previous experiences, the quality of researchers and a wide range of interactions, but also due to luck in research. Many sources of innovation are connected with inter-firm procedures and cultural habits that make it difficult to define specifically the relationship between investments in R&D funds and innovation-based growth. Usually, new inventions reduce the impact of older innovations on economic growth and decrease the level of invested capital return. Although there have been attempts to model the effect of new innovation in reducing the effects of older ones (Aghion and Howitt, 1992), we should remember that new innovations can also increase the value and role of previous innovations and their impact on economic growth. There is also a problem with finding proper indicators which describe the level of economical innovativeness. The number of patents is often used as an indicator of useful inventions. But this can be distorted if generating patents is used to evaluate researchers' activity. Patents may then become not an indicator of a useful invention but an opportunistic response to evaluation procedures. Despite this, patents indicators are commonly used in analysis.

6.5 Conclusion

Kalecki treated technical progress as a factor of long-run investment and supporting long-run growth trends. In his opinion, innovation is one of the 'development factors' which prevent the system from settling to a static position According to him, the innovation process is a chain of short-term decisions of entrepreneurs concerning their innovative activities. Kalecki connected the role of investment in stimulating economic growth with the marginal productivity of capital, where planned investments generate higher demand and in effect larger profits. Amongst the impacts of technical progress described by him were an increase in the productivity of labour, lowering the general level of prices and keeping the inducement to invest higher than it would be otherwise. He stressed that the effect of technical progress is not to increase output but to save labour. Kalecki claimed that innovation made some types of investments more profitable than others.

Notes

1. The first centred in 1750–1830 from the inventions of the steam engine and cotton gin through the early railroads and steamships. The second from 1870–1900 connected with electric light and a workable internal combustion engine. The third associated with the invention of the web and internet around 1995 but in practice connected with replacing routine and repetitive work from 1960 because of electronic computers.
2. If it is disregarded, the effect of technical progress upon the degree of oligopoly is to stimulate innovative investment off-setting the pressure of increasing labour productivity on the general level of prices.

References

Aghion, P. and Howitt, P. (1992) 'A model of growth through creative destruction', *Econometrica,* March, 60(2): 322–352.

Courvisanos, J. (2012) *Cycles, Crises and Innovation: Path to Sustainable Development – A Kaleckian-Schumpeterian Synthesis*, Cheltenham, UK and Northampton, US: Edward Elgar.

Freeman, C. and C. Perez (1988) 'Structural crises of adjustment, business cycles and investment behaviour', in G. Dosi, C. Freeman, R. Nelson, G. Silverberg and L. Soete (eds), *Technical Change and Economic Theory*, London: Pinter, pp. 38–66.

Gordon, R.J. (2012) 'Is US economic growth over? Faltering innovation confronts the six headwinds', *CEPR Policy Insight* No. 63.

Harrod, R.F. (1936)*The Trade Cycle, An Essay*, Clarendon Press, Oxford.
Harrod, R.F. (1948) *Towards a Dynamic Economics*, London: Macmillan.
Kaldor, N. (1957) 'Model of Economic Growth', *Economic Journal*, 67(268): 591–624.
Kalecki M. (1941/1991) 'A theorem on technical progress', *Review of Economic Studies*, 8(3), 1940–1941: 179–184, in *Collected Works of Michał Kalecki* (1991), Vol. 2, ed. J. Osiatyński, Oxford: Clarendon Press, pp. 107–116.
Kalecki M. (1943/1991) *Studies in Economic Dynamics*, in *Collected Works of Michał Kalecki* (1991), Vol. 2, ed. J. Osiatyński, Oxford: Clarendon Press, pp. 118–190.
Kalecki M. (1954/1991) *Theory of Economic Dynamics: An Essay on Cyclical and Long-Run Changes in Capitalist Economy*, London: Allen & Unwin, reprinted in *Collected Works of Michał Kalecki* (1991), Vol. 2, ed. J. Osiatyński, Oxford, Clarendon Press, pp. 205–348.
Kalecki, M. (1962) 'Observations on the theory of growth', *Economic Journal*, 72: 134–153.
Kalecki, M. (1963/1993) Introduction to the *Theory of Growth in a Socialist Economy* (original book published in Polish in Warsaw: PWN), in *Collected Works of Michał Kalecki* (1993), Vol. 4, ed. J. Osiatyński, Oxford: Clarendon Press, pp. 4–110.
Kalecki, M. (1968) 'Trend and business cycle reconsidered', *The Economic Journal*, 78(310): 263–276.
Kennedy, C. (1961) 'Technical progress and investment', *Economic Journal*, 71(282), Jun.: 292–299.
Nelson, R.R. and S.G. Winter (1982) *An Evolutionary Theory of Economic Change*, Cambridge, Mass.: Harvard University Press.
Osiatyński, J. (1990) *Collected Works of Michał Kalecki*, Vol. 1, Oxford: Clarendon Press.
Robinson, J. (1936) 'The long period theory of employment', *Journal of Economics*, 7(1): 74–93.
Romer, P.M. (1986)'Increasing returns and long run growth', *Journal of Political Economy*, 94: 1002–1037.
Romer, P.M. (1990) 'Endogenous technological change', *Journal of Political Economy*, 98: S71–S102.
Sawyer, M.C. (1985) *The Economics of Michał Kalecki*, New York: M.E. Sharpe Armonk.
Schumpeter, J.A. (1939) *Business Cycles: A Theoretical, Historical and Statistical Analysis of the Capitalist Process*, 2 Volumes, New York: McGraw-Hill.
Silverberg, G. and B. Verspagen (1998) 'Economic growth and economic evolution: a modelling perspective', in F. Schweitzer and G. Silverberg (eds), *Evolution and Self-Organization in Economics*, Jahrbuch für Komplexität in den Natur-, Sozial und Geisteswissenschaften, Band 9, Berlin: Duncker & Humblot.
Solow, R.M. (1956) 'A contribution to the theory of economic growth', *Quarterly Journal of Economics*, 70: 65–94.
Steindl, J. (1968) 'Educational planning and economic growth', in OECD, *Educational Policy and Planning: Austria*, OECD: Paris.
Steindl, J. (1981) 'Ideas and concepts of long run growth', reprinted in J. Steindl (1990): *Economic Papers 1941–88*, Basingstoke: Macmillan.

7
'Dr Kalecki' on Mr Keynes

Hanna Szymborska and Jan Toporowski

This chapter presents Kalecki's interpretation of the *General Theory*, contained in his review of the book from 1936. The most striking feature of this interpretation is that, despite criticizing a great deal of Keynes's analysis, particularly regarding the determinants of investment, Kalecki was highly impressed by Keynes's theory showing the effect of changes in investment on global employment, income and production levels. Kalecki's review and restatement of the key ideas of the *General Theory* is superior to the original due to a clearer and more concise account of the causes of changes in investment and their influence on the short-run equilibrium position, taking into consideration the distribution of income between capitalists and workers. But the review also criticized Keynes's methodology and does not even mention key elements of his analysis (notably his monetary and financial analysis).

Kalecki's review of the *General Theory* was published in the third quarter of 1936 in Polish in the journal *Ekonomista* (*Economist*) and was humbly entitled 'Some remarks on Keynes's theory' ('Parę Uwag o Teorii Keynesa'). The fact that it was not available in English until 1982 (translated by Targetti and Kinda-Hass) may be one of the key reasons why Kalecki's 'version' of the effective demand theory did not initially gain as much recognition as it deserved, given the acclaimed superiority of his findings over Keynes's.

Kalecki himself emphasized the precedence of his conclusions on the role of investment and demand on several occasions. In the introduction to his 1971 *Selected Essays on the Dynamics of the Capitalist Economy* he stated that the three papers written in 1933, 1934 and 1935 ('Outline of a theory of the business cycle', 'On Foreign Trade and "Domestic Exports"' and 'The Mechanism of the Business Cycle', respectively) contain the 'essentials' of the *General Theory* (Kalecki, 1971, p. vii). Furthermore,

Kalecki remarks in a couple of footnotes to his 1936 review that his earlier ideas regarding the causality running from investment to savings rather than the opposite are 'analogous' to the implication contained in the *General Theory* (Kalecki, 1936/1990, p. 228). According to G.C. Harcourt, Kalecki's review is conclusive evidence for his independent derivation of the key propositions of Keynes's work, albeit through different reasoning (Harcourt, 2006, p. 21). Kalecki began the paper with words of high appreciation of Keynes's book, describing that book as: 'without any doubt, a turning-point in the history of economics', although Kalecki himself was far from being an expert in the history of economic thought (Kalecki, 1936, p. 223).

In his interpretation Kalecki distinguished between two parts of Keynes's theory: firstly, the determination of a short-term equilibrium with a given level of investment and given 'production apparatus'; and secondly, the determination of the level of investment (1936, p. 223). While he expressed his overall satisfaction with the way in which Keynes handles the first issue, Kalecki was more critical of the 'serious deficiencies' characterizing Keynes's analysis of the determinants of investment.

Despite a certain similarity between their conclusions, Kalecki and Keynes followed fundamentally different assumptions due to methodological differences. For the purposes of exposition, Kalecki temporarily adopted certain underlying assumptions of Keynes, analysing a closed economy with no government over a short period. Further, Kalecki maintained Keynes's proposition regarding the existence of a reserve army of the unemployed workers, although he remained sceptical about the use of wage unit as a basic unit of measurement. Nevertheless, he retained this premise for expositional purposes.

In addition, Kalecki used the assumption typical of his own analysis, namely that workers do not save because living standards only allow them to consume whatever they earn, and that the economy is operating at less than full capacity. Contrary to the assumption of perfect competition in the *General Theory*, he considered the general case of imperfect competition, without assuming any particular market structure.

Kalecki interpreted the first part of Keynes's proposition through an analysis of distribution. He identified the short-period equilibrium output for a representative, vertically integrated firm by reference to a marginal value-added curve, in which marginal value-added is the marginal product of labour times the price of that product. Having established that the short-run equilibrium (B in Figure 7.1) is determined by the intersection of the marginal value-added curve (MVA) with the

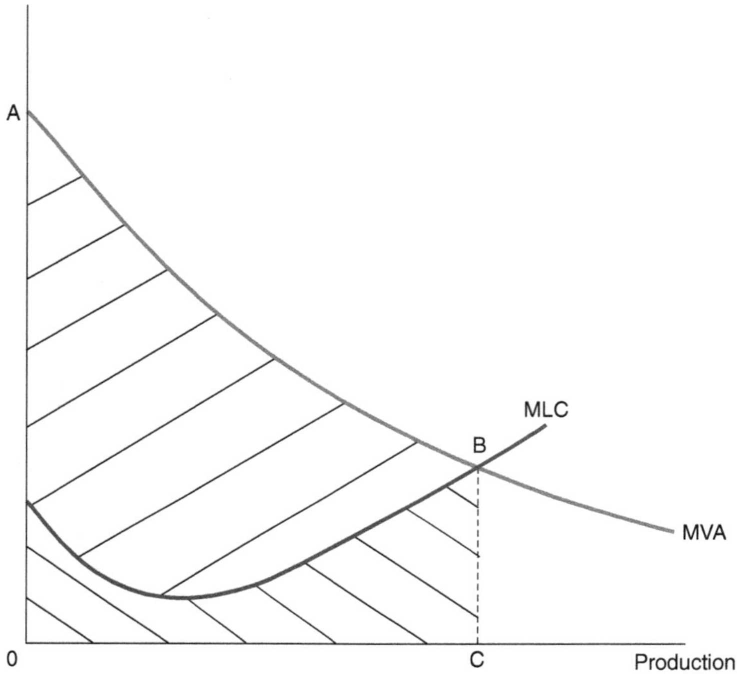

Figure 7.1 Determination of short-run equilibrium in Kalecki's interpretation
Source: Kalecki, 1936/1990.

marginal labour cost (MLC), Kalecki noted that the total value-added indicates the size of 'social income', comprising of capitalist expenditure and workers' consumption (lined area ABCO in Figure 7.1). Since workers' expenditure is determined by their wage income, no spontaneous change in workers' spending can take place. Kalecki therefore examined the consequences of an increase in capitalist spending. He argued that the expansion of capitalist production expenditure leads to increased marginal revenue in the short-run, shifting the equilibrium point to B′ (Figure 7.2). Subsequently, income and hence consumption of the wage-earners rises, resulting in higher incomes of the capitalist and demanding expansion in the economy as a whole, in the area A′B′C′0 (Kalecki, 1936, p. 226).

In this way Kalecki showed the crucial role of capitalist consumption and investment decisions in the determination and persistence of short-run equilibrium (1936, p. 227). This conclusion is critical in

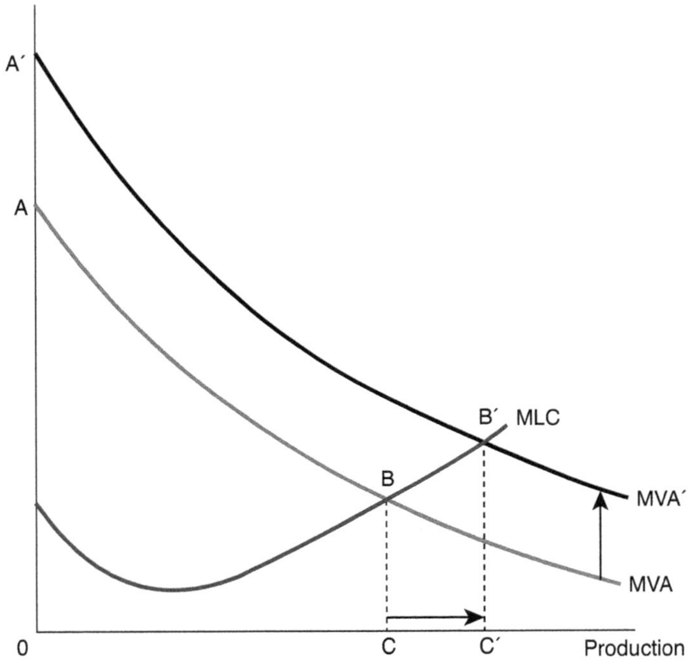

Figure 7.2 Impact of an increase in capitalist expenditure on the short-run equilibrium in Kalecki's interpretation

Source: Kalecki, 1936/1990.

Kalecki's evaluation of Keynes. Because capitalist expenditure consists of consumption and investment, and capitalist income is devoted to consumption and saving, Kalecki directly inferred that it is investment which forces an equal amount of savings and exerts the most significant impact on the process of equilibrium formation. He further showed that his proposition holds even if the Keynesian assumptions of closed economy, perfect competition and constant money wages are relaxed. Investment therefore has a direct and exclusive effect on the levels of social income and employment in the economy (1936, pp. 228–229). Given the volume and composition of the production apparatus, employment (Y) is an increasing function of investment (I) (Equation 7.1). He reformulated this relationship into the Keynesian multiplier (Equation 7.2), implying that investment is a decisive factor influencing the short-term equilibrium and labour absorption at a given point in time (1936, p. 228).

$$Y=f(I) \tag{7.1}$$

$$dY/dI=f'(I) \tag{7.2}$$

As previously mentioned, Kalecki's criticism was focused on the issue of investment determination contained in what he regarded as the second part of the *General Theory*. In the review, he identified two fundamental flaws of Keynes's marginal efficiency of investment approach. Kalecki argues that the approach could only explain the *ex post* level of investment, ignoring the *ex-ante* investment *decisions*, which are more relevant in determining the investment level in Kalecki's view (1936, p. 230). The weakness of Keynes's analysis was seen by Kalecki as a consequence of an inappropriate *static* approach attempting to explain an inherently *dynamic* issue (1936, p. 231), a view that was subsequently taken up by other critics (see, for example, Leontief, 1948). Kalecki noted that the initial investment decisions will rarely yield an equal level of actual investment due to certain realization problems and that therefore any short-period equilibrium is bound to move from period to period. He identified Keynes's lack of understanding of the inherent *disequilibrating* nature of investment, as waves of optimism associated with investment expansion divert its marginal efficiency away from the interest rate level, disturbing the equilibrium.

Kalecki's summary of Keynes's fundamental theoretical insight (the determination of output and employment by the level of investment) also allowed Kalecki to demonstrate later on an essential element of Keynes's critique of 'the classics' that Keynes had the most difficulty in expounding: a difficulty that provided the loophole of the re-establishment of pre-Keynesian ideas, first under the 'neo-classical synthesis' and subsequently in New Classical macroeconomics and the 'new neoclassical synthesis'. This concerns the extent to which price and wage flexibility can bring an economy to full employment. The notion that the forces of supply and demand will bring an economy to full employment, if only wages will show sufficient flexibility, is an article of faith in pre-Keynesian macroeconomics, Austrian economics and in neoclassical economics today. It is also a fallacy that both Kalecki and Keynes sought to expose. Keynes attempted this in Chapter 19 of the *General Theory* and subsequently in his 1939 paper on 'Relative Movements of Real Wages and Output' (Keynes, 1936, Chapter 19; Keynes, 1939). Kalecki had done it in his earlier paper 'Three Systems', which was not published in English until 1990 (Kalecki, 1934).

In his review, Kalecki showed the fallacy of flexible wages and employment with virtually irrefutable simplicity. If there is a general reduction in wages, then, in conditions of perfect competition, prices should fall proportionately. The fall in prices will leave real wages more or less where they were before. The change in prices will lower the MVA curve by a similar amount, leaving output and employment approximately where they were before. If, however, there is imperfect competition, then prices will not fall proportionately to wages. In that case, real wages will fall, and with it real consumption, output and employment. In this way Kalecki was able to demonstrate that wage reductions have either no effect on output and employment, or reduce them, depending on the degree of competition in the economy.

The fact that Kalecki was able to present Keynes's theory through his own formulation in a much simpler way is evidence for his genius as an economist. Perhaps his single greatest achievement in interpreting the *General Theory* was to restate Keynes' theory, accounting for the distribution of income amongst the social classes, namely workers and capitalists. Furthermore, by distinguishing between investment decisions and actual investment, Kalecki's interpretation reflects a more accurate and robust understanding of the role of investment and its impact on employment, which is proved by the fact that his exposition holds without the restrictive assumptions that Keynes had made. Moreover, Kalecki's account of Keynes's theory is more concise and his use of terms more comprehensive than Keynes's, making Kalecki's version of the theory presented in the review much more appealing and convincing than the original.

Another advantage of Kalecki's analysis is the logical reasoning he presented in the review, accompanied by less flamboyant language. He was concerned with objective factors in explaining decline in investment and employment. This stands in sharp contrast with Keynes, who stressed the subjective and hence less straightforward aspects, such as expectations and uncertainty. Furthermore, while Keynes was largely averse to the use of technical tools, Kalecki possessed a good command of mathematics and statistics. This led Moggridge, the editor of Keynes's collected works, to admit that Kalecki was more useful in providing analytical tools; he even recalls daring attempts to label Keynes as an important post-Kaleckian rather than Kalecki a 'left Keynesian' (Moggridge, 1993, p. 167; King, 2002, p. 50). Moggridge further emphasized the disparity of fundamental interests of the two men: Kalecki aimed at thoroughly understand the determinants and mechanisms of economic processes, while Keynes was motivated by his 'desperate desire to influence policy' (Moggridge, 1993, p. 23). Paradoxically, it is Kalecki's analysis which relies more on the interplay of socio-political and economic factors than Keynes, providing a more realistic dimension to his exposition.

The more in-depth account of the effective demand theory confirms Sawyer's (1985, p. 179) observation that Kalecki was operating within his own macroeconomic framework, differing in many aspects from the approach represented by Keynes. The basic disparities are apparent in Kalecki's review. Apart from the fundamental methodological differences ('a deviationist from Marx' examining 'a deviationist from Marshall' who had come to similar conclusions – Kaldor, 1989, p. 8), the nature of the theoretical investigation itself has a visibly different focus. Kalecki was predominantly concerned with the product markets, reflected for example in his use of measures such as value-added and his overall dissatisfaction with Keynes' adoption of wage unit as a numéraire. In contrast, Keynes' analysis in the *General Theory* treats the labour market in a more ambiguous way, holding onto his assumption of the wage unit as a numéraire, for the sake of his monetary analysis, while seeking to obtain from that analysis a theory of employment. Nevertheless, Keynes seems to have been rather ignorant of Kalecki's genius. The correspondence between Kalecki, Keynes and Robinson in 1937 betrays Keynes's sense of superiority over Kalecki (Moggridge, 1983). Methodological differences then caused Kalecki's resignation from Keynes's Cambridge Research Project in 1939 (Toporowski, 2011, p. 5).

It is clear that it was Kalecki who truly broke with the traditional theory. In contrast, Keynes's breach with the classics was rather vague and, in places, rhetorical rather than analytical, as was noted by many of his contemporaries (Backhouse, 1999). In fact, Keynes's work ultimately became orthodoxy itself, even if academic economists have not ceased to argue about the meaning of that work. Keynes believed in the possibility of full employment by means of government economic policy rather than by institutional change. However, Kalecki considered full employment a special case, related to military spending (Kalecki, 1944) and subject to the class conflict inherent in the capitalist economy (Kalecki, 1943).

However, a striking omission from Kalecki's review is any mention of money and finance, except in passing to state that, in Keynes's theory, the rate of interest is not determined by the demand and supply of new capital, but the supply of and demand for means of payment. This is a view that is not original to Keynes, but goes back to the monetary theory of Wicksell. However, Kalecki was able to draw from this the conclusion that investment effectively pays for itself.

7.1 Conclusion

Kalecki's review of Keynes's *General Theory* is unusual for its simple exposition of Keynes's view of the determination of output and employment, the basic composition of aggregate demand and the distribution of income. It is unusual too for identifying the key weaknesses and inconsistencies in Keynes's theory, while recognizing its seminal refutation of 'classical' theory. This gives Kalecki's review a unique position in 20th-century macroeconomics, and unique relevance to the macroeconomics of the 21st century.

References

Backhouse, R. (ed.) (1999) *Keynes: Contemporary Responses to the General Theory*, Bristol: Thoemmes Press.

Harcourt, G.C. (2006) *The Structure of Post-Keynesian Economics. The Core Contributions of the Pioneers*, Cambridge: Cambridge University Press.

Kaldor, N. (1989) 'Personal recollections on Michał Kalecki' in M. Sebastiani (ed.), *Kalecki's Relevance Today*, New York: St. Martin's Press.

Kalecki, M. (1934/1990) 'Three Systems' in J. Osiatyński (ed.), *Collected Works of Michał Kalecki: Vol. I: Business Cycles and Full Employment*, Oxford: Clarendon Press, 1990.

Kalecki, M. (1936) 'Some remarks on Keynes's theory' in J. Osiatyński (ed.), *Collected Works of Michał Kalecki: Vol. I: Business Cycles and Full Employment*, Oxford: Clarendon Press, 1990.

Kalecki, M. (1943) 'Political Aspects of Full Employment' in J. Osiatyński (ed.) *Collected Works of Michał Kalecki: Vol. I: Business Cycles and Full Employment*, Oxford: Clarendon Press, 1990.

Kalecki, M. (1944) 'Three ways to full employment' in J. Osiatyński (ed.), *Collected Works of Michał Kalecki: Vol. I: Business Cycles and Full Employment*, Oxford: Clarendon Press, 1990.

Kalecki, M. (1971) *Selected Essays on the Dynamics of the Capitalist Economy 1933–1970* Cambridge: Cambridge University Press.

Keynes, J.M. (1936) *The General Theory of Employment, Interest and Money*, London: Macmillan.

Keynes, J.M. (1939) 'Relative Movements of Real Wages and Output', *Economic Journal*, 49(193), March: 34–51.

King, J.E. (2002) *A History of Post Keynesian Economics since 1936*, Northampton, MA: Edward Elgar Pub.

Leontief, W. (1948) 'Postulates: Keynes's *General Theory* and the classicists' in S. Harris (ed.) *The New Economics*, New York: Knopf, reprinted in W. Leontief *Essays in Economics Theories and Theorizing Volume One*, Oxford: Basil Blackwell, 1976.

Moggridge, D.E. (ed.) (1983) *The Collected Writings of John Maynard Keynes. Vol. XII, Economic Articles and Correspondence: Investment and Editorial*, London: Macmillan.

Moggridge, D.E. (1993) *Keynes*, Houndsmill, Basingstoke: Macmillan.

Sawyer, M.C. (1985) *The Economics of Michał Kalecki*, Basingstoke: Macmillan.

Toporowski, J. (2011) 'Shared ideas amid mutual incomprehension: Kalecki and Cambridge' in P. Arestis (ed.) *Microeconomics, Macroeconomics and Economic Policy: Essays in Honour of Malcolm Sawyer*, Basingstoke: Palgrave.

Part II

Kalecki and Crisis in the 21st Century

8

Michał Kalecki's Capitalist Dynamics from Today's Perspective

D. Mario Nuti

8.1 Premise

Fifty years ago, I sat in the first row of Michał Kalecki's lecture courses, both on capitalist dynamics and on the growth of the socialist economy, at the Warsaw SGPiS (the Higher School of Planning and Statistics, as it then was, now the Higher School of Commerce). At the time there was a thriving school of economics in Poland, with eminent representatives – besides Kalecki – such as Oskar Lange, Kazimierz Łaski, Włodzimierz Brus, Ignacy Sachs and many others. In 1962, freshly graduated in Economics from the University of Rome 'La Sapienza' and queueing for a scholarship to go to Cambridge the following year, I decided to go to Warsaw in the meantime, braving the coldest winter of the century, and learn more *in corpore vili* about comparative economic systems, which were to become my main research and teaching interest of a lifetime.

I learned Polish fast, and by September I was attending Kalecki's and Lange's lectures, as well as their courses that that year were being held at SGPiS in English for students from developing countries. A year later I went to King's College, Cambridge, where I was to remain for the following fourteen years; there I heard Joan Robinson repeatedly lavish praise for Kalecki's anticipation of Maynard Keynes's *General Theory* (1936).

8.2 Kalecki and Keynes

'It must be rather annoying for you' – Joan Robinson wrote to Kalecki in 1937 – 'to see all this fuss being made over Keynes when so little notice was taken of your own contribution' (reproduced in Patinkin, 1982; she also wrote similar acknowledgements in 1964, 1976 and elsewhere).

She was not alone in making this claim on Kalecki's behalf: 'Kalecki's greatest achievement, among many, was undoubtedly his complete anticipation of Keynes' *General Theory*' (Lawrence Klein, 1975, as well as 1966; see also Lange, 1939). In fact Michał Kalecki published in Polish (1933, 1934; reprinted in English in Kalecki, 1971) and in English (1935) before Keynes' *General Theory*, a demand-determined theory of national income and employment, centred on investment, with an expenditure multiplier, similar to those of Keynes. But his intellectual roots, methodology and arguments were original – and so were Keynes's. There are many very significant differences between the two (see Nuti, 2004).

First, money and the money interest rate, that figure prominently in Keynesian theory and in the very title of the *General Theory*, have no role in Kalecki, for whom only the long-term interest rate is relevant, within the limits set by the principle of increasing risk of credit-financed investment.

Second, Keynes had a view of the volatility of expectations and the dependence of investment on 'animal spirits' as well as 'the state of the news'. Kalecki's investors, instead, simply looked at the degree of capacity utilization (a flexible accelerator or capital-stock adjustment) and projected the current profit rate into the future.

Third, Keynes had no particular views about income distribution – in spite of post-Keynesian developments in this area – while Kalecki had two distribution theories, one based on the relative propensities to consume of capitalists and workers – 'workers spend what they earn, capitalists earn what they spend' – akin to the post-Keynesian approach, and one based on the average degree of monopoly aggregated over all producers.

Fourth, Keynes's approach lent itself to be combined with an accelerator to produce economic cycles, which is what Roy Harrod did, followed by many others; Kalecki had a whole armoury of complete models of economic cycles.

Finally, both Kalecki and Keynes made outstanding contributions to other areas of economic thought. Keynes's ranged from probability theory to fiscal policy to the design of the international monetary system; Kalecki's from the theory of growth of the capitalist economy, to the theory and practice of socialist economic planning, to original criteria for the selection of investment projects.

Both Kalecki and Keynes were great economists on their own account and merits; stressing the relatively small overlapping of their demand-determined theory of employment and income – no matter how important – unnecessarily detracts from their greatness.

8.3 Kalecki's political cycle

Besides his mathematical models of the economic cycle, Kalecki (1943) produced a model based on the political economy of government fiscal policy and of capitalists' behaviour.

In theory full employment could be achieved via additional government expenditure, were it not for the government and capitalists' need to reproduce labour unemployment in order to keep wage rates and labour discipline under control.

In a nutshell, 'A solid majority of economists is now of the opinion that, even in a capitalist system, full employment may be secured by a government spending programme, provided there is in existence adequate plan[t] to employ all existing labour power, and provided adequate supplies of necessary foreign raw-materials may be obtained in exchange for exports'. As long, of course, as such government spending programme is 'financed by borrowing and not by taxation'.

However, 'we may expect the opposition of the leaders of industry [to such a policy of full employment] on three planes: (i) opposition on principle to government spending based on a budget deficit; (ii) opposition to this spending being directed either towards public investment – which may foreshadow the intrusion of the state into the new spheres of economic activity – or towards subsidizing mass consumption; iii) opposition to maintaining full employment and not merely preventing deep and prolonged slumps'. Such objections subside in the slump, and are revived in the boom.

With lasting full employment workers would 'get out of hand' and the 'captains of industry' would be anxious to 'teach them a lesson'. Moreover, the price increase in the upswing is to the disadvantage of small and big *rentiers*, and makes them 'boom-tired' and ready to ally with capitalists. Their pressure would probably induce the government to return to the orthodox policy of cutting down the budget deficit. 'A slump would follow in which government spending policy would again come into its own'. (Kalecki, 1943)

8.4 Today's world

Seventy years later, what has changed in economic theory and in the state of the world? At least three fundamental things: first, labour markets have become globalized; second, the fiscal constraints on the sustainability of sovereign government debt have tightened; and third, the economic profession's consensus about the possibility of achieving full employment has gradually faded – at least until 2008–2010.

Since Kalecki's times there has been an increasing integration of international trade and movements of production factors especially since about 1970, with a single temporary decrease of the average import-export share in world GDP in 2009, immediately reversed. The globalization of world labour markets – through international migrations, de-localization of output to lower-wage locations, but primarily through international trade – has led to a deterioration of labour shares in national incomes: in 1985–2005 in advanced countries by 10 percentage points from 65 per cent to 55 per cent (IMF, World Economic Outlook, 2007), without its parallel, offsetting increase in emerging countries where labour is still relatively abundant.

The global crisis has made unemployment a cyclical worldwide phenomenon; conversely, global calls for expansionary fiscal and monetary policies have been made (for instance, in November 2008 at the G20 under IMF leadership) and implemented, though short-lived and subjected to premature reversal. In other words, Kalecki's political cycle is still there, but it has grown globally synchronized and possibly weakened on average by both the general weakening of the power of organized labour and by persistent international divergences in the timing of the cycle.

The second feature that today differs markedly from Kalecki's time and framework is the record high level of sovereign debt. How can fiscal stimulus be feasible and sustainable in this situation? Kalecki expected interest rates on public debt to be contained by monetary policy (as it was at the time of his writing and would be today were it not for the so-called 'spread' that distances the cost of credit in the Southern members of the Eurozone from that in the more virtuous and credible Nordic members like Germany). In any case Kalecki envisaged interest on public debt to be financed out of a recurring capital tax – a solution technically unimpeachable though politically unpopular; therefore, the persistence of unemployment continues to be the result of political obstacles to alternative policies.

Finally, the economists' consensus on the effectiveness of expansionary fiscal policy, that Kalecki could confidently assert in 1943, was challenged soon after the War, at least until 2008–2010, on an escalation of arguments.

8.5 From deficit spending to expansionary contraction

First, it was argued that government expenditure would 'crowd out' private investment (see Blanchard's, 2008a, review of the argument).

The idea neglects the possibility of private investment on the contrary 'crowding in' additional expenditure due to the activation of its accelerator effect of higher primary demand. On the contrary, Dennis Robertson (in a talk given at Princeton in 1953, Robertson 1954) argued that at least some of the additional savings out of the income generated by government spending would not represent a leakage but would be channelled into additional investment, and called this 'the Kalecki effect'.

Second, Ricardian equivalence was invoked, tentatively put forward by David Ricardo in the 1820s and re-discovered by Robert J. Barro in 1974. When government expenditure is raised, funded by borrowing, economic agents discount the future payments of higher taxes that they anticipate having to pay to service the higher debt. The effect is the same as it would be if expenditure was funded directly by an immediate higher tax: lower private consumption offsetting higher government expenditure.

Third, in the early 1970s the theory of so-called rational expectations was introduced by Lucas (1976) and others, which was a tendentious misnomer. They should have been called expectations *successful by definition*. The efficient utilization of all information available, by all economic agents, makes markets efficient. Nobody is ever surprised. Multipliers could then be lower than unity.

The final blow to the full employment feasibility consensus invoked by Kalecki was given by the concept of an 'Expansionary Fiscal Contraction', indeed an 'expansionary *extreme* fiscal contraction'. In the 1990s and 2000s a series of empirical studies purported to show that closing the budget deficit via higher taxes and/or lower expenditure can be and by and large is expansionary: see Giavazzi and Pagano (1990, 1996); Alesina and Perotti (1997); Alesina and Ardagna (2010). Blanchard (1990, then a Professor at MIT, before joining the IMF as Chief Economist in 2008) explained how this was due to the promotion of private sector-led growth, for the reasons already mentioned above: Ricardian equivalence, increasing confidence, a favourable impact on expectations, declining borrowing costs, a weaker currency.

Giavazzi and Pagano (1990, 1996) showed that fiscal consolidations are sometimes correlated with expansions in private consumption within one year. They presented evidence based on case studies and regressions of private consumption on cyclically-adjusted government revenue and spending for a panel of OECD economies.

Similarly, using case studies, Alesina and Perotti (1995) found that fiscal consolidations are sometimes correlated with rapid output growth, particularly if implemented by cutting government spending rather than by increasing taxes. These findings were confirmed by subsequent research based on larger samples of countries and years, including a more recent paper of Alesina and Ardagna (2010).

But the culmination of the expansionary fiscal consolidation thesis, supported by the so-called '"austerians" – advocates of fiscal austerity, of immediate sharp cuts in government spending" (Krugman's definition Krugman 2012, p. 5) – is a paper by Harvard economists Carmen Reinhart and Kenneth Rogoff, 'Growth in a Time of Debt' (2010). On the basis of a new dataset of 44 countries spanning about two hundred years, incorporating 'over 3,700 annual observations covering a wide range of political systems, institutions, exchange rate arrangements, and historic circumstances', Reinhart and Rogoff find that 'the relationship between government debt and real GDP growth is weak for debt/GDP ratios below a threshold of 90 percent of GDP. Above 90 percent, median growth rates fall by one percent, and average growth falls considerably more' (2010, p. 23).

The notion that government debt exceeding 90 per cent of GDP has a significant negative effect on economic growth became a decisive supportive argument for austerity by national and international leaders, from ex-vice-presidential candidate Paul Ryan, chairman of the USA Congress budget committee, to EC Commissioner Olli Rehn and authoritative commentators. Thus Keynes's proposition that 'the boom, not the slump, is the right time for austerity' was falsified, austerity becoming a good policy for all seasons in highly indebted countries.

8.6 The tide is turning...

The proposition of 'Expansionary Fiscal Consolidation' was immediately subjected to many criticisms and was gradually discredited both on theoretical and on empirical grounds.

Already in November 2008 the IMF Managing Director Dominique Strauss-Kahn took the initiative for a sizeable global fiscal stimulus of the order of 2 per cent of Global GDP. In an interview with IMF Survey Online on 29 December 2008, Olivier Blanchard – by then IMF Chief Economist – and Carlo Cottarelli, Chief of the IMF Fiscal Affairs Department, called for bank recapitalization (time consuming) and monetary expansion (ineffective at low interest rates) and made the case for fiscal stimulus: 'In normal times, the Fund would indeed be recommending to many countries that they reduce their budget deficit and their public debt. But these are not normal times, and the balance of risks today is very different.' 'If no fiscal stimulus is implemented, then demand may continue to fall. And with it, we may see some of the vicious cycles we have seen in the past: deflation and liquidity traps, expectations becoming more and more pessimistic and, as a result, a deeper and deeper recession. If, instead, a fiscal stimulus is implemented but proves unnecessary, the risk is that the economy recovers too fast. Surely, this risk is easier to control than the risk of an ever deepening recession' (Blanchard, 2008b). The IMF raised its lending, increased its own resources and relaxed somewhat its conditionality, but its commitment was intermittent and short-lived. The European Central Bank, under the leadership of Mr Trichet, soon was advocating an early exit strategy from both monetary expansion and fiscal stimulus.

In October 2010, Chapter 3 of the IMF World Economic Outlook examined 'the effects of fiscal consolidation – tax hikes and government spending cuts – on economic activity.' It found that fiscal consolidation typically reduces output and raises unemployment in the short term, especially if it occurs simultaneously across many countries, and if monetary policy is not in a position to offset them. Only in the longer term can interest rate cuts, a fall in the value of the currency and a rise in net exports usually 'soften' but not offset the contractionary impact.

Baker (2010) criticizes Alesina and others (1995, 2006) for their use of cyclically adjusted deficits while policy-driven deficit adjustments behave in a Keynesian fashion and the argument by Broadbent and Daly (2010) on the ground that known cases of expansionary consolidation occurred for very narrow output gaps relatively to the large ones that have occurred in the current crisis.

The January 2012 IMF Fiscal Monitor Update warned that 'too rapid consolidation during 2012 could exacerbate downside risks': 'Further tightening during a downturn could exacerbate rather than alleviate market tensions through its negative impact on growth' IMF 2012 p. 5. In 2012 Carlo Cottarelli stressed the 'schizophrenic' attitude of investors with regard to fiscal consolidation manoeuvres: their initial enthusiasm is followed by the fear of consequent recession, so that governments are 'damned if they do, damned if they don't'.

The IMF World Economic Outlook (October 2012) contains a Box by its chief economist Olivier Blanchard and Daniel Leigh arguing that fiscal multipliers have probably been under-estimated by IMF forecasts and policy documents, by the OECD and the European Commission. Recent IMF research suggests that fiscal multipliers are in the range 0.9 to 1.7, rather than the customary assumption of their being around 0.5. In other words, the cost of fiscal consolidation has been grossly under-estimated. In January 2013 Blanchard and Leigh presented a paper expanding their argument at the American Economic Association Annual Conference. However, according to the authors 'More research is needed'.

But more research was already available to the IMF: Guajardo, Leigh and Pescatori (2011) investigated 'the short-term effects of fiscal consolidation on economic activity in OECD economies.' They explain, 'We examine the historical record, including Budget Speeches and IMF documents, to identify changes in fiscal policy motivated by a desire to reduce the budget deficit and not by responding to prospective economic conditions. Using this new dataset, our estimates suggest fiscal consolidation has contractionary effects on private domestic demand and GDP. By contrast, estimates based on conventional measures of the fiscal policy stance used in the literature support the expansionary fiscal contractions hypothesis but appear to be biased toward overstating expansionary effects.' (Guajardo, Leigh and Pescatori, 2011, p. 1)

And Batini, Callegari and Melina (2012) discredit the need for cutting public/social expenditure. Especially in a downturn, expenditure multipliers can be up to *ten* times larger than tax multipliers. They find absolute values for multipliers of the order of 2.5 instead of 0.9–1.7 as in the IMF World Economic Outlook (2012) and conclude that aggressive consolidation may be much more expensive in terms of GDP than gradual consolidation.

In May 2013 Jeffrey Frankel (2013) criticized Alesina and Giavazzi (2013), Alesina and Ardagna (2010) and a further 2012 paper by Alesina with Favero and Giavazzi, all claiming that fiscal consolidation is not contractionary in a recession. Frankel criticizes the methodology of Alesina's original co-author, Perotti, and points out that some of the fiscal consolidations used by Alesina were announced by governments but never implemented. Thus Frankel concludes that Alesina 'has not been receiving his fair share of abuse' (Frankel, 2013). Alesina and Giavazzi (2013) softened very considerably their original position. In May 2013 they actually recommended the Italian government to overstep the 3 per cent deficit threshold for two years – for 'that three per cent should not be a taboo' – offering the EC in exchange immediate tax reductions on labour incomes and planned gradual and permanent expenditure cuts in the following three years. The European Commission would not close the excess deficit procedure for Italy at the end of May but should be willing to approve such a plan and verify its implementation. At the same time, credit to households and enterprises should resume through bank re-capitalization conditionally funded by the EMS.

The Reinhart-Rogoff notion of a critical 90 per cent threshold of the debt/GDP ratio was immediately criticized by Irons and Bivens (2010) who argued that causation runs backwards, in that slower growth leads to higher debt-to-GDP ratios rather than the other way round. Moreover 'there is no compelling reason to believe...that gross debt of about 90% will necessarily lead to slower economic growth....In fact, the greatest threat to economic growth is policy inaction fuelled by deficit fears.'

The final blow to the Reinhart-Rogoff 90 per cent debt/GDP dogma came from Herndon, Ash and Pollin (2013), who replicated the analysis by Reinhart and Rogoff (2010) using the original data. They found that coding errors, selective exclusion of available data and unconventional weighting of summary statistics had led Reinhart and Rogoff to serious errors: 'when properly calculated, the average real GDP growth rate for countries carrying a public-debt-to-GDP ratio of over 90 percent is actually 2.2 percent, not 0.1 percent as published in Reinhart and Rogoff' (Herndon, Ash and Pollin, 2013, p. 1). It turns out that 'average GDP growth at public debt/GDP ratios over 90 percent is not dramatically different than when debt/GDP ratios are lower' (Herndon, Ash and Pollin, 2013, p. 1).

Reinhart and Rogoff (2013) admitted some of their errors and omissions but argued that these do not alter their ultimate austerity-justifying conclusion: excessive debt depresses growth. But two subsequent studies have claimed that, on the contrary, slow growth appears to cause higher debt (as Irons and Bivens, 2010, had already argued). Dube (2013) finds that growth tends to be slower in the five years before countries have high debt levels. In the five years after they have high debt levels, there is no noticeable difference in growth at all, certainly not at the 90 per cent debt-to-GDP level regarded by Reinhart and Rogoff as the threshold of non-sustainability. Kimball and Wang (2013) present similar findings. This point is accepted by Reinhart and Rogoff (2013): 'The frontier question for research is the issue of causality.'

8.7 ...but suicidal policies persist

Such an amazing, cumulative and final discrediting of the alleged expansionary (severe at that) fiscal contraction approach, and the associated 90 per cent threshold to debt sustainability, does not appear to have had much impact on actual policies, especially on German-led European policies, with the European Union and especially countries in the European Monetary Union tied to a 'suicide pact' (Joseph Stiglitz) of so-called Growth and Stability (*The Telegraph*, 17 January 2012).

The latest EU Fiscal Compact or TSCG – Treaty on Stability, Coordination and Governance – demanded a balanced budget provision to be inserted in member states' national constitutions, subject to a maximum structural deficit of 0.5 per cent of GDP. There are penalties and automatic adjustments in case of inobservance, subject to the verification and rulings of the European Court of Justice. Financial assistance programmes under the ESM – the European Stability Mechanism that came into operation in March 2012 – from March 2013 are conditional on prior TSGC ratification.

From 2014, countries exceeding the statutory debt/GDP ceiling of 60 per cent, required by both the Maastricht Treaty and the Stability and Growth Pact, are expected to reduce the excess debt by 1/20 of the current gap every year until the ceiling is reached – which for a country like Italy at over 130 per cent involves a budgetary surplus of over 3.5 per cent a year for 20 years.

Recently the IMF criticized the Troika's [EC, ECB, IMF] handling of the Greek crisis over the last four years, but concluded that all was for the best and their policies would not be any different today in the same circumstances. In July 2013 a conference of German economists advocated that a debt/GDP ratio of 90 per cent – Reinhart and Rogoff's fated but dubious threshold – should trigger automatic debt re-structuring and bail-in.

In conclusion, the Keynesian-Kaleckian view of capitalist dynamics is alive and well. The IMF itself has been reviving it and providing theoretical and empirical backing for it, by stressing the high cost of fiscal consolidation, but at the same time continuing to officially recommend and impose such fiscal consolidation. While providing the strongest case for a fiscal stimulus, IMF research is being used even by their more enlightened officials to recommend gradual fiscal consolidation, instead of the fiscal stimulus that would be appropriately needed. Obstacles to full employment policies are still of a political nature today (resistance to a capital tax to service exceptionally high sovereign debt, in addition to the drive to maintain workers' discipline through unemployment). The time for a Kaleckian (and Keynesian) over-due revival is now, but until it takes place we are all condemned to suffer from the impoverishment and the unemployment caused by the deepest man-made economic crisis in human history.

References

Alesina, A. and S. Ardagna (2010) 'Large changes in fiscal policy: taxes versus Spending' *Tax Policy and the Economy,* Vol. 24, Cambridge Mass.: National Bureau of Economic Research.

Alesina, A., S. Ardagna and F. Trebbi (2006) 'Who adjusts and when? The political economy of reform', *IMF Staff Papers*, 53, Special Issue, Washington.

Alesina, A., Favero and Giavazzi (2013) 'The Output Effects of Fiscal Consolidations' *Working Paper* No. 18336, National Bureau of Economic Research.

Alesina, A. and F. Giavazzi (2013) 'Crescita, una proposta alternativa: Quel tre per cento non sia un tabù', *Corriere della Sera*, 17 May.

Alesina, A. and R. Perotti (1995) 'Fiscal expansion and adjustments in OECD economies', *Economic Policy*, 21: 207–247.

Baker, D. (2010) 'The myth of expansionary fiscal austerity', Centre for Economic Policy Research, October.

Barro, R.J. (1974) 'Are government bonds net wealth?', *Journal of Political Economy* 82(6): 1095–1117.

Batini, N., G. Callegari and G. Melina (2012) 'Successful austerity in the United States, Europe and Japan', Working Paper 12/190, July, Washington: International Monetary Fund.

Blanchard, O.J. (1990) 'Can severe fiscal contractions be expansionary? Tales of two small European countries: a comment', *NBER Macroeconomics Annual* Vol. 5, Cambridge, Mass.: MIT Press, pp. 111–116.

Blanchard O.J. (2008a) 'Crowding Out', *The New Palgrave Dictionary of Economics*, London: Palgrave.

Blanchard, O.J. (2008b) 'Interview with Oliver Blanchard', *IMF Survey Online* 12 February.

Broadbent, B. and K. Daly (2010), 'Limiting the fall-out from fiscal adjustments', *Goldman Sachs Global Economics Paper* 195.

Cottarelli, C. (2012) 'Fiscal adjustment: too much of a good thing?', Posted on 29 January by *iMFdirect*.

Dube, A. (2013) 'A note on debt, growth and causality', *Economist's View*, May 30.

Frankel, J. (2013) Eurointelligence.com, 22 May 2013.

Giavazzi, F. and M. Pagano (1990) 'Can severe fiscal contractions be expansionary? Tales of two small European countries', *NBER Macroeconomics Annual* Vol. 5, Cambridge, Mass.: MIT Press.

Giavazzi, F. and M. Pagano (1996) 'Non-Keynesian effects of fiscal policy changes: international evidence and the Swedish experience', *NBER Working Papers* 5332, National Bureau of Economic Research, Inc.

Guajardo, J., D. Leigh and A. Pescatori (2011) 'Expansionary Austerity: New International Evidence, *Working Paper* 11/158, Washington: International Monetary Fund.

Herndon, T., M. Ash and R.E. Pollin (2013) 'Does high public debt consistently stifle economic growth? A critique of Reinhart and Rogoff', *Working Paper* No. 322, Amherst: Political Economy Research Institute, 15 April.

Irons, J. and J. Bivens (2010) 'Government debt and economic growth: overreaching claims of debt "threshold" suffer from theoretical and empirical flaws', Briefing Paper No. 271, Amherst: Economic Policy Institute, 26 July.

International Monetary Fund (IMF) (2007) *World Economic Outlook*, Washington.

International Monetary Fund (IMF) (2010) 'Will it hurt? Macroeconomic effects of fiscal consolidation' *World Economic Outlook*, Chapter 3, Washington.

International Monetary Fund (IMF) (2012) *Fiscal Monitor Update,* 24 January, Washington.

Kalecki, M. (1933) *Proba teorii koniunktury [An Essay on the Theory of Business Cycle]*, Warszawa: Instytut Koniunktur Gospodarczych i Cen, Warsaw, published as 'Outline of a theory of the business cycle', in Kalecki (1971).
Kalecki, M. (1934) 'On foreign trade and "Domestic Exports"', translated from Polish in Kalecki (1971).
Kalecki, M. (1935) 'A macrodynamic theory of business cycles', *Econometrica*, 3(July): 327–344.
Kalecki, M. (1943) 'Political aspects of full employment', *The Political Quarterly*, 14(4): 322–330.
Kalecki, M. (1971) *Selected Essays on the Dynamics of the Capitalist Economy 1933–1970*, Cambridge: Cambridge University Press.
Keynes, J.M. (1936) *The General Theory of Employment, Interest and Money*, London: Macmillan.
Kimball, M. and Y. Wang (2013) 'After crunching Reinhart and Rogoff's data, we've concluded that high debt does not slow growth', *QUARTZ*, 29 May.
Klein, L. (1966) *The Keynesian Revolution*, Revised edition, New York: Macmillan.
Klein, L. (1975) *Foreword* to George R. Feiwel (1975), *The Intellectual Capital of Michał Kalecki*, Knoxville, Tenn.: University of Tennessee Press.
Krugman, P. (2012) *End this Depression Now.* New York: W.W. Norton.
Lange, O. (1939) 'Neoklasyczna szkola w ekonomii' [The neoclassical school of economics], reprinted in Lange, *Dziela* [Works], Vol. III, edited by T. Kowalik, Warszawa: Państwowe Wydawnictwo Naukowe, 1975, pp. 64–92.
Lucas, R.E. (1976) 'Econometric policy evaluation: a critique', *Carnegie-Rochester Conference Series on Public Policy*, 1(1): 19–46.
Nuti, D.M. (2004) 'Kalecki and Keynes re-visited', in Z.L. Sadowski and A. Szeworski (eds), *Kalecki's Economics Today*, London and New York: Routledge.
Patinkin, D. (1982) *Anticipations of the General Theory?*, Oxford: Basil Blackwell.
Reinhart, C.M. and K.S. Rogoff (2010) 'Growth in a time of debt' *NBER Working Paper* No. 15639, January.
Reinhart, C.M. and K.S. Rogoff (2013) 'Responding to our critics', *The New York Times*, 25 April.
Robertson, D. (1954) 'Thoughts on meeting some important persons', *Quarterly Journal of Economics*, 68: 181–190.
Robinson, J.V. (1964) 'Kalecki and Keynes', in P.A. Baran, et al. (eds), *Problems of Economic Dynamics and Planning: Essays in Honour of Michał Kalecki*, Warszawa: Państwowe Wydawnictwo Naukowe.
Robinson, J.V. (1976) 'Michael Kalecki: a neglected prophet', *New York Review of Books*, 23, 4 March: 28–30.

9
Kalecki's Profits Equation after 80 Years

Kazimierz Łaski and Herbert Walther

Keynes and Kalecki both assumed that private investment determines (but is not determined by) private saving. For Keynes, the desired level of saving is an increasing function of GDP, somehow related to the psychology of the society; 'autonomous' shifts of investment are determined by the state of long-term expectations. For Kalecki, the saving propensity depends on the income distribution in a capitalist society, while investment expenditures are determined by past investment decisions. The causality link between investment and saving runs through profits. We take a look at short-run and long-run aspects of Kalecki's fundamental profit equation: (1) We argue that the short lag between investment decisions and expenditures is an essential element of any meaningful interpretation of Kalecki's profit equation. This lag has critical implications for the interpretation of the multiplier, for the story of 'wage-led versus profit-led growth' and for the various tax paradoxes related to the Kaleckian profit equation. (2) We argue that an excess of desired long-term saving over investment, which might be caused by demographic ageing in Western economies, can only be eliminated by accepting the necessity of a permanent primary public deficit and/or active redistributive policies.

9.1 Kalecki versus Keynes

Keynes and Kalecki both assumed that private investment determines (but it is not determined by) private savings. However, the link between savings and GDP is not the same for both. For Keynes the desired level of saving is an increasing function of GDP, somehow related to the psychology of the society. Adjustment of aggregate demand and income – the expenditure 'multiplier' – induces ex-post equality of saving to pre-determined investment. For Kalecki the causality link between investment and saving is the same, but the link to GDP goes through profits, the driving force of a capitalist economy. And it turns out that the relation between savings and GDP is more complicated than assumed by Keynes.

9.1.1 Kalecki's profit equation with outside savings

As a sum of incomes we have for a closed economy without the state:

$$Y = P + B + W \tag{9.1}$$

where P = (gross) profit, including depreciation, rent and interest; B = overheads, mostly salaries and income of management and non-manual workers, that is, fixed labour costs; W = wages of manual workers, assumed to be a share ($0 < \alpha < 1$) of Y, representing variable labour costs.

National income can be presented also as the sum of expenditures:

$$Y = I_P + C_c + C_E \tag{9.2}$$

where I_P = expenditure of firms on gross private capital formation; C_c = expenditure of 'capitalists' on consumption; C_E = consumption expenditure out of 'earned income', that is, out of the sum of wages, W, and salaries, *B*.

From (1) and (2) we get:

$$P + B + W = I_P + C_c + C_E \tag{9.3}$$

By definition,

$$P = I_P + C_c - (B + W - C_E) \tag{9.4}$$

$$P = I_P + C_c - S_E \tag{9.5}$$

where S_E (= $B + W - C_E$) is saving out of 'earned incomes'. Assuming *SE* = 0 Kalecki gets the identity

$$P = I_P + C_c \tag{9.6}$$

according to which profits are equal to the sum of private investment and capitalists' consumption. The fundamental Kaleckian equation of profit generation (9.5) can be extended (as will be done below) by adding government deficits and current account surplus.

The most important macroeconomic question concerns the causality in this equation. Kalecki's explanation runs like this: capitalists can decide to invest or consume next year more than this year, but they cannot decide to earn more profits; hence their profits are determined by I_P and C_c and not vice-versa. It is no exaggeration to say that this thesis is the very core of the theory of effective demand.[1]

That the right hand side (r.h.s.) of equation (9.5) determines the left hand side (l.h.s.) does not contradict the possibility that investment and consumption decisions of capitalists are – by some vague behavioural regularities – linked to past profits generating the possibility of positive feed-back mechanisms. But even under such conditions, the causality in Kalecki's profit equation does not change. The issue of 'causality versus simultaneity' will become important again, when we discuss the possibility of a 'profit-led growth' scenario (Bhaduri and Marglin, 1990).

When $S_E > 0$ we get (9.5), according to which profits suffer when part of earned incomes is saved. Indeed, in this case for pre-determined I_P and C_c, profits, P, are the smaller the higher S_E, savings out of earned income, are.

9.2 The Marxian reproduction scheme

The role of 'outside saving' can be best understood when – disregarding overheads – a Marxian reproduction scheme is used with three vertically integrated sectors producing investment goods (sector I), consumption goods for capitalists (sector II) and consumptions goods for workers (sector III) as final goods. The value added produced in every sector is equal to the sum of wages W_i and Profits P_i, (i = I, II, III). Indeed, the sum of wages in the sectors I and II (= $W_{\text{I}} + W_{\text{II}}$) represents an external demand for sector III. This external demand generates profits in sector III, which represents a surplus of goods produced in the sector III above W_{III}, the internal sales of consumption goods for workers produced in sector III. P_{III} will therefore match $W_{\text{I}} + W_{\text{II}}$ when no savings out of these wages are made.

$$W_I + W_{II} = P_{III} \tag{9.10}$$

By adding to both sides P_{I} and P_{II} we get

$$(W_I + P_I) + (W_{II} + P_{II}) = P_I + P_{II} + P_{III} \tag{9.11}$$

$$I_P + C_c = P \tag{9.12}$$

which is again Equation (9.6). When some savings out of $W_{\mathrm{I}} + W_{\mathrm{II}}$ denoted S_E are made, then

$$W_I + W_{II} - S_E = P_{III} \tag{9.13}$$

We can prove in the same way that profits, *P*, would be smaller than $I_P + C_c$ by the amount of S_E according to Equation (9.5). Hence the output of sector III – given output of sectors I and II – depends upon the size of S_E. The smaller S_E and the higher external demand for the goods surplus in sector III, the higher the saleable output of this sector. This is how the principle of effective demand can be explained – it is the demand created by spending in sectors I and II that drives the supply in sector III. Of course, this implies the existence of not fully utilized capacity in this sector. But idle capacity and unemployment are basic features of a capitalist economy. Goods, especially consumer goods, 'queue' here for buyers, and workers 'queue' for jobs while in opposition to this in centrally planned economies buyers 'queued' for goods and jobs for workers.

9.3 A simple extension of Kalecki's profit equation

Let P_R designate 'retained profits', and P_D be distributed profits. Therefore

$$P_R + P_D = P \tag{9.14}$$

Let us assume that the managers and the boards of corporate firms decide upon the share of retained profits $0 < \rho < 1$.

$$P_R = \rho\, P \tag{9.15}$$

Corporate gross profits are partly retained and partly distributed to an extremely heterogeneous group of share and bond holders – ranging from rich 'capitalists' (hedge-fund managers or some corporate managers) to retired (non-manual) workers. In the system of financial capitalism the latter group receives small supplementary 'funded pensions' in addition to social security.

From a political point of view, the economic interests of this heterogeneous category of capital income recipients (with respect to anti-inflationary policies, anti-welfare state policies, etc.) are at least partly aligned to those of the genuine, classical 'capitalists'. This explains why a shift to 'funded pensions' and the dismantling of the 'pay as you go' system is so vigorously and partly successfully propagated by the 'Wall Street' lobbies and the financial sector.[2] Given the highly concentrated nature of the household distribution of capital income, it seems nevertheless to be justified to differentiate between the saving propensity out of distributed profit and the saving propensity out of wages and/or salaries. In the age of financial capitalism, the managerial power of determining ρ has been challenged by the governance of investment fund representatives in the board of corporate firms – presumably acting in the interest of an anonymous mass of non-entrepreneurial 'rentiers'. The parameter ρ becomes the outcome of a bargaining struggle between entrepreneurial and fund managers.

The consumption of 'capitalists' (or alternatively 'rentiers'), C_c, is based on expected profit, $\hat{P}$

$$C_c = (1-\sigma_c)(1-\rho)\hat{P} \tag{9.16}$$

where σ_c is the marginal and average propensity to save out of distributed profits. Following Kalecki, consumption of capitalists will be characterized by a high degree of inertia relative to fluctuations in current profits. First, this is because corporate profits can only be distributed with a lag. Secondly, this is because profit expectations will adjust to changes in current profits rather slowly. And thirdly, because the absence of liquidity and credit constraints implies that the wealthy can smooth consumption much more easily across time.

Let us further assume that saving out of wages, W, is equal to zero. Therefore, saving out of earned income, S_E, is equal to saving out of fixed income, B. Let σ_B be the marginal and average propensity to save for salary recipients.

$$S_E = S_B = \sigma_B B \tag{9.17}$$

Kalecki assumed that the current level of investment expenditure is predetermined since there will be a natural and unavoidable lag between investment decisions and the execution of those decisions. Therefore, in any particular historical period, profits will be determined by the predetermined r.h.s. of Equation (9.18).

$$P=I_P + C_C - \sigma B \tag{9.18}$$

Usually there will be involuntary saving/dissaving of firms and/or of capitalists since expectations with regard to profits are always uncertain.

Hypothetical equilibrium profit requires that profit expectations of capitalists are fulfilled $\hat{P} = P^*$. Then,

$$P^* = I_p + (1-\sigma_c)(1-\rho)P^* - \sigma_B B \tag{9.19}$$

Rearrangement of Equation (9.19) shows that this condition is tantamount to the Keynesian equality of desired saving to investment:

$$\rho P^* + \sigma_c(1-\rho)P^* + \sigma_B B = I_p \tag{9.20}$$

Solving for equilibrium profits gives:

$$P^* = \frac{I_P - \sigma_B B}{\rho + \sigma_C(1-\rho)} \tag{9.21}$$

Contrary to Keynes (and far ahead of most economists of his time) Kalecki had already developed a theory of the share of 'variable labour costs', α, which is related to the 'degree of monopoly' in the economy (Kalecki, 1939).

If α is determined by the 'degree of monopoly', then by definition,

$$P = Y - W - B \tag{9.22}$$

$$P = (1-\alpha)Y - B \tag{9.23}$$

Therefore,

$$Y^* = \frac{P^* + B}{1-\alpha} \tag{9.24}$$

Substituting for P^*, we get an expression for equilibrium income Y^*.

$$Y^* = \frac{1}{1-\alpha}\frac{I_P + B(\rho + \sigma_C(1-\rho) - \sigma_B)}{\rho + \sigma_C(1-\rho)} \tag{9.25}$$

9.4 Some implications

It is interesting to compare the implications of Kalecki's extended 'investment-saving' equilibrium with the standard investment-saving presentation of Keynesian economics popularized by Samuelson and still a cornerstone of introductory macroeconomics courses. Let A be the autonomous consumption and s be the marginal propensity to save, then

$$-A+sY = I_P \tag{9.26}$$

$$Y^* = \frac{I_P + A}{S}$$

First, let us note that the formally analogous component to the 'autonomous' consumption ('autonomous' dissaving), part of the Keynesian model appearing in Equation (9.25), can only be positive (negative) if

$$\rho + \sigma_C(1-\rho) > \sigma_B \tag{9.27}$$

which can – and will from now on – be safely assumed. The aggregate "Kaleckian' counterpart to the Keynesian aggregate saving function can be written as

$$S = -B(\rho + \sigma_C)((1-\rho)-\sigma_B) + (1-\alpha)(\rho+\sigma_C(1-\rho))Y \tag{9.28}$$

Contrary to the Keynesian aggregate saving function, it is not possible to separate neatly changes of the marginal propensity to save from shifts of 'autonomous' consumption. Note also that the 'marginal propensity to save' in the economy is not related to any (more or less vague) 'fundamental psychological law', but to the 'degree of monopoly' and to the retention ratio of profits. These are essential characteristics related to the power structure of a modern capitalist economy, linked to the price-setting power of firms on the one hand, and to the whole institutional framework regulating the power of unions and the interests of the managerial and the capitalist classes on the other hand.[3]

The Kaleckian determination of output shown in Equation (9.25) has richer implications than the simple Keynesian income-expenditure model (analytical derivations can be found in the Appendix):

9.4.1 If the saving rate of salary recipients, σ_B, rises (perhaps due to a shift from 'pay as you go' to 'funded' retirement saving), profits, aggregate demand and equilibrium output decrease.

9.4.2 If the saving rate out of distributed profits, σ_C, rises, profits, aggregate demand and output fall.

9.4.3 If all firms simultaneously try to increase the ratio of retained profits, ρ, (because managers wish to 'deleverage'), demand and output fall.

9.4.4 If the aggregate income of salary recipients, B, falls, profits rise (because of lower household savings), while aggregate demand and output fall.

9.4.5 If the share of variable labour costs, α, falls, output and demand decrease, while profits remain constant (as can be seen from equations (9.25) and (9.21)).

9.5 The graphical summary

In Figure 9.1 we have illustrated the latter case (9.4.5). A lower α reduces the slope and the intercept of the linear relationship between income and profits (constructed according to Kalecki's theory of the degree of

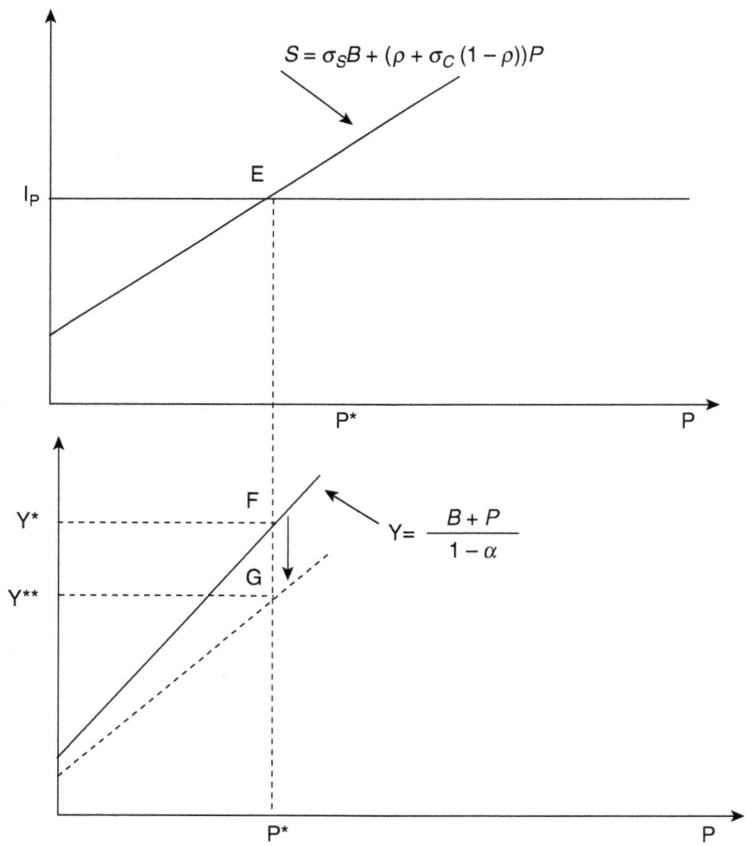

Figure 9.1 Lowering the wage share

monopoly (Kalecki, 1939a). In accordance with Equation (9.24) lowers aggregate demand and output is reduced from Y* to Y** at the same level of profits.

It is possible to condense Figure 9.1 to a single diagram (Figure 9.2), which illustrates the 'Kaleckian cross' implicit in our equations, analogous to the 'Keynesian cross'. In Figure 9.2, private investment is equal to desired aggregate saving at the income level Y*. Retained profits (P_R) as a function of Y are shown by the dashed line with slope $\rho\ (1–\alpha)$ and a constant term $- \rho B$. Adding saving of capitalists, S_c, to retained profits, P_R, gives a solid line with steeper slope $\rho + \sigma_C(1–\alpha)$ and the smaller constant term $- (\rho\ \sigma_C + (1 - \alpha)B)$, showing total savings out of profits.

At the equilibrium level desired savings from profits (S_C+P_R) plus the desired savings of salary recipients ($\sigma_B B$) must be equal to predetermined investment expenditure, I_P. As can be seen, this is the case at the income level, Y^*, where the horizontal line $I_P - S_B$ cuts the S_C+P_R line (at point E). The equilibrium values of P_R, S_C, C_C and P are given by the distances Y *F, FE, EG and Y*G, respectively. Household saving is equal to Sc + S_B, which is equal to the vertical difference between the horizontal I_p-line

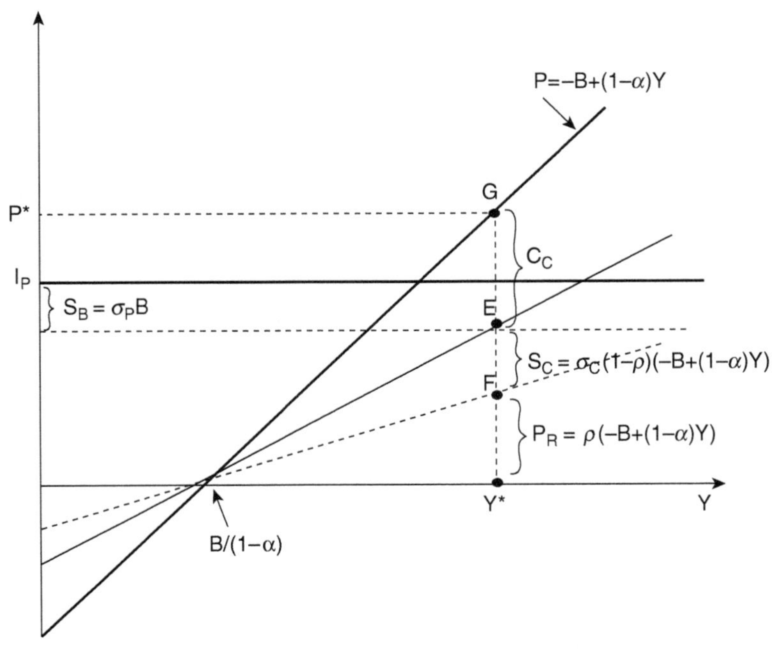

Figure 9.2 The Kaleckian cross

and the dashed line of retained profits, P_R. Obviously, total household saving must also be equal to external finance of investment.

It is immediately apparent that a higher saving rate of non-manual workers, σ_B; a higher saving rate of capitalists, σ_c; or a higher retention rate, ρ, lowers equilibrium profits and income.

Note that the Kaleckian profit equation $C_C + I_P - S_B = P$ can be made visible in Figure 9.2 by adding up distance EG (= C_C) and Y*E (= $I_P - S_P$) to Y*G (= P).

9.6 Profit-led versus wage-led growth

Insights (9.4.4) and (9.4.5) raise some doubts with respect to potential 'profit-led' growth, as suggested by Bhaduri and Marglin (1990), following Rowthorn (1981), Dutt (1984), Taylor (1985), Blecker (1989; 2011). Let K be the capital stock and let us assume that private investment depends in a very general way on profitability and the utilization ratio.

$$I_P = j\left(\frac{P}{K}, \frac{Y}{K}\right) \tag{9.29}$$

If α, the share of wages of manual workers falls, for profit-led growth to evolve, investment or consumption of capitalists must rise immediately and more than necessary to compensate for lower consumption of workers. If, however, as Kalecki assumes, investment and consumption of capitalists react with a lag to changes in profits and aggregate demand, after the reduction of α, profits remain constant first, while aggregate demand and output decrease. In the second period, consumption of capitalists might still remain constant, while lower investment (9.29) reduces profits (and aggregate demand declines even further).

What happens if only salaries, B, are reduced? Profits rise, as

$$\frac{\partial P}{\partial B} = \frac{-\sigma_B}{\rho + \sigma_C(1-\rho)} < 0 \tag{9.30}$$

while simultaneously a 'profit-led slump' develops.

$$\frac{\partial Y}{\partial B} = \frac{\rho + \sigma_C(1-\rho) - \sigma_B}{(1-\alpha)(\rho + \sigma_C(1-\rho))} > 0 \tag{9.31}$$

Consequently, a hypothetical profit-led growth requires that the effect of higher profitability on investment expenditures dominates the counteracting effect of lower capacity utilization.

Any simple comparative static extension of our analysis (by integrating Equation (9.29) into the model and studying the signs of derivatives) can be seriously misleading, however: Due to the Kaleckian lag between investment decisions and investment spending, avoidance of the 'profit-led slump' solution in Equation (9.31) requires that private investment decisions react to lower B in advance. This, however, is only possible if private investors expect that profits will rise as a consequence of lowering B in the future. However, a 'wait and see' attitude of investors is much more plausible under such circumstances, but not sufficient for reversing the sign of Equation (9.31).

The whole argument in favour of 'profit-led growth' becomes even weaker, if one takes into account that lowering B will only be feasible, if – due to high unemployment – the bargaining power of entrepreneurs is sufficiently strong. Even if this is the case and even if profits slightly rise in response to lower B, when capacities are already underutilized any further decline of Y will act as a powerful brake against any rise of investment.

Nevertheless, the idea of 'profit-led growth', while particularly inappropriate as a policy strategy during a global depression, might have a kernel of truth – under extreme conditions in the very long-run – albeit this is a completely different issue.[4] Clearly, to compensate for entrepreneurial risk, the rate of profit cannot fall below a minimum bound. It is important that long-run wage and income policies do not violate this long-run profitability barrier. Raising an (appropriately adjusted) level of real wages in accordance with the increase of labour productivity (and avoiding the failure of procyclical wage policy!) is probably the best compromise to stabilize investors' state of confidence with regard to long-term profitability on the one hand and aggregate consumption of employees (as much as possible) on the other hand.

Distinguishing between the 'long-run' and the 'short-run' perspective is also highly relevant for the alternative – equally dubious – 'wage-led growth' strategy. Clearly, if α or B are already 'too high', threatening to violate the minimum profit rate barrier, any further rise might have severe negative effects on investment, so that aggregate demand (and consumption of workers) might even collapse – contrary to what we have derived in the preceding section.[5] We conclude that neither a short-sighted 'profit-led' nor an aggressive 'wage-led' growth strategy can be useful substitutes for vigorous anticyclical fiscal policy during a deep crisis and for labour productivity oriented long-run wage policy.

9.7 The government sector

Let us extend the model to include a government sector. How does this change the fundamental equation of profit determination? Let G be the government expenditures for goods and services. Now, gross profits, P, and salaries, B, are defined gross of taxes.[6] Expenditure must be equal to revenues, therefore, by definition

$$P + B + W = I_P + G + C_c + C_E + C_W \tag{9.32}$$

Total government revenues are the sum of corporate taxes, T_c, and income taxes, T_i, calculated net of transfers and interest on public debt.

$$T = T_c + T_i \tag{9.33}$$

The income tax rate (net of transfers) $0 < \theta < 1$, is assumed to be the same for salaries and distributed profits. Corporate profits are taxed at a rate $0 < \theta_C < 1$. Workers do not pay net taxes, but salary recipients and capitalists pay net income tax. Then, total net tax revenues, T, are the sum of revenues from income tax, T_i, and corporate tax revenues, T_c.

$$T = T_i + T_c \tag{9.34}$$

$$= \theta[B + (1-\rho)(1-\theta_C)P] + \theta_C P \tag{9.35}$$

Gross profits are the sum of retained profits, distributed profits and corporate taxes:

$$P = P_R + P_D + T_c \tag{9.36}$$

Assuming $C_W = W$, and subtracting B, T and P_D from both sides of Equation (9.32) gives

$$P - P_D - (T_c + T_i) = I_P + D + C_c + C_E - (P_D + B) \tag{9.37}$$

where $D = G - T$ is the primary government deficit. Adding now the sum of distributed profits and tax revenues on both sides,

$$P = I_P + D + T_c + P_D - (P_D + B - T_i - C_c - C_E) \tag{9.38}$$

$$= I_P + D + T_c + P_D - S_H \tag{9.39}$$

the modified Kaleckian profit Equation (9.39) can be derived. Gross profits are the sum of private investment, the budget deficit, corporate taxes and distributed profits minus household saving. Any observable change in the empirical level of gross profits must therefore – by definition – find its counterpart somewhere at the r.h.s. of Equation (9.39).

Is it still possible to argue that in any particular period the r.h.s. of (9.39) is causally determining the l.h.s.? The answer is yes because it can be easily shown (see Appendix) that Equation (9.39) is tantamount to

$$P = I_P + G + C_C - B[1-(1-\theta)(1-\sigma_B)] \tag{9.40}$$

Similar to investment, there is a considerable lag between budgetary decisions and government expenditures.

Equation (9.39) can be written as the Keynesian equality of private saving, that is, the sum of retained profits plus household saving to private investment plus government deficit:

$$P_R + S_H = I_P + D \tag{9.41}$$

By definition, distributed profits, P_D, are

$$P_D = (1-\rho)(1-\theta_C)P \tag{9.42}$$

Consumption of capitalists, based on expected profits is equal to

$$C = b\hat{P} \tag{9.43}$$

where

$$b \equiv (1-\sigma_C)(1-\theta)(1-\theta_C)(1-\rho) \tag{9.44}$$

is the marginal propensity to consume of capitalists, which depends on the retention ratio, the corporate tax rate, the income tax rate and the saving rate. Let us again assume that profit expectations are fulfilled ($P = P = P^*$). Substituting in Equation (9.39) the expressions for corporate and income taxes (9.35), for desired saving of capitalist ($= \sigma_C P_D$) and salary recipients ($=\sigma_B B$), as well as (9.42) for distributed profits, P_D, the modified expression (9.39) can be solved to determine gross profits:

$$P^* = \frac{G + I_P - B\left[1-(1-\theta)(1-\sigma_B)\right]}{1-b} > 0 \tag{9.45}$$

Similarly, equilibrium output and government deficit are determined by

$$Y^* = \frac{B+P^*}{(1-\alpha)} > 0 \tag{9.46}$$

$$D^* = G - \theta B - [\theta(1-\rho)(1-\theta_C)] + \theta_C > 0 \tag{9.47}$$

If government expenditures increase by one euro, profit increases by $(1–b)_{-1}$, output by $[(1–\alpha)(1–b)]^{-1}$ and the government deficit by

$$\Delta D^* = 1 - \frac{\theta(1-\rho)(1-\theta_C)+\theta_C}{1-b} \tag{9.48}$$

Obviously, the deficit does not increase by the full amount of additional government spending.[7]

9.8 Kalecki's corporate tax paradox

Let us assume that the government raises the corporate tax rate, *Bc*, and simultaneously adjusts government expenditure by the full amount of additional tax revenues. Therefore,

$$G = T + D_O \tag{9.50}$$

where D_O is the fixed budget balance. Substituting in first Equation (9.45) in the r.h.s. of Equation (9.50) and then *T* as defined in Equation (9.35), we can solve again for P^*

$$P^* = \frac{1}{1-\theta_C}\left[\frac{I_P + D_0 - B\sigma_B(1-\theta)}{\rho+\sigma_C(1-\rho)(1-\theta)}\right] \tag{9.51}$$

$$(1-\theta_C)P^* = \frac{I_P + D_0 - B\sigma_B(1-\theta)}{\rho+\sigma_C(1-\rho)(1-\theta)} \tag{9.52}$$

The implications for varying θ_c are straightforward: any rise in θ_c, leading to higher tax revenues (as demonstrated above) and accompanied by an equivalent rise in government spending, raises profits gross of taxation by an amount just necessary for net profits $(1 - \theta_c)P$ to remain constant, as can be seen immediately from Equation (9.52), where the r.h.s. is independent of θ_c and *P* and exogenously given.

Several qualifications – already brought forward by Kalecki – are important. First, capitalists might expect falling net profits and react by increasing the degree of monopoly. Secondly, consumption of capitalists might react in response to lower expected income.[8]

9.9 A Kaleckian income tax paradox

We can check in a similar way the effects of an increase of the income tax rate, *B*, if additional tax revenues are fully spent by the government. Varying θ in (9.51), profits before and after corporate tax rise, as can be seen in (9.53):

$$\frac{\partial P^*}{\partial \theta} = \frac{1}{1-\theta_C}\left[\frac{\sigma_C(1-\rho)(I_P + D_0) + B\rho\sigma_B}{(\rho+\sigma_C(1-\rho)(1-\theta))^2}\right] > 0 \tag{9.53}$$

This result raises the question, whether net distributed profits after corporate and income tax could also rise (or remain at least constant) under such circumstances.

It can be shown (for proof see Appendix) that distributed profits net of all taxes ($= (1-\theta)(1-\theta_C)(1-\rho)P$) fall after a rise of the income tax, if and only if

$$\frac{\sigma_B(1-\theta)B}{I_P + D_0} < \frac{\rho}{(2\rho+\sigma_C(1-\rho)(1-\theta))} \tag{9.54}$$

Given (9.54), the overall tax burden for capitalists rises, in spite of higher net corporate profits. If, however, the saving out of net salaries is sufficiently high relative to the sum of investment and government deficit, a rise of the income tax rate might even increase net distributed profits.

Intuitively, under such circumstances, higher θ becomes more powerful to reduce private saving and income tax financed expansionary fiscal policies become more powerful. Note that the successful fight of investment fund managers for lower retention ratios and the political pressure towards funded pension schemes designed for salary recipients (raising σ_B) increase the odds for switching to a positive sign in (9.54).

9.10 The current account

While exports can be seen as an exogenous variable for the present purpose of analysis, import demand will be part of the final demand for goods and services. The marginal propensity to import will probably be the highest for investment goods and exports, lower for consumption of capitalists and salary recipients and even lower for government expenditures and consumption of workers. It should be kept in mind that the marginal propensity to import relevant for the fiscal multiplier can therefore be much lower than the average propensity, which is particularly relevant for an economically correct interpretation of the fiscal multiplier (Łaski, Osiatyński and Zięba, 2010).

For the sake of simplicity, let us assume that the marginal propensity to import (mpi) of workers is zero; the mpi for investment demand plus exports is $0 < mx < 1$, the mpi for consumption of capitalists is $0 < m_c < m_x < 1$, and for salary recipients
$0 < m_B < m_c < 1$. Therefore

$$M = m_x(I_P + X) + m_B B + m_C(1-\theta)(1-\rho)(1-\theta_C)P \tag{9.55}$$

Expenditure net of imports must be equal to gross income:

$$P + B + W = I_P + G + C_C + C_B + C_W + X - M \tag{9.57}$$

Similar manipulations like above give us the modified Kaleckian profit equation:

$$P = I_P + D + P_D + T_C + X - M - S_H \tag{9.57}$$

Substituting Equation (9.55) and expressions for D, P_D, T_c and S_H allows to solve for P^*,

$$P^* = \frac{G + (X + I_P)(1 - m_x) - B\left(1 - (1-\theta)(1-\sigma_B)(1 - m_B)\right)}{1 - b(1 - m_C)} \tag{9.58}$$

where b is again the marginal propensity to consume of capitalists, Equation (9.44). The fiscal multiplier now becomes

$$\Delta P = \frac{\Delta G}{1 - b(1 - m_C)} \tag{9.59}$$

Output and demand rise by

$$\Delta Y = \frac{\Delta G}{(1-\alpha)(1-b(1-m_C))} \tag{9.60}$$

The higher the marginal import propensity, m_c, and the lower the share of wages, α, the lower becomes the multiplier.

An export surplus fulfils a similar function as an internal government deficit by raising profits without the necessity to increase public debt or to reduce household saving (9.61).

$$\Delta P = \frac{(1-m_x)\Delta X}{1-b(1-m_C)} \tag{9.61}$$

Equation (9.57) is equivalent to the following, familiar one, which shows the sectorial financial balances of the private sector, the government sector and the foreign sector:

$$S_H + (P - T_C - P_D) - I_P + (T - G) = X - M \tag{9.62}$$

$$(S_P - I_P) + (T - G) = X - M \tag{9.63}$$

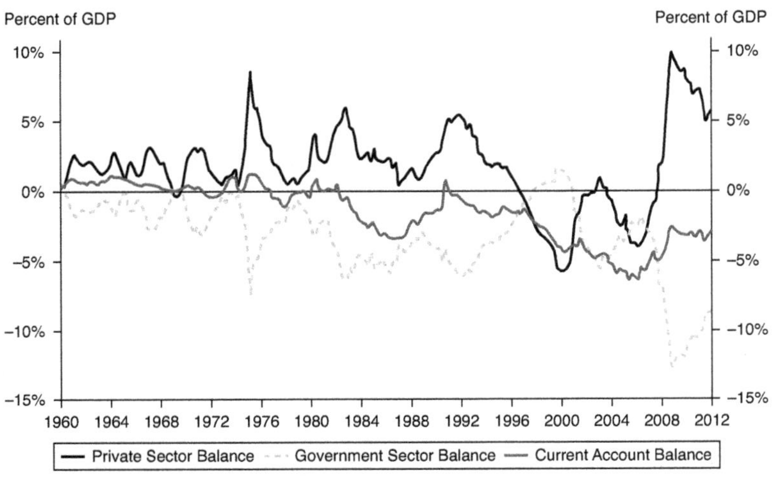

Figure 9.3 US sectoral financial balances

Source: US Department of Commerce and US Federal Reserve.

Figure 9.3 illustrates the empirical side of this equation for the US. When the surplus of private saving, S_P, over private investment, I_P, rises, aggregate demand suffers lowering imports and income; therefore, the balance of the foreign sector improves and the government balance deteriorates.

9.11 The long-term problem of full-employment

Kalecki (1945) asked the interesting question, whether a policy of stimulating private investment via lower interest rates can be a sustainable policy or whether capitalism might suffer from a rate of accumulation, which is structurally (not cyclically) too low for maintaining full employment.

Kalecki's argument can be presented in a nutshell as follows: To maintain full employment, that is, for aggregate demand to be permanently equal to full employment output, *Yf*, the following conditions must be fulfilled: The economy must start from a state of full employment and the rate of accumulation of capital, $\Delta K/K$, must be equal to the growth rate of potential output, which is equal to the sum of the growth rates of population, n, and labour productivity, m. Gross investment, $I_p > \Delta K$, must also include depreciation (= δK). Therefore,

$$\frac{\Delta K}{K} = n + m \tag{9.64}$$

$$\frac{I_P}{K} = n + m + \delta \tag{9.65}$$

The condition expressed in Equation (9.65) implies that capital-productivity, $Y_f\,/K = v$ remains constant over time and the capital stock per capita rises with the rate of labour productivity. Consequently, for full employment to be maintained, the share of gross investment must be equal to $(n + m + \delta/v)$

$$\frac{I_P\,/\,K}{Y_f\,/\,K} = \frac{I_P}{Y_f} = \frac{n + m + \delta}{v} = \frac{S}{Y_f} \tag{9.66}$$

If and only if the desired gross saving rate out of full employment income, S/Y_f is equal to this gross investment share, a steady-state growth with full employment might be possible.

Now, let us assume that, starting from such a situation, the degree of monopoly rises and remains forever at the higher level. Desired gross saving would rise above gross investment, and demand and output would fall, as we have shown above. If investment is stimulated by lower interest rates, so that the share of investment rises sufficiently to compensate for the leakage of higher saving, the rate of accumulation rises above $n + m + \delta$: however, capital productivity and the rate of profit must fall. Contrary to the neoclassical model of Solow, where v smoothly adjusts via capital deepening to a lower equilibrium level (and everything is fine again at a lower level of marginal productivity of capital), for Kalecki a decrease of capital productivity is tantamount to an increase of unused capacity – which has a negative impact on investment. The interest rate would have to fall again and again to boost investment. This cannot be a sustainable policy (but might lead to temporary, dangerous and illusionary relief via repeated asset price bubbles).

If higher investment is not sufficient to compensate for the higher leakage of saving, alternative routes might be the following ones:

9.11.1 Raising public deficits to close the gap between (excessive) desired full employment saving and capital accumulation. This strategy raises the question of the long-run sustainability of public debt. The revival of orthodox economic thinking after the inflationary 1970s had propagated the fatal dogma that real interest rates on government bonds should be – on average – at least as high as the growth rate of GDP, so that governments are forced to respect an intertemporal budget constraint like private agents. Obviously, this type of thinking denies the possibility of a structural gap between the desired saving rate at full employment and the steady-state rate of capital accumulation. Actually, the average annual growth rate of real GDP in the US had been 3.1 per cent after the war, while the real interest rate on long-term government bonds had been approximately 2 per cent (Bradford DeLong and Magin, 2009) or even less.[9] The prescription given by orthodox economics is therefore at odds with historical realities. But it is also at odds with institutional realities in the US, where public debt can always be monetized by the Fed, cancelling the necessity to pay interest at all. Therefore, to close a long-term structural saving/investment gap via primary deficits is not only viable, but also recommendable (provided a country has the power to manage its own currency).

9.11.2 Generating structural export surplus via 'beggar my neighbour' policies (the German, mercantilist strategy), is an unsustainable way, however, as can be seen in the Euro-crisis.
9.11.3 Lowering household saving by stimulating indebtedness of households and creating virtual wealth (Bhaduri, Łaski and Riese, 2006) via asset price bubbles (the US route during the 1990s) will not be sustainable either.
9.11.4 Lowering household saving by redistribution (higher corporate taxes, higher income taxes, higher inheritance taxes, higher wealth taxes) and increasing government expenditures for welfare.

Only (9.11.1) and (9.11.4) seem to be economically meaningful and sustainable (and had been the basis for preventing a recurrence of the Great Depression after the Second World War in the 1950s and 1960s), but in a capitalist economy political resistance against both routes is – for obvious reasons – strongest.

9.12 The rise of 'financial capitalism'

While Kalecki never had been a Marxist, his thinking was obviously influenced by the Marxian reproduction schemes and by the idea that class conflicts are important – theoretically and empirically. The background of his ideas was been the intellectual and social world of the 1930s. The world, however, has changed considerably since that time. To put the extension of his basic model, into a historical perspective, it is necessary to take a short look at the changing historical conditions of capitalism.

In the period after the Second World War, modern capitalism has undergone a significant transformation. Somewhat simplified, one can say that from the 1950s to the 1970s a system of 'managerial capitalism' dominated, while since the 1980s a system of 'financial capitalism' has evolved. In the first period retained profits provided the basis for the accumulation of equity by and for loyal, long-term shareholders, while external finance primarily relied on similarly long-term credit relationships. Financial capitalism, which evolved due to the deregulation of financial markets and the rise of investment and pension funds, weakened long-term relationships, fostered lower corporate taxes and higher dividends at the expense of internal accumulation and tried to strengthen the weight of external finance (not only via credits, junk bonds, etc., but also via newly issued shares).

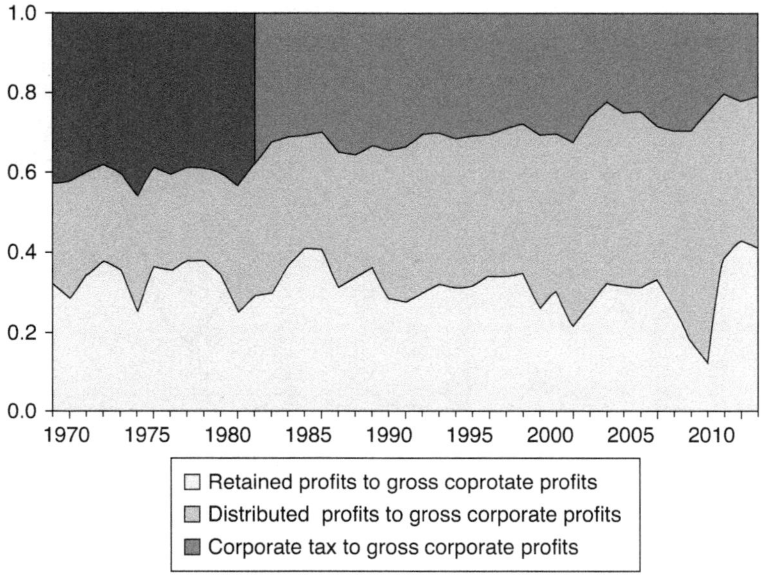

Figure 9.4 The uses of gross corporate profits
Source: Bureau of Economic Analysis; calculation by the authors.

Figure 9.4 illustrates these trends for the US. While the ratio of corporate taxes to gross corporate profits dramatically decreased between 1969 and 2011 from 42 per cent to 21 per cent, the share of net dividend payments to gross corporate profits shows a clear upward trend from below 30 per cent to more than 50 per cent just before the great financial crises.

The theoretical basis behind these shifts had been the ideologically biased faith in the importance of capital mobility as a manager's discipline device to maximize the shareholder value.

One of the negative implications of the strengthening of 'rentier interests' had been a shift towards extreme 'short-termism' of managerial decision making at many levels (profit maximization, portfolio shifts, employment policies, mark to market valuations, etc.).[10]

Another consequence had been a trend towards higher leverage ratios to raise the returns on equity, pointing to the ongoing relevance of Kalecki's famous 'principle of increasing risk' (and the dangers of financial fragility for the stability of the system as a whole.)

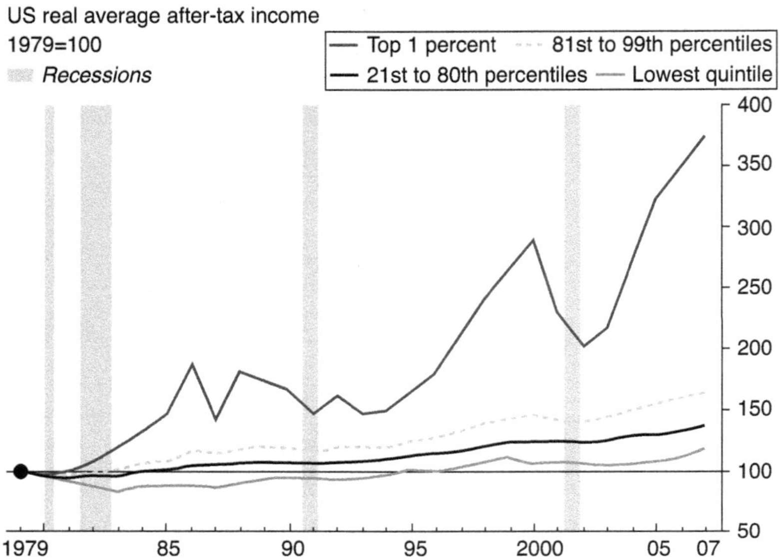

Figure 9.5 Increasing income inequality in the US

Deregulation, liberalization and the rise of financial capitalism (starting in the 'Reagan/Thatcher era' of the early 1980s) had been simultaneously a cause and a consequence of rising income inequality: On the one hand, the freedom for industry to switch locations in search of the lowest wage costs (and lowest tax bills) on earth dramatically increased the economic and political bargaining power of corporations. On the other hand, rising inequality of income (see Figure 9.5) and wealth became a genuine source of demand for sophisticated financial services – besides shifting political power even further in favour of their interests. Increasing concentration of savings and financial wealth in the higher and highest income groups implies a shrinking market for consumer goods and weaker stimuli for private investment, however.

Changes in the distribution of income are not the only factor in strengthening the role of finance in relation to the real economy. In Europe after two world wars and the great crisis of the 1930s that devastated financial assets, a long period of peace unknown on this continent succeeded. Hence conditions have been created for the appearance of a first generation of inheritors. Young private households very often do not start from scratch but inherit some wealth after their parents. The heritage is in turn not consumed but used for financial investment. Their value increases with time and is passed further to the next generation. As a consequence, rentier interests in society expand. Last but not least the ageing of society in Europe caused both by higher longevity and smaller fertility has been used as a pretext to substitute the old, cheap 'pay as you go' system through the expensive capital-funded system. It is, of course, true that in an ageing society the relation between pension payments and pension rewards must – and would – deteriorate. No changes in the pension system can solve this difficulty since it depends upon demography, not the method of its financing. But the gradual substitution of the 'pay as you go' system by a capital-funded system in many European countries has well served the world of finance. On the one hand, pension funds came into existence as additional great players on the capital market; on the other hand, the old 'pay as you go' system must continuously be serviced and when payments do not come in, it is the government budget that is forced to fund pensions through deficits and public debt.

As a result of these changes the position of finance in relation to the real economy has further strengthened. Financial investors require rates of return which disregard the possibilities of the economy. If the latter increases by 2–3 per cent per annum and rates of return (measured in per cent of capital) are more or less of the same order, then a double-digit rate of return on financial instruments cannot be achieved. What remains possible are speculative bubbles that may increase as long as the capital gains remain notional, that is, are not realized on a larger basis; however, sooner or later such bubbles explode and cause havoc in the whole economy. It should be stressed that the dominant position of finance and the increase of rentiers' savings influence negatively the rentability of the real economy. First, real investment suffers because the internal capital of a firm increases more slowly and firms themselves often get involved in financial speculation. Second, at a given private investment level, profits decrease when rentiers savings increase. Both factors lower profits and ceteris paribus the rate of return of the real economy. Thus the contradiction between the real economy and finance deepens and would lead to a catastrophe if the real economy would not regain the upper hand it used to possess in the past.

Appendix

The modified Kaleckian profit equation:

$$P = I_P + D + T_C + P_D - S_H \tag{9.67}$$

$$= I_P + G - T_C - T_{I,C} - T_{I,B} + T_C + P_D - S_C - S_B \tag{9.68}$$

$$P = I_P + G + C_C - S_B - T_{I,B} \quad (9.69)$$

$$= I_P + G + C_C - B(1-(1-\theta)(1-\sigma_B) \quad (9.70)$$

All variables on the r.h.s. of (9.70) can be considered as predetermined in a given period.

The Kaleckian income tax paradox: Distributed profits net of taxes are

$$P_D = (1-\theta)(1-\theta_C)(1-\rho)P \quad (9.71)$$

Therefore

$$\frac{\partial P_d}{\partial \theta} = -(1-\rho)(1-\theta_C)P + (1-\theta)(1-\rho)(1-\theta_C)\frac{\partial P}{\partial \theta} \quad (9.72)$$

Substituting for P Equation (9.51), for BP/BB Equation (9.53) and simplifying, we get

$$\frac{\partial P_d}{\partial \theta} = (1-\rho)\frac{\sigma_B(1-\theta)\left(2\rho + \left(\sigma_C(1-\rho)(1-\theta)\right)\right)B - \rho(I_P + D_0)}{(\rho + \sigma_C(1-\rho)(1-\theta))^2} \quad (9.73)$$

The sign of (9.73) can be negative or positive. Net distributed profits after tax fall if and only if the nominator in (9.73) is negative or

$$\frac{\sigma_B(1-\theta)B}{I_P + D_0} < \frac{\rho}{2\rho + \sigma_C(1-\rho)(1-\theta)} \quad (9.74)$$

Notes

1. This can be seen by linking C_c,t to past profits. That is,

   $$C_{c,t} = bP_{t-1} \qquad 0 < b < 1 \quad (9.7)$$

   If in period 1 investment changes permanently to $I_1 = I_O + \Delta I$, the corresponding immediate effect on profits in period 1, 2, ... t–1 is

   $$P_t - P_O = \Delta I + b\Delta I + b^2\Delta I \ldots + b^{t-1}\Delta I \quad (9.8)$$

   As $t \rightarrow \infty$

   $$\Delta P = \Delta I/(1-b) \quad (9.9)$$

   Even if consumption of capitalists (or some investment) is partly dependent on past profits, autonomous shifts of the propensity to invest or to consume remain the fundamental factor determining profits in any particular period. The critical nature of 'causality versus simultaneity' is often ignored in modern macroeconomics, as can be seen by the illogical 'Keynesian' textbook story of the simultaneous determination of the aggregate price level (via aggregate supply and demand curves) on the one hand and effective demand, output, interest and employment on the other hand. (See Bhaduri, Łaski and Riese, 1999)

2. The counter-revolution against Keynesianism and the revival of the orthodox policy during the late 1970s confirmed Kalecki's scepticism regarding the political viability of long-term full employment policies in capitalist economies (Kalecki, 1943). Those developments had their political roots in the rise of the new rentier class.
3. The alternative explanation offered by orthodox theory – 'explaining' saving via utility maximization based on intertemporal preferences executed by a representative agent – looks like an absurd fairy tale in comparison to Kalecki's deep insights.
4. 4 For an overview of the empirical literature, see Stockhammer and Onaran (2013). They conclude: 'One striking common finding stands out in this empirical literature: most studies conclude that domestic demand is wage-led – that is, the effect of a pro-capital redistribution of income on the sum of private consumption and private investment is negative because consumption is much more sensitive to an increase in the profit share than is investment. Thus demand is profit-led only when the effect of distribution on net exports is high enough to offset the effects on domestic demand, and this is likely only in small open economies.' We would like to add: this is, however, profit-led growth in the sense of net-export led growth; in this case no time lag exists between lowering unit labour cost cum prices and increased international competitiveness (Stockhammer and Onaran 2013, p. 78).
5. Such a situation might have existed in the Netherlands in the 1970s, when during the 'Dutch disease' period the profit share declined below 20 per cent. After a severe investment crisis, wage moderation was implemented in the Dutch Wassenar agreement of 1982.
6. In modern accounting terms, gross profits would be equivalent to 'gross economic surplus' (= gross profits + mixed income), while B + W is tantamount to the concept of 'compensation of employees' in the primary balance of income.
7. As an example, let us assume that $\sigma_c = 0.2$, $\rho = 0.2$, $\theta = 0.4$, $\theta_c = 0.25$. Then $\Delta D = 0.31$.
8. This point was also brought forward by Keynes in a letter to Kalecki: 'It is only if they have read your article and are convinced by it that their profit will rise by the amount of the tax that they will maintain their spending as before' (Osiatyński, 1990, p. 559). Ironically, a similar argument can be made with regard to Keynes' thesis that lower nominal wages will not increase employment and output, or the budget deficits do not induce crowding out of public investment...Contrary to Keynes, Kalecki argued that it is much more plausible that consumption reacts with a lag to actual changes of income.
9. As the average maturity of public debt is lower than ten years, real interest rates on government debt were even lower.
10. See Lazonick, W. (2013) for an interesting analysis of the problems associated with shareholder value maximization in the US economy.

References

Bhaduri, A. and S. Marglin (1990) 'Unemployment and the real wage: the economic basis for contesting political ideologies', *Cambridge Journal of Economics*, 14: 375–393.

Bhaduri, A., K. Łaski and M. Riese (2006) 'A model of the interaction between the real and the virtual economy', *Metroeconomica*, 57: 412–427.

Bhaduri, A., K. Łaski and M. Riese (1999) 'Effective Demand versus Profit Maximization', in 'Aggregate demand/supply analysis: a dynamic perspective', *Banca Nazionale del Lavoro Quarterly Review*, 210, September 1999: 281–293.

Bradford DeLong, J. and K. Magin (2009) 'The U.S. equity return premium: past, present and future', *Journal of Economic Perspectives*, 23(1): 193–208.

Blecker, R. (1989) 'International competition, income distribution and economic growth' *Cambridge Journal of Economics*, 13: 395–412.

Blecker, R. (2011) 'Open economy models of growth and distribution', in E. Hein and E. Stockhammer (eds) *A Modern Guide to Keynesian Macroeconomics and Economic Policies* Cheltenham: Edward Elgar.

Dutt, A. (1984) 'Stagnation, income distribution and monopoly power', *Cambridge Journal of Economics*, 8: 25–40.

Kalecki, M. (1937) 'The principle of increasing risk', in *Collected Works of Michał Kalecki Volume I Capitalism, Business Cycles and Full Employment*, (ed.) J. Osiatyński Oxford: Clarendon Press, 1990, pp. 274–285.

Kalecki, M. (1939) 'Essays in the theory of economic fluctuations' in, *Collected Works of Michał Kalecki Volume I Capitalism, Business Cycles and Full Employment*, ed. J. Osiatyński Oxford: Clarendon Press, 1990, pp. 235–252.

Kalecki, M. (1943) 'Political aspects of full employment', *Political Quarterly*, 14/4, 1943: 322–331.

Kalecki, M. (1945) 'Full employment by stimulating private investment?', *Oxford Economic Papers*, NS, 7: 83–92.

Łaski, K., J. Osiatyński and J. Zięba (2010) 'The government expenditure multiplier and its estimates for Poland in 2006–2009' *Working Paper*, The Vienna Institute for International Economic Studies, (63), March.

Lazonick, W. (2013) 'From innovation to financialization: how shareholder value ideology is destroying the US economy' in E. Epstein and M. Wolfson (eds), *The Handbook of the Political Economy of Financial Crises*, Oxford: Oxford University Press.

Osiatyński, J. (ed.) (1990) *Collected Works of Michał Kalecki Volume I Capitalism, Business Cycles and Full Employment* Oxford: Clarendon Press, 1990.

Rowthorn (1981) 'Demand, real wages and economic growth', *Thames Papers in Political Economy* Autumn.

Stockhammer, E. and O. Onaran (2013) 'Wage-led growth: theory, evidence, policy', *Review of Keynesian Economics*, 1(1): 61–78.

Taylor, L. (1985) 'A stagnationist model of economic growth', *Cambridge Journal of Economics*, 9: 383–403.

10

Kalecki and Kowalik on the Dilemma of 'Crucial Reform' in the United States and Poland

Gary A. Dymski

10.1 Introduction

This chapter reflects on one of the recurrent themes in the work of Michał Kalecki and Tadeusz Kowalik – the challenge of the 'crucial reform.' During World War II, Kalecki posed the question of whether capitalist growth would face a limit due to constraints emanating from tensions between capitalists and workers regarding the conditions for political consent and the conditions for sustained growth. One possibility to avoid the threatened slowdown in economic growth would be a 'crucial reform' in the political and economic configuration underlying the capitalist economy. In the post-war period, this crucial reform was undertaken, making possible the period of relatively sustained growth and rising wages that is often termed the 'golden age of capitalism' (Marglin and Schor, 1991). As events unfolded in the 1970s and 1980s, 'golden age' growth was undermined, and the question was posed whether another 'crucial reform' would be possible. This same time period brought the socialist economies of Eastern Europe face-to-face with their own need for a 'crucial reform'.

The idea of a 'crucial reform', unique to these writers, is that circumstances at certain historical conjunctures throw the continuation of the core model of accumulation and growth, whether capitalist or socialist, into question. At such moments, the controlling interests – whether capital, labour or the state – can remain in control only if they are able to make key adjustments in the political realm – either by adjusting the mechanisms of political control or renewing the bases of popular consent. If this is not done, the current model of accumulation cannot be sustained. As Kowalik put it:

> 'Crucial reform' is a process of transition from one economic system to another, e.g. from free market capitalism to regulated capitalism, or – and precisely that is the main theme of this study – the transition from the 'command economy' to an economy with a regulated market, but still within the framework of 'real socialism'.
>
> ...Social pressure is indispensable, but if the crucial reform is to be carried out, the language of the dialogue, agreement, consensus and social contract has to be used. (Kowalik, 1986, pp. 3, 44)

Note that the distinguishing aspect of this definition is that the political sphere puts pressure on the economic sphere – accumulation depends on either continued political consent or on continued political control, or on the shift from one political mode to the other.

Our exploration of this concept unfolds as follows. Section 2 reviews Kalecki's notion of the political business cycle and shows how it suggests the existence of both upper speed limits (emphasized by Kalecki) and lower speed limits (implicit in his arguments). Section 3 reviews the ideas of Kalecki and Kowalik about the 'crucial reform' of capitalism. Section 4 takes up the reflections of these authors on the crisis of 'really-existing socialism' and the need – in the post-1980 world – for a 'crucial reform' that might preserve its desirable aspects but permit its survival even in a transformed world system.

These arguments about 'crucial reform' suggest that the economic dog is wagged by the political tail. However, this notion that political pressures can drive economic outcomes has not been borne out in the post-1980 world. In capitalist economies, increased unemployment did not lead in any systematic way to worker resistance; the floor on capitalist accumulation did not hold. Further, in the socialist countries, the crisis of reproduction of social and economic relations of the late 1980s did not lead to systemic demands by an empowered 'people' for a more responsive – because democratically controlled – economy.

Sections 5 and 6 explore why the pressures that had come to bear in the 1980s on both capitalist and formerly socialist economies did not lead to new 'crucial reforms', preserving the conditions for the pre-existing economic growth dynamic, as the Kalecki-Kowalik view suggests it should have (or could have). We conjecture that the reason for this failure of further reform is the impact of the neoliberal global economy on labour-market conditions in both socialist and capitalist economies.

Data from the United States and Poland are used to illustrate the argument. Section 7 concludes.

10.2 Kalecki's 'political business cycle'

Michał Kalecki focused attention in much of his published work on the problem of investment and employment fluctuations in capitalist economies. His formal models (Kalecki, 1954) highlighted that cyclical fluctuations in capitalism are driven by investment spending: given that workers largely spend their incomes and capitalists largely save it, profits – and the pace of economic growth – vary directly with the rate of investment. Since capitalists control the latter, then (as the Keynesian aphorism has it) they earn what they spend. This leads to insights unfolded in one of Kalecki's non-technical papers, 'Political Aspects of Full Employment' (1943). Capitalists' willingness to invest depends on the profit they might expect to earn from so doing. If productivity (output per hour of labour) is constant and workers' income is reliably and substantially spent on domestically produced goods, then investment spending does reliably convert into profit. But if productivity declines – and/or if workers' spending flows to goods produced elsewhere – this simple relationship breaks down.

Kalecki linked this insight to the idea that as a given economy approaches full employment, productivity may slow down. With falling unemployment, worker effort may arguably fall; further, workers may be able to extract higher real wages and improved working conditions as they negotiate new contracts. So capitalists will feel coerced into wage bargains that compromise profitability, to hire workers whose effort levels are suboptimal. So the profit rate depends on a labour-effort/output trade-off, which becomes more severe as the economy approaches full employment. This danger can be averted only if the economy operates below full employment.

So if workers unite in social democratic parties that demand full employment as a political goal, the very legitimacy of the powers and rights of the owners of the means of production will be threatened. Capitalists' loss of control then leads to reducing investment and even to moving production elsewhere: shifts that will initiate an economic downturn.

Thus, Kalecki warned of an upper limit to capital accumulation. However, as Dymski (2012) points out, Kalecki's work also suggests that there exists a lower limit on growth. If unemployment levels become very high, the working class may agitate for reforms through the political system. High unemployment may legitimize arguments that constraints should be placed – via political action – on the free movement of capital, and/or that unemployment benefits should be increased (and paid by firms), and/or that capital should pay higher taxes (for example, via wealth taxes or profit taxes). That is, an economically aggrieved working class may seek compensation for damages through political means. This may lead to a political business cycle, wherein macroeconomic growth fluctuates between these upper and lower limit points.

10.3 'Crucial reform' of the post-war capitalist economy

Kalecki's 1943 essay did not propose the idea of a 'crucial reform': it focused on forces that would hasten or slow economic activity, not on the sustainability of the institutional arrangements undergirding these fluctuating equilibria. This notion that the system might have a fatal institutional flaw was, however, considered by Kalecki and his colleague Kowalik some 25 years later. The upheavals and protests of the late 1960s had awakened a new spirit of radicalism among working-class people and parties. It seemed possible that political agitation fuelled by this spirit and movement might lead toward a socialist reorganization of capitalist economies. But in the 1930s, too, it had seemed that working-class fuelled political and workplace activism might dethrone capitalism, and before that had been the agitation linked to the cataclysmic losses of World War I and to the Russian Revolution. Capitalism had survived these threats, prompting Kalecki and Kowalik to reflect on why. They argued as follows:

> the strong pressure of the masses leads to such a radical reform of the system, in spite of the opposition of the ruling class, that, without abolishing existing relations of production, a new value is opened for the development of forces of production. There will then be a paradoxical situation: a 'crucial reform' imposed on the ruling class may stabilize the system, temporarily at least. (Kalecki and Kowalik, 1991, p. 467)

The use of the Marxian categories of relations and forces of production to describe the possibilities that follow from a 'crucial reform' is provocative. The term 'forces of production' refers to the physical and technological means of production, together with the labour power that brings them together in production; the 'relations of production', by contrast, are comprised of the methods that are deployed at any point in time to combine labour and the means of production in actual production processes. In traditional readings of Marxian theory (such as Cohen, 1978), advances in the forces of production drive developments in the relations of production: new ways of working are possible when there are new technologies with which to work.

What Kalecki and Kowalik proposed here is a kind of inversion: a 'crucial reform' can permit further technological advances without overturning existing relations of production. In traditional readings, contradictions between the (continually evolving) forces of production and the relations of production will lead to rifts and contradictions that eventually require the creation of new social relations more conformable to the new phase of development of the forces of production. The idea that the forces of production can be spurred ahead precisely by interventions that preserve (at least the key aspects of) the existing relations of production represents, then, an innovation in the theory of historical materialism. Using this theoretical framework to articulate this idea, in turn, reaffirmed these authors' commitment to the idea of a Marxian conception of history as a remorseless process of conflict and change.

In what did this 'crucial reform' consist, and from whence did it come? We take these questions in reverse order. The authors suggest it comes from 'outside' the system of production taken as a whole, including the nucleus of relations binding capital and labour. This notion of a reform from outside clearly has in mind – although it is not stated in so many words – the state sector. This sector's reform could presumably involve either its role as a fiscal (spending and taxing) entity, its role as a productive entity (organizing one or more production sectors), its role in regulating markets per se (such as financial markets), or its role in regulating the relations between capital and labour per se (terms and conditions of hiring, working conditions, security and tenure of employment and so on).

This idea thus introduces a further inversion in orthodox or traditional readings of historical materialism (the theory of history derived from Marx's economic theory): for the state is regarded in such readings as part of a 'superstructure' of social relations that surround and support (but do not affect) the social relations of production at any point in time. In effect, the arrows of causation flow – in orthodox readings – from forces of production to relations of production to superstructural relations. The idea that shifts in superstructural relations (for example, state interventions that provide stricter guidelines about the procedures for firing workers) could spur technological advances as a feedback effect, again, provides an innovative way of looking at trajectories of historical possibility.

What then is the substance of this 'crucial reform'? Kalecki and Kowalik argued that one key component is the stabilization of aggregate demand. They interpreted war and armaments expenditures (including World War II) from this viewpoint, as they do the efforts of governments in capitalist nations to 'limit unemployment to a few percent' (ibid., p. 470) via the expansion of social security and other measures. In effect, this 1969–1970 paper adds a third alternative to the two alternatives identified by Kalecki in 1943: capitalists can avoid the labour-effort/output trade-off and a profit squeeze due to the exhaustion of the reserve army of the unemployed, if they support adequate safety-net provisions and obtain workers' acquiescence in supporting the expansion of the military-industrial complex (and the associated project of national military dominance).

Kalecki and Kowalik warned that this situation is unstable. On the one hand, workers are willing to accept the build-up of military spending, as well as other contingencies, if these maintain high rates of employment. This has indeed led to a 'transformation of the working class, which ... became radically reformist in its attitude toward capitalism' (ibid., p. 470). On the other hand, workers will react adversely if the 'rules of the game' – the exchange of loyalty to the capitalist system for low unemployment – are violated. Thus, 'relative stability ... depends on a high degree of social conformity' (ibid., p. 476). Capitalists, for their part, are happy to have had the realization problem solved, but not at the expense of their profit rates. And while it was not stated in so many words, these authors' depiction of the steps leading to the 'crucial reform' of post-war capitalism indicates the steps that would be needed to undue or to augment it: shifts in the state's provision of stabilizing demand and of regulatory oversight, followed by an expansion in the forces of production that would create opportunities for new relations of production (and of enhanced profit rates).

10.4 'Crucial reform' of the post-war socialist economy?

Kalecki and Kowalik were deeply involved in planning for and analysing the construction of the 'mixed' socialist economies of Poland (and of other Eastern European nations) in the post-war period. Both economists engaged in debate with Lange, Brus and other economists over core issues involved in the construction and operation of these economies, such as the balance between centralized and local production and consumption decisions.[1] By the 1980s, change was in the air in Eastern Europe: heavy-handed political manipulation of these nations' economic and political systems, punctuated by several forceful Soviet-army interventions, had created widespread (if cautiously expressed) popular dissent.

This tension between the people and the ruling elites threw open the question of the political sustainability of the 'real socialist' economies of these nations. As with the capitalist economies at mid-century, the problem involved the interweaving of political consent and economic outcomes. With the capitalist economies, as Kalecki observed, the problem was to operate the capitalist economy in such a way that the two political force vectors on either side of the unemployment/labour-extraction nexus would not bind: capital strike with unemployment too low and worker revolt with unemployment too high. Capitalism would run best as what David Schulman of Salomon Brothers termed, in 1992, a 'Goldilocks' economy – not too hot, not too cold. The problem was different for socialist Eastern Europe. There was insufficient political support for the status-quo operation of these nations' economies; indeed, political resistance was growing by the month. The question was how to restore political consent for the economies of Eastern Europe in a way that would leave them recognizably socialist. In effect, the moment for a 'crucial question' was at hand.

Kowalik laid out his thinking in this question in his 1986 paper, 'On Crucial Reform of Real Socialism Economy', written for a Vienna think-tank. Here he defined the possibility of a 'crucial reform' question for the socialist economy as involving 'the transition from the "command economy" to an economy with a regulated market, but still within the framework of "real socialism"', which means, *inter alia*, 'abandonment of central planning' (Kowalik, 1986, p. 3) and the independence of the enterprises regarding the three main problems of production: what to produce, how much and how.

Socio-institutional and political change were the critical steps in achieving a 'crucial reform'. The arguments for economic decentralization in the 1950s had already recognized the need to challenge the 'power of the party and state elite' (Kowalik, 1986,p. 7). By the 1980s the problem of political power had reached the boiling point; in Kowalik's view, plans for the reform of socialism such as Kornai's (Kornai, 1986) which ignore 'the role of the party and other political institutions in regulating the economy' (Kowalik, 1986, p. 9) had not grasped the central problem.

Kowalik appealed to Keynes' ideas from the interwar period in making this case. Keynes' ideas about large-scale government intervention (and the welfare state) provided the crucial reform that sustained capitalism even while it 'appeared to undermine the whole capitalist system' (Kowalik, 1986, p. 13). Therefore, in the socialist economies then present, the crucial reform that is apparently unthinkable involves a displacement of the central role of the party: 'extra-party pluralism [is]...an indispensable component of the "crucial reform"... [because the] sound functioning of the economy with a regulated market requires the articulation and defence of the different social groups' interests' (p. 31).

Kowalik argued that 'a clear distinction should be made between an option for capitalism as a social system and allowing for the co-existence of capitalist enterprises with the socialized sector, and the restoration of the private sector, that is, of private handicrafts and trade, small-scale industrial production units and family farms' (p. 35). State socialism involves one-party political rule and overemphasizes concentration in production. Kowalik advocated 'democratic socialism' which 'must be pluralistic in three respects':

- there should be a variety of forms of ownership, but state ownership should not be dominant (other forms include self-management ownership, co-operatives, municipal and private forms of ownership);
- autonomy of the economic units;
- unrestricted opportunities for self-organisation of various groups for the protection of their interests. (p. 40)

In Kowalik's vision, democratic socialism involves self-organization and advocacy in two spheres, the economic and the political. One key is '[p]luralism of ownership,... [which] widens the scope for...social activity... [and] constitutes a barrier to bureaucratization and "leviathanization" of the state' (p. 42). And, while state overreach must be arrested, a strong state presence is needed to protect what might be termed the public interest. In the economic realm, this would involve ensuring that the goods needed for basic living standards are available, and that core infrastructure and investment in strategically important industries is protected:

> There exists an economic, social and political rationale behind the pluralism of the forms of ownership. To put it in a nutshell, I see the scope for different forms of ownership in the following way: state ownership seems to be most justified in the key industries, such as mining and energy. Part of the infrastructure can be based on municipal ownership (local transport). Manufacturing industry can be an

> area of competition between different types of enterprises: ... self-management ... co-operatives, joint stock companies, ... individualized private capital or on mixed capital. (Kowalik, 1986, p. 41)

In the civil realm, this would involve suppressing socially harmful developments in the market and looking after public welfare. This would be done by planning 'based on broad participation in the decision-making process ... mediating contradictory interests of different social groups.' This in turn 'presupposes ... politically independent organizations [and] freedom of speech, publications and meetings. For economic life ... political pluralism is of paramount importance' (ibid., p. 42).

Ironically, this democratization of planning and political participation could only go forward with the commitment to these reforms of these nations' ruling elites. Kowalik argued that the mid-century 'crucial reform' of capitalism had involved precisely the surrender of powers by the ruling elite (capitalists):

> The mainstay of the capitalist system – private ownership – [was] limited and ... the economic rules of the game were altered. The logic of this change contradicted ... traditional liberal doctrine. ... But it was precisely the radical reform which secured stability of the Western world for over a quarter of a century. (ibid., p. 48)

Crucial reform in real socialism must 'take opposite character and direction' (ibid., p. 47): permitting enterprises to operate on the basis self-management and self-financing, with minimal state control; a reduction in the decision-making prerogatives of the state, and its embrace of differentiated forms of ownership, control and competition in the provision of public services; and finally, 'accepting social pluralism and institutionalizing it in a diversity of non-party forms' (ibid., p. 48). The state, in shifting from a command to a coordination function, 'would then more closely resemble its counterpart in the contemporary Western economies than in the majority of the communist countries before the reform' (ibid., p. 50).

Kowalik hastened to add that he was not calling for 'a turn from omnipresent collectivism to individualism'; but he noted that his call for crucial reform could easily be misinterpreted and manipulated, both by 'people in power [in the current socialist state], capable of mobilizing big collectives to serve the interests of that narrow group, ... [and by] the ruled ones, who do not identify themselves with big, anonymous collectives that they frequently joined against their own will' (ibid., pp. 48–49). In other words, a 'restitution of conditions to real collectivism' (ibid., p. 49) requires the ruling elite to set aside some of its own privileges and prerogatives, thereby salvaging real socialist society by embracing its democratization.

10.5 The 'crucial reform' of capitalism undermined in the neoliberal era: the US case

We can readily see that Kowalik's effort to sketch out a 'crucial reform' for socialism appealed to the logic of the 'crucial reform' of capitalism that had been installed four decades earlier. But the ruling elites of the socialist nations did not undertake reforms that would have permitted them to closely resemble the social-democratic capitalist societies of the quarter-century after World War II. It may be that the enmity between the peoples and ruling elites was too far advanced to leave any policy space for the shifts that Kowalik hoped to see. But any such argument that the well was already poisoned has to be set against the election by huge majorities, at the end of the 1980s and in the early 1990s, of hugely popular reform figures such as Lech Wałęsa (in Poland) and Vaclav Havel (in Czechoslovakia).

Another factor in the failure of socialist 'crucial reform' is that, at just the time that Kowalik (among others) was calling for US/Western European-style reforms, the preconditions for maintaining the US/Western-European 'crucial reform' had been so far undermined that the capital-labour accord (in the phrase of Weisskopf, Bowles and Gordon (1983) was coming undone. The destruction of peaceful coexistence between capital and labour and the consequent deindustrialization, at the nation-state level, was linked to the rise of the global factory and the deregulation of financial markets, at the global level. And the global mobility of capital and of production, the increasing freedom of movement of finance and the rise of least-cost competition for manufactured goods all undercut the capacity of Eastern European political elites and economic planners to orchestrate a transition to a more democratic and decentralized, but still recognizably socialist (full-employment) society. In effect, the coming of the neoliberal era not only put the Western European and US welfare states at risk; it also prevented transition paths in that direction by the Eastern European economies.

The remainder of this section presents a truncated analysis of the forces that undermined the 'Goldilocks' logic of business-cycle dynamics, and hence the 'crucial reform' capital-labour accord, in the capitalist nations. This is done via a case study of the United States. Section 6 then analyses the failure of the 'crucial reform' of socialism in this same neoliberal era, focusing on the case of Poland.

10.5.1 The decline of US global hegemony and the rise of the global factory and globally-mobile finance.

The changing level of US global hegemony holds the key to the 'softening' of Kaleckian political business-cycle constraints, and thus to the collapse of the capitalist 'crucial reform'. While this argument can be made for a significant number of global-North nations, here the focus is on the experience of the US economy.

It is readily seen that in any nation, a capital-labour accord – with decent wages and low unemployment levels, on one side, and with high profit rates and dependable markets, on the other – depends on several pre-conditions. First, there must be no opportunity for capital to look elsewhere for cheaper labour. This in turn depends on the existence of strict rules preventing capital from moving jobs abroad (and creating a 'global factory') and/or on the absence of suitable locations abroad for relocating production. Second, there must exist market demand for the goods and services created in high-wage industries. These preconditions existed in the Bretton Woods period, in most global-North nations (Armstrong, Glyn and Harrison, 1991): capital mobility was restricted, finance was heavily regulated, and there was a high rate of unionization. Verdoorn cycles obtained in production: high-wage workers, in effect, bought goods made by other high-wage workers, encouraging rising productivity (Verdoorn, 1980).

The US facilitated the stability of these macroeconomic conditions in the immediate post-war period, as Kindleberger (1973, 1974) pointed out, by playing the role of a global hegemon. The US dollar was fixed against gold, and most currencies were fixed against the dollar; the US Federal Reserve functioned implicitly as the global lender-of-last-resort. These arrangements helped provide stability in the international financial system, which the US guaranteed by playing the role of a global hegemon. Critical to the preservation of internal financial stability, as well, were tight restrictions on global capital movements, against which Kindleberger had warned in the midst of the Great Depression (Kindleberger, 1937).[2]

However, these arrangements began to fall apart in 1971, when the convertibility of the dollar into gold was ended. When the dollar began to float against other currencies, it immediately fell in value; two oil-price shocks soon thereafter, as well as the US defeat in Vietnam, highlighted the decline of US power. By the end of the 1970s, the US economy was in disarray. This led to a shift in US economic policies – away from a welfarist, regulationist state and toward marketization and deregulation. The US banking system was opened to market forces and consolidation. US workers were exposed to new risks, pay cuts and dislocation. Paul Volcker (1979) baldly described the agenda: 'a controlled disintegration in the world economy is a legitimate objective for the 1980s'.

The Reagan Administration took office in 1981 and implemented a macroeconomic policy that imposed tight money and high interest rates as a means of attacking inflation, on the one hand, and expansionary fiscal policy as a means of stimulating demand, on the other. The result was a rapid rise in the value of the dollar and a rapid deterioration of the US current account. Overseas wealth-owners bought dollar-denominated assets. The 1980s and 1990s were characterized, in developing markets, by occasional debt crises and periods of macroeconomic stagnation. US economic growth was slower than in the 1960s, but the steady inflow of capital into Wall Street (a by-product of chronic current-account deficits) permitted US financial markets to gather strength and US-based financial firms to gain market share in global markets.

The 1990s brought relatively steady macroeconomic growth and led to the rise of the digital 'new economy'. Events in the first decade of the 2000s contradicted the term adopted in the 1990s to characterize this period of growth, 'the Great Moderation': the 'new economy' was hit with an equity-market collapse in 2001, followed by a housing-market bubble and a wave of predatory and speculative lending that led into a housing-market collapse (2006) and then a full-blown financial-system collapse (2008).

10.5.2 Shifts in the political business cycle

Kalecki's political business-cycle model suggests that unemployment outcomes should moderate in the wake of the 'crucial reform'. And indeed, a comparison of empirical evidence from the pre- and post-War period shows more moderate lows and highs in the latter than in the former era.

However, after 1980, the hot-cold balance in Kalecki's political business-cycle has been upset: capital increasingly secured higher growth rates for profits not by extracting labour from labour-power in domestic markets, but via aggressive globe-spanning investments in production and assembly facilities in lower-wage hubs. This eased the lower-bound constraint on the unemployment rate, even while the growth in redundant workers – and the competition among regional governments for manufacturing or service employment – reduced the political penalties associated with high unemployment rates.

This 'boundary shift' can be seen in the drift of cyclical US unemployment rates over time. In business cycles prior to the 1980s, unemployment rates peaked after cyclical troughs were reached (in GDP growth), but then dropped significantly due to the government's commitment to countercyclical policy; see the cyclical patterns in US quarterly data analysis in Dymski (2012). In the 1980s, this pattern began to change. The 1991 and 2001 expansions were different: unemployment rates dropped very little during the run of the cycle. Thus far, in the expansion that began in 2009, unemployment rates have barely moved. Figure 10.1 shows cyclical patterns for annual post-1980 business cycles: after the 1982 trough, the unemployment rate moved downward dramatically; but in the 1991 and 2001 expansions, little downward shift is evident – and in the 2009–2010 period, the unemployment rate remained virtually unchanged.[3] Figure 10.2 shows that long-term unemployment has not improved after the 1991 and 2001 business-cycle troughs; and it has gone up after the 2009 trough.

Another way of evaluating the evolution of the forces shaping the Kaleckian business cycle in the post-war era is to decompose the sources

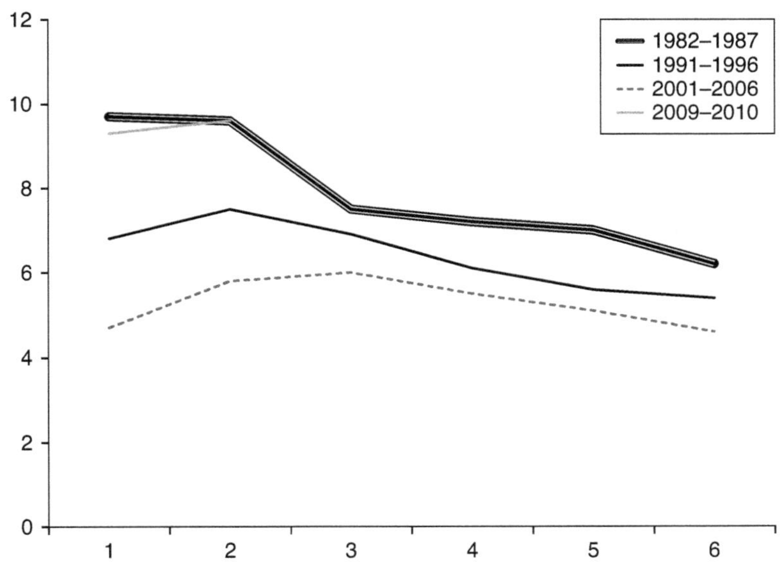

Figure 10.1 Annual US unemployment rates in post-1980 expansions, trough to peak (truncated at 6 years)

Source: World Bank – www.data.worldbank.org/country/.

Note: The unemployment rate shown is for adults ages 15–64 who are active labour force participants. Data are shown beginning in the year that constitutes the trough of cyclical expansion.

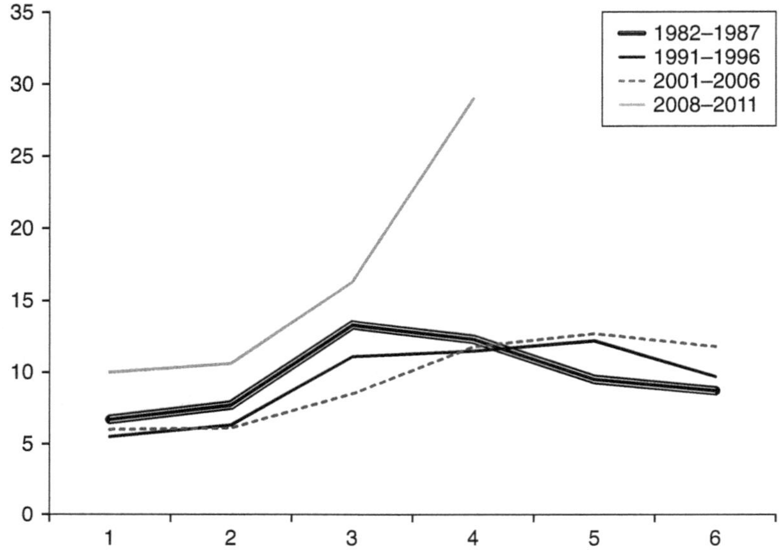

Figure 10.2 Annual US long-term unemployment rates in post-1980 expansions, trough to peak (truncated at 6 years)

Source: World Bank – www.data.worldbank.org/country/.

Note: The long-term unemployment rate shown is for adults ages 15–64 who are active labour force participants but have not worked for 15 or more weeks. Data are shown beginning in the year that constitutes the trough of cyclical expansion.

of real GDP growth into their component parts. The level of GDP for any given year can be decomposed as follows:

Real GDP = (Real GDP/Employed Worker)(Employed Worker /Labour Force) (Labour Force/Working-Age Population)(Working-Age Population)

The change in GDP from one year to the next can be interpreted as approximately equal to the sum of the changes in these terms (using a time-derivative approach and ignoring cross-effects). Evaluating the percentage change in each of the above ratios gives an indication of whether real GDP growth is attributable, respectively, to productivity growth, the rate of employment, the rate of labour-force participation or the growth of the working-age population per se.

In the 1950s and 1960s in the US, productivity growth (real GDP/ employed worker) accounted for most of real GDP growth; almost all the remaining growth in GDP can be attributed to a growing working-age population. The 1970s marked a break in pattern: population growth itself drove GDP growth, as productivity growth fell to less than 30 per cent and there was substantial labour-force entry by working-age adults. This labour-force entry effect continued into the 1980s, as productivity growth strengthened somewhat while the working-age population effect weakened substantially.

Figure 10.3 depicts annual percentage-change data for the above ratios for the 1990s and 2000s. The 1990s brought a virtual repeat of the 1960s: more than half of GDP growth was driven by productivity growth, and one third by labour-force growth. In the 2000s, however, both productivity growth and population growth slowed in influence; these factors were heavily offset by a shrinkage in the ratios of labour-force to working-age population and of employed workers to labour force. Only in the 1970s was this decade-long decline in the employed-worker/labour-force ratio duplicated.

From a Kaleckian perspective, maintaining labour peace involves generating sufficient productivity growth to spread income gains between workers and capitalists. The growth of the working-age population spreads income across households as long as these households' members enter into the labour force and then into paid employment at steady rates. If these rates of labour-force participation and/or of

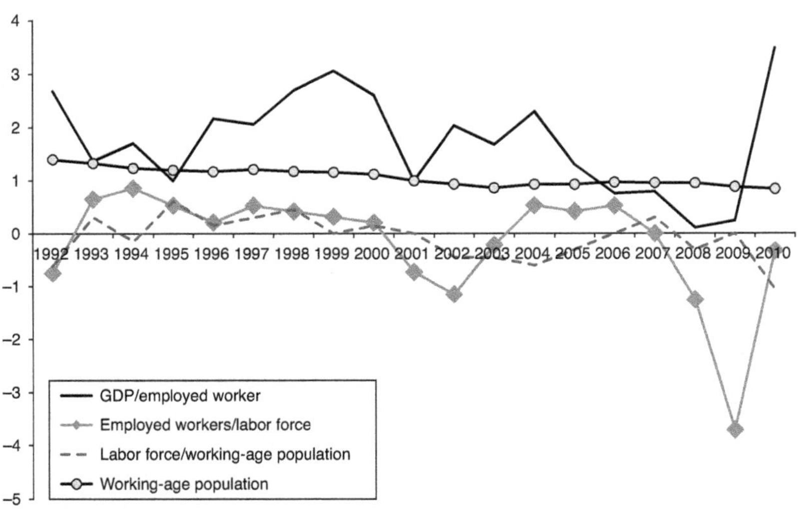

Figure 10.3 Annual percentage changes in components of US GDP growth, 1992–2010

paid employment are reversed, then the spread of income across households is made more difficult; it requires transfer mechanisms outside of the capital-labour relation in the private sector. An increasing pace of labour-force participation, as in the 1970s and 1980s, puts pressure on the upward bound: the number of unwaged adults shrinks and the economy must run hotter to satisfy heightened income/employment demands. A reduced level of labour-force participation, on the other hand, relaxes the lower-bound constraint on the business cycle: the economy can perform worse without triggering political demand from labour/popular coalitions for public-welfare expenditures.

10.5.3 The undoing of the 'crucial reform' in the neoliberal era.

Some of the factors that emerged with the coming of the neoliberal era and softened the lower-bound constraint on employment have already been introduced above: the weakening of US trade unions and the relocation of much US-based manufacturing offshore. US manufacturing survived only with lower wages and reduced labour standards: virtuous Verdoorn cycles were a thing of the past. This shift was one of several factors pushing the US economy toward greater inequality during the neoliberal period (Wolff, 1995, 1998); another was the growth in financial-sector incomes. This push both softened the Kaleckian political constraint and eliminated the possibility of the high-wage-for-high-profits trade-off that constituted the core of the 'crucial reform'.

The data for the US suggest that the 1990s brought a return to 1960s-type growth patterns. But for this decade's growth pattern to make possible a new 'crucial reform' – or a restoration of the implicit terms and conditions of the post-War 'reform' – would have required more than a few years' reversal of developments in the 1970s and 1980s that had eliminated union jobs, outsourced production and decimated many of the institutions of the US welfare state. In fact, the Clinton Administration's two signature accomplishments – the 1996 welfare reform and several financial deregulation acts – moved the US further in the direction of destroying the structures of financial-market control and of broad-based welfare provision. And in any case, the 2000s brought business cycles that involved less pressure from labour on capital than had been the case in the previous four decades. As productivity growth fell below its Golden Age peak, there were fewer gains to share; but labour-force participation trends meant that labour made weaker demands on capital to share its gains.

10.6 The 'crucial reform' of socialism undermined in the neoliberal era: the Polish case

We turn now to the question of why a 'crucial reform' of the socialist economy and polity did not occur. While this moves us backward in time to the late 1980s and early 1990s, Section 5 has provided a critically important context for this discussion: for during the 1980s and 1990s, the US and most Western European democracies were busily dismantling or disabling the signature features of the governance model toward which Kowalik was trying (along with others) to pull Eastern Europe. Why should Poland not liberalize its financial institutions, when the West was doing just that? Why should it maintain its safety-net provisions, when the West was insisting that families and individuals functioned best when they were primarily responsible for their own welfare?

In any event, we can recall that Kowalik's (1986) reflections on socialist reform were penned against the backdrop of a quickening pace of conflict and change in the Eastern bloc. Solidarność was founded in 1980, and anchored an anti-bureaucratic, pro-worker social movement that gathered force and led to a political transition to a democratically elected government. Lech Wałęsa was elected President in 1990, and free parliamentary elections were held in 1991. In November 1995, Wałęsa was defeated by Aleksander Kwaśniewski in Poland's second post-war free presidential election. Debate raged in these years over what economic shifts should accompany the political transition.

The remarkable actions of the 1989–1995 period led to deep disagreements about what economic changes were needed and how they should be achieved. Kalecki's economics of socialism leads to the conclusion that 'errors of economic strategy and, in particular, weak planning of investment, rather than an absence of markets, [led] to the 'Collapse of Communism' at the end of the 1980s' (Toporowski, 1999, p. 227). And as we have seen, Kowalik (1986) emphasized the importance of balancing centralized planning with firm-level and political democratization.

But alongside these views were many voices emphasizing problems that could be attributed to the absence of markets. One view emphasized the need to modernize production methods and to deepen work discipline. Another view emphasized the need to reform or eliminate state managers' control of process and output decisions. For example, Balassa (1973) and Kornai (1986) argued that state managers are incapable of thinking beyond their own gratification and gain, thus an external force to discipline the planner's allocation process was needed. The only question for some commentators was whether the state control of the economy should be disciplined or eliminated. Balcerowicz (1992), for example, espoused Hayek's critique of socialist planning as impossible to implement, as well as the view that efforts to maintain a mixed economy would end being implausible. He viewed the freedom to establish private firms and the privatization of state enterprises to represent the inevitable endpoint of the centrally planned economy.[4]

It was Balcerowicz's 'Shock Therapy' Plan – opposed by Kowalik – which won the day; it was implemented in October 1989. This view was based on an overly rosy assessment of the superiority of market incentives in allocating resources.[5] It was also based on the view of Kornai (1986) and others that proofs of the plausibility of central planning – chief among them, Lange (1936) – required the existence of omniscient, benevolent planners who could never be found in any real world. Kowalik (1992) criticized Kornai (1986), arguing that Lange, Kalecki and Brus saw price-setting and the control of investment as critical components of the socialist model, and that the 'countervailing power towards bureaucracy' should be provided by 'workers' councils' (Kowalik, 1992, p. 170).

This plan pushed aside the gradualist approach of the Round Table of February–April 1989, which had provided the basis for a peaceful transition from Communist Party rule by emphasizing consultative deliberations and bargaining among stakeholders representing different economic sectors. The 'Shock Therapy' or 'Polish Big Bang' put in place later that year, and approved as a stabilization program by the IMF in December 1989, took precisely the opposite approach – immediate, large-scale economic transformation via a series of non-negotiable top-down decisions. These changes included the introduction of a bankruptcy mechanism for state-owned firms, the end of special access to credit for state-owned companies, restrictions on wage increases and so on.

Kowalik (1996) pointed out that the IMF program delivered rates of unemployment higher than in other Eastern European countries, and it was based on the false premise that Poland required the same sort of primitive accumulation (via the reallocation of ownership rights and the amassing of a pool of savings that could seek out new investment opportunities) as might a developing country. This false premise provided a justification for radical across-the-board actions, such as the attack on the 'welfare state' provisions that had been part of Poland's socialist system. These acts of social dismantling and the power to reallocate given to new actors were consequences of seeing Poland as a developing – and not a transitioning – society.

Kowalik (1997) refers to this as a tragicomedy – the 'largest labour movement in Europe' bringing about one of the most inequitable societies in Europe (p. 26). He argues that Solidarność squandered its popular mandate due to a conjuncture of factors. Chief among them was the inability of its leadership to see that the Balcerowicz program of privatization and market-opening embodied a neoliberal program whose logic would undercut the working-class alliance that was the root of their success.

10.6.2 Cyclical employment and labour-force trends in Poland in the transition period

Figures 10.4–10.8 provide some empirical evidence for why the possibility of a 'crucial reform' was lost. Irrespective of the disputes among Polish and non-Polish intellectuals, the situation on the ground was difficult. In discussing the Kaleckian business cycle during the 'crucial reform' period of Western capitalist economies, we noted the importance of the lower-bound limit on unemployment: too many workers unemployed creates the conditions for mass protests calling on the state to defend workers' rights that capitalist firms are abusing or disregarding. There is arguably a lower-bound dimension to the 'crucial reform' moment for the socialist economies, as well, but it plays out differently. If the economy maintains a high rate of employment security, workers will have reason to rally around it, but if employment security and the level of employment fall, then workers will look for other options.

This was a fundamental problem in Poland – even leaving aside the fact that workers had been organizing fierce resistance against precisely the bureaucrats who controlled the economy. Figure 10.4 shows that unemployment stood at over 12 per cent when the first democratic elections were being held.[6] This period witnessed a large decline in the rate of labour-force participation (Figure 10.5), and youth unemployment rates were double those of the overall labour force (Figure 10.6). Further, those who lost work had little hope of avoiding long-term unemployment, throughout the 1990s (Figure 10.7). With brutal shrinkages in state-enterprise workforces, widespread privatization, and other austerity measures, economic growth resumed through productivity increases (Figure 10.8); only in the middle of the first decade of the 2000s did employment rates recover and help to spur economic growth.

These data demonstrate, then, that the Polish employment scenario was replete with problems of unemployment (especially for youth) and labour-force participation just when the first opportunity was being presented to make democratic choices about how the state should

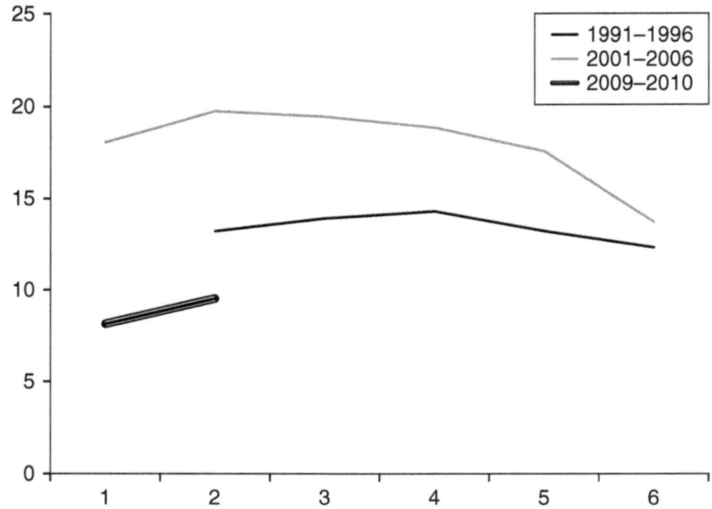

Figure 10.4 Annual Polish unemployment rates in post-1990 expansions, trough to peak (truncated at 6 years)

Source: World Bank – www.data.worldbank.org/country/.

Note: Unemployment rate consists of all unemployed adults 15–64 as a share of the overall labour force ages 15–64. Data are shown beginning with the year that constitutes the trough of cyclical expansion.

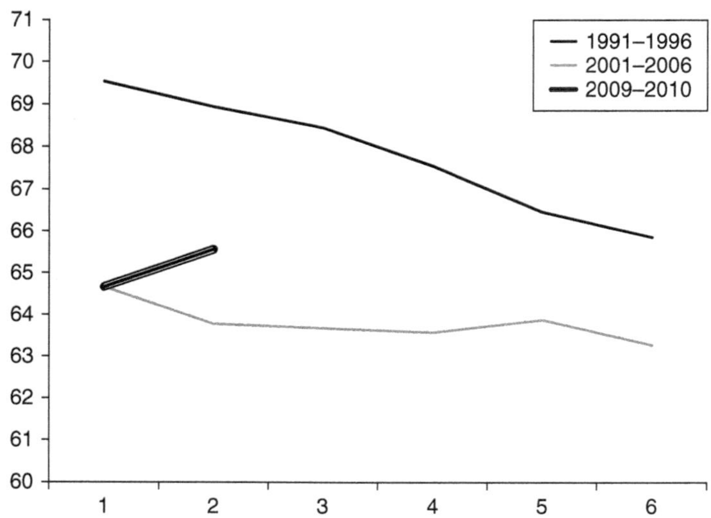

Figure 10.5 Annual Polish labour-force participation rates in post-1990 expansions, trough to peak (truncated at 6 years)

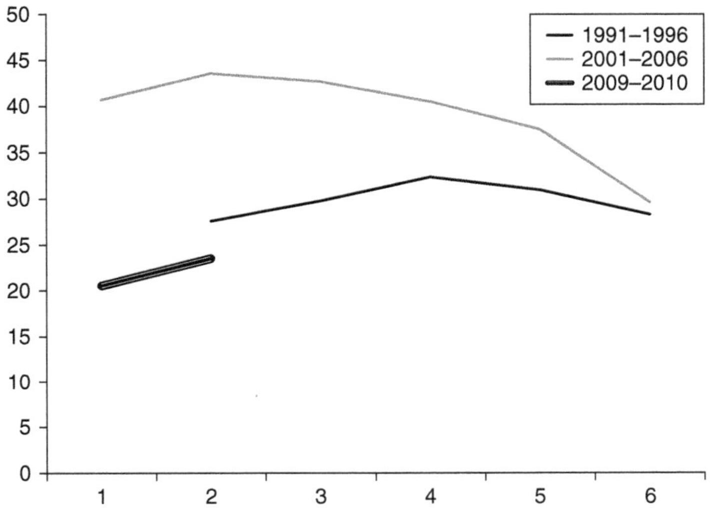

Figure 10.6 Annual Polish youth unemployment rates in post-1990 expansions, trough to peak (truncated at 6 years)

Source: World Bank – www.data.worldbank.org/country/.

Note: The unemployment rate shown is for adults ages 15–24 who are active labour force participants. Data are shown beginning in the year that constitutes the trough of cyclical expansion.

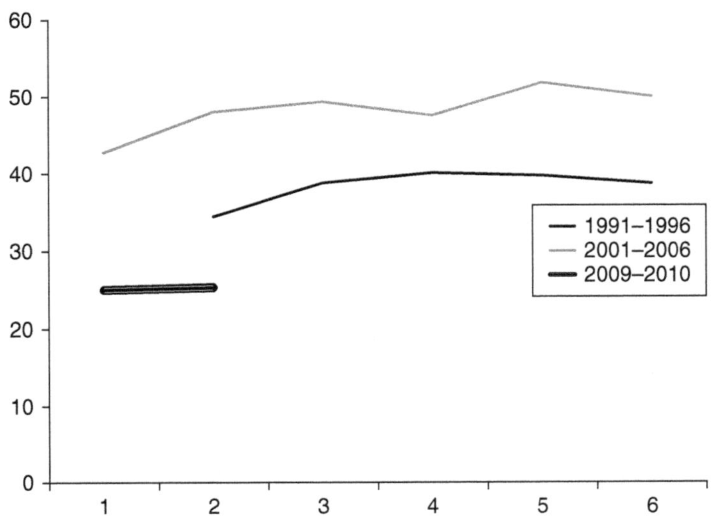

Figure 10.7 Annual Polish long-term unemployment rates in post-1990 expansions, trough to peak (truncated at 6 years)

Source: World Bank – www.data.worldbank.org/country/.

Note: The long-term unemployment rate shown is for adults ages 15–64 who are active labour force participants. Data are shown beginning in the year that constitutes the trough of cyclical expansion.

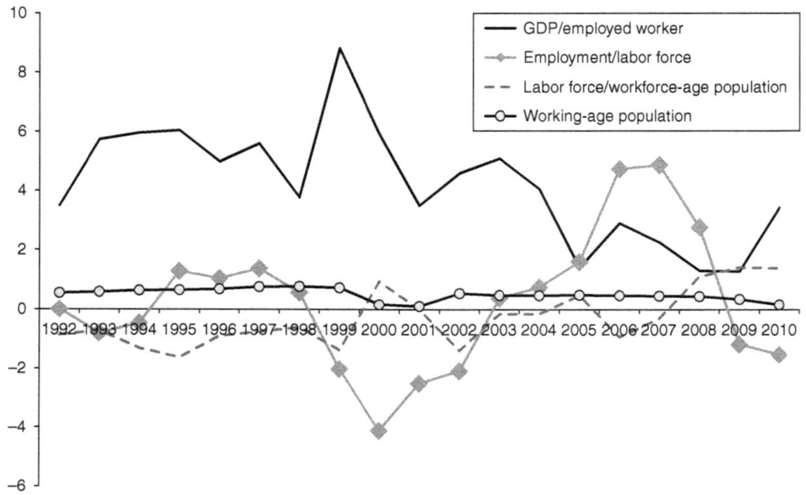

Figure 10.8 Annual percentage changes in components of Polish GDP growth, 1992–2010

guide the economy. The thematic of dismantling – a thematic fed by a decade of righteous protest against unresponsive bureaucrats – overwhelmed Kowalik's urging that strategic reforms of the socialist system could preserve the positive features of socialism while embedding the democratic guidance and participation that had been missing under the Soviet-led regime.

10.6 Conclusion

This essay has investigated the reasons for the dual failures of efforts at 'crucial reforms' of both the capitalist and socialist economic systems in the past half-century. The 'crucial reform' of capitalism enacted in many Western democracies after World War II represented an implicit response to Kalecki's fears that full employment could never be realized (or even approached) under capitalism. For approximately a quarter-century, it seemed that capitalists could earn adequate returns to their capital even while paying high real wages to heavily organized workforces. But the conditions that supported this state of affairs melted away with the end of fixed exchange rates, oil price shocks and the ascendancy of a macroeconomic and regulatory policy agenda that favoured attacks on unionized labour, reductions in welfare-state supports and broad-based deregulation (especially in the realms of finance). The period that many heterodox economists refer to as the 'golden age of capitalism' lasted only a few brief years.

But if the 'crucial reform' that created the possibility of a prosperous working class cooperating with a satisfied capitalist class, and overseen by democratically-elected governments, lasted only a short time, the 'crucial reform' that might have permitted the 'real socialist' economies of Eastern Europe to offer their own variants of democratic voice and worker prosperity never came into being. Ironically, the collapse of the form of capitalism created under its mid-century 'crucial reform' constituted a key reason why a parallel 'crucial reform' of socialism had become an impossibility in the historical moment when it could have been feasible.

Kalecki gave us, first of all, an understanding of the limits that the capitalist economy could approach – limits that suggested unremitting conflict between the state and capital. He then, along with Kowalik, provided a vision of how these limits could be surpassed – along with the warning that the 'crucial reform' he envisioned might prove unstable. Kowalik, in turn, sketched out a vision of an alternative path for socialism, one that would avoid the conflict between capital and state by leaving the state in control – democratic control – of investment and growth. These visions of alternative and more benign capitalisms and socialisms have not come to pass; instead we are left, in the post-subprime, Eurozone crisis era, with a scenario of unremitting conflict between state and capital, state and markets. No end is in sight, nor are there new visions of 'crucial reforms' that might break the global trends toward more macroeconomic stagnation and increasing worker insecurity and joblessness.

Notes

1. Dymski (2012) summarizes Kalecki's and Kowalik's participation in and reaction to these debates.
2. Kindleberger had described capital movements as destabilizing in these terms: 'capitalists seek to avoid the country of business of depression and avoid the possibility of national bankruptcy' a process that can end only with drastic action, such as an overnight devaluation, banking system collapse, a debt moratorium, foreign exchange controls, or the 'accession of a "strong man" to power' (Kindleberger, 1973, pp. 170–172).
3. The figures shown in this chapter are drawn from the World Bank country databases, which have more restricted years of data for the United States than are available from the Bureaus of Labor Statistics and Economic Analysis. Dymski (2012) uses data from the latter sources, and thus covers more years of

US experience than are shown here. Since the data used herein for Poland are drawn exclusively from the World Bank database, all figures shown for the US here are based only on data from that source as well.

4. Leszek Balcerowicz is an influential Polish economist who was affiliated with Solidarność. He served as deputy prime minister and twice as finance minister. He rationalized his plan in Balcerowicz (2000), arguing that '*extreme... inherited macroeconomic instability calls for the rapid implementation of a tough stabilization* program' (p. 233; italics in original).
5. Alec Nove (1992) points out that the neoclassical model which Balcerowicz regarded as a superior tool for real-world economies was itself based on implausible and unrealistic ideas about economic behaviour.
6. Unfortunately, the World Bank data for Poland that were used to construct Figures 10.4–10.7 begin, in almost all cases, with observations for 1990 or 1991.

References

Armstrong, P., A. Glyn and J. Harrison (1991) *Capitalism since 1945,* London: Basil Blackwell.

Balcerowicz, L. (1992) 'The "socialist calculation debate" and reform discussions in socialist countries', in J.M. Kovács and M. Tardos (eds), *Reform and Transformation in Eastern Europe,* London: Routledge, pp. 5–18.

Balcerowicz, L. (2000) 'Understanding post-Communist transitions' in W. Kostecki, K. Żukrowska and B.J. Góralcyzk (eds), *Transformations of Post-Communist States.* London: Macmillan, pp. 225–242.

Cohen, G.A. (1978) *Karl Marx's Theory of History: A Defense.* Princeton: Princeton University Press.

Dymski, G.A. (2012) 'Can the US economy escape the law of gravity? A Minsky-Kalecki approach to the crisis of neoliberalism', in K. Yagi, N. Yokokawa, S. Hagiwar, and G.A. Dymski (eds), *The Crisis of 2008 and the Future of Capitalism,* London: Routledge, pp. 222–246.

Kalecki, M. (1943) 'Political aspects of full employment', *Political Quarterly,* 14(4): 1–9.

Kalecki, M. (1954) *Theory of Economic Dynamics.* London: Allen and Unwin.

Kalecki, M. and T. Kowalik (1971) 'Observations on the "crucial reform"' in *Collected Works of Michał Kalecki, Volume 2. Capitalism: Economic Dynamics,* Oxford: Clarendon Press, 1991, pp. 467–476.

Kindleberger, C.P. (1937) *International Short-Term Capital Movements,* New York: Columbia University Press.

Kindleberger, C.P. (1973) *The World in Depression, 1929–1939.* Berkeley: University of California Press.

Kindleberger, C.P. (1974) *The Formation of Financial Centers: A Study in Comparative Economic History.* Princeton: International Finance Section, Princeton University.

Kornai, J. (1986) 'The Hungarian reform process: visions, hopes, and reality', *Journal of Economic Literature,* 24, December: 1687–1737.

Kowalik, T. (1986) 'On crucial reform of real socialism' No. 122, *Forschungsberichte* Nr. 122, Wien: Wiener Institut für Internationale Wirtschaftsvergleiche, October.

Kowalik, T. (1992) 'Reform economics and bureaucracy' in J.M. Kovács and M. Tardos (eds), *Reform and Transformation in Eastern Europe*, London: Routledge, pp. 164–176.

Kowalik, T. (1996) 'On the transformation of post-Communist societies: the inefficiency of primitive capital accumulation', *International Political Science Review*, 17(3), Traditions in Pluralist Thought, July: 289–296.

Kowalik, T. (1997) 'The Polish revolution', *Dissent*, 44, Spring: 26–30.

Lange, O. (1936) 'On the economic theory of socialism', *Review of Economic Studies*, 4(1): 53–71.

Marglin, S.A. and J.B. Schor (eds) (1991) *The Golden Age of Capitalism: Reinterpreting the Post-War Experience*. Oxford: Oxford University Press.

Nove, A. (1992) 'Soviet reforms and western neo-classical economics' in J.M. Kovács and M. Tardos (eds) *Reform and Transformation in Eastern Europe*, London: Routledge, pp. 103–119.

Toporowski, J. (1999) 'Kalecki, Marx and the economics of socialism' in M.C. Sawyer (ed.), *The Legacy of Michał Kalecki, Volume 2*. Cheltenham: Edward Elgar, pp. 227–244.

Volcker, P.A. (1979) 'The political economy of the dollar', *Federal Reserve Bank of New York Quarterly Review*, Winter 1978–1979: 1–12.

Weisskopf, T.E., S. Bowles and D.M. Gordon (1983) 'Hearts and minds: a social model of U.S. productivity growth', *Brookings Papers on Economic Activity* 2: 381–441.

Wolff, E.N. (1995) *Top Heavy: A Study of Increasing Inequality of Wealth in America* New York: Twentieth Century Fund Press.

Wolff, E.N. (1998) 'Recent Trends in the Size Distribution of Household Wealth' *Journal of Economic Perspectives* 12(3): 131–150.

11
A Kaleckian Perspective on Changes in the Aggregate Income Distribution in the US

Tracy Mott and Mark Evers

11.1 Kalecki on the determinants of the income distribution

In Michał Kalecki's (1954/1991) major article on the distribution of the national income between wages and profits, he wrote that national income is measured as value added minus the cost of material inputs and as a result,

natonal income = aggregate wages + Overheads + profits

Overheads + profits are equal to the aggregate of the percentage mark-up of prices over direct costs minus the aggregate sum of these costs, which are wages plus materials costs. The *relative shares* of wages, profits and overheads in national income will then be determined, Kalecki showed, by the *mark-up*, the ratio of materials to wage costs and the *composition of industry*, which affects relative shares since different industries have different mark-ups and ratios of materials to wage costs.

Since material inputs are produced in the domestic economy, they represent proceeds to some and costs to others, which net out in the aggregate. The way in which they should influence the distribution of income then has to do with Kalecki's distinction between 'cost-determined' and 'demand-determined' prices. Since *raw* materials' prices are 'demand-determined', rising demand for them, relative to supply, will raise profits at the expense of wages somewhat in a way that will not show up as a higher mark-up in the national income statistics if the mark-up is measured by data from the industries in which prices are cost-determined. Changes in the composition of industry affecting distribution should or should not be expected to show up in the measurement of the aggregate mark-up, depending upon the methods used to measure it.

What should be done about overheads when examining the aggregate distribution between profits and wages? If these expenses represent overhead labour, such as non-production staffing, they represent labour income, through perhaps mostly higher, salaried incomes than production and non-supervisory labour. Often we describe overhead costs as those which do not vary as the scale of production varies over a given amount of plant and equipment. Along with the salaried staff, within these must be the cost of maintaining the existing production and distribution capacity of the firm. A lot of the non-labour overhead expenses surely must be debt service, and one could even think that the existing dividend pay-out could be thought of as a kind of overhead expense by the firm's management since firms are loathe to cut the dividend due to the likely effects on the firm's shares.[1] These surely represent capital income, whether dividends or interest payments, and so count in the profit share.

Kalecki held that the major factor determining the relative distribution should be the mark-up, which he argued to be determined by the degree of monopoly, and this in turn is determined by the following four factors: the level of industrial concentration, selling costs, overheads and trade union strength. Since the mark-up on direct costs is thought to vary with the need to cover the average amount of overhead cost on a per-unit basis, here is a way in which overheads can affect distribution, but to the extent that these expenses represent salaries, they will go to the wage share, and to the extent that they represent capital payments, they will go to the profit share. Because they are payments for maintenance of existing capacity, they will go somewhat towards labour and somewhat to other firms' revenues, which will be divided between wages and profits. Kalecki listed selling costs as a separate expense, but it can be seen as an overhead expense of a particular type, which ultimately resolves itself into wages and profits.

Since overheads affect the size of the mark-up, they will shift the income distribution away from wages, except insofar as these overheads represent payments to labour. If they do not give rise to higher mark-ups, higher overhead labour as a percentage of national income can affect the distribution by raising the wage share.

11.2 What happened in recent decades in the US?

This chapter focuses on the issue that, from 1983 on, real wages in the US did not keep up with productivity gains, except during 1998–2000, and asks why this happened and how did it affect the distribution of income over this period.[2] The changes in income and productivity are shown in Table 11.1.

The first column shows the percentage change in US productivity as measured by output per hour. The second column gives the percentage change in non-farm business real hourly compensation (including benefits) for production and non-supervisory workers. The third column shows the difference between the two or what might be described as the productivity-wage gap.

Table 11.2 shows that, from the 1970s onwards, unemployment in the US was higher on average than before, except for 1998–2000, and that the level of interest rates was higher on average than before for most of this period.

We also see in Figure 11.1 that the percentage of the US workforce that is unionized has declined precipitously to 11.2 per cent of employed wage and salary workers in the US, a level not seen since 1916 (Greenhouse, 2013). This is of course, one of the factors identified by Kalecki as affecting the mark-up.

Lawrence Mishel, et al., in *The State of Working America, 2012*, examine the evidence and the myriad of explanations offered to explain this compensation-productivity divergence and the growth in wage-inequality over this period. Evidence of consumer prices rising faster than overall output prices, rising wage-education differentials and a movement toward lower-paying industries internationally have tended to support a story that shifts in technology and increased globalization of production have punished lower-skilled workers in the US. Mishel, et al., (2012) are sceptical about the Skills Based Technology (SBT) explanation, arguing that while demands for higher skilled workers have risen, the workforce has also become more educated. They find that the wage gap that has arisen is between the very highest wage-earners and everyone else, not between higher-skilled middle-income earners and lower-skilled lower-wage earners. Alternatively, they believe that the decline in trade union strength since the 1970s, the erosion of the real value of the minimum wage and higher levels of unemployment provide better explanations. They also note that when the unemployment rate came down in the late 1990s, real wage growth at all levels of the distribution rose.

Table 11.1 Labour Income and Productivity in the US

Year	% Change in Productivity	% Change in Hourly Compensation	Productivity-Wage Gap
1948	2.8	0.9	1.9
1949	3.4	3.9	–0.6
1950	6.6	4.7	1.9
1951	2.7	0.8	2.0
1952	1.8	3.1	–1.4
1953	2.3	4.8	–2.5
1954	1.9	2.8	–0.9
1955	4.2	3.9	0.3
1956	–0.7	4.6	–5.3
1957	2.6	2.3	0.2
1958	2.2	1.2	1.0
1959	3.8	2.9	0.9
1960	1.2	2.8	–1.6
1961	3.1	2.2	0.9
1962	4.5	2.8	1.7
1963	3.5	2.1	1.4
1964	2.9	1.8	1.1
1965	3.1	1.7	1.4
1966	3.6	2.8	0.7
1967	1.7	3.0	–1.2
1968	3.4	3.4	0.0
1969	0.2	1.3	–1.1
1970	1.5	1.2	0.3
1971	4.0	2.0	1.9
1972	3.3	3.1	0.2
1973	3.2	1.8	1.4
1974	–1.6	–1.1	–0.5
1975	2.7	0.8	2.0
1976	3.3	2.5	0.8
1977	1.6	1.6	0.0
1978	1.3	1.7	–0.4
1979	–0.4	–0.1	–0.3
1980	–0.3	–0.4	0.1
1981	1.4	0.1	1.3
1982	–1.1	1.0	–2.0
1983	4.4	–0.1	4.4
1984	2.0	–0.1	2.1
1985	1.6	1.0	0.6
1986	3.1	3.4	–0.3
1987	0.3	0.3	0.0
1988	1.6	1.3	0.3
1989	0.8	–1.6	2.4
1990	1.8	1.1	0.7

Continued

Table 11.1 Continued

Year	% Change in Productivity	% Change in Hourly Compensation	Productivity-Wage Gap
1991	1.5	1.6	0.0
1992	4.0	2.8	1.2
1993	0.5	-0.5	1.0
1994	1.0	-0.3	1.3
1995	0.4	-0.3	0.7
1996	2.6	0.6	2.0
1997	1.5	0.9	0.6
1998	2.9	4.5	-1.6
1999	3.3	2.1	1.2
2000	3.3	3.9	-0.6
2001	3.1	1.8	1.3
2002	4.5	1.5	3.0
2003	3.7	2.4	1.3
2004	2.7	0.7	2.0
2005	1.7	0.7	1.1
2006	0.9	0.5	0.4
2007	1.5	1.1	0.4
2008	0.6	-0.4	1.0
2009	2.9	1.8	1.2
2010	3.1	0.3	2.8
2011	0.6	-0.6	1.2
2012	0.9	-0.1	1.0

Source: US Bureau of Labor Statistics and Federal Reserve Bank of St. Louis Economic Database (FRED).

Table 11.2 Unemployment in the United States

Year	US Unemployment Rate	Federal Funds Rate	10 Year Treasury Bond Rate
1955	4.4	1.79	2.82
1956	4.1	2.73	3.18
1957	4.3	3.11	3.65
1958	6.8	1.57	3.32
1959	5.5	3.31	4.33
1960	5.5	3.22	4.12
1961	6.7	1.96	3.88
1962	5.5	2.71	3.95
1963	5.7	3.18	4
1964	5.2	3.5	4.19
1965	4.5	4.07	4.28
1966	3.8	5.11	4.92
1967	3.8	4.22	5.07
1968	3.6	5.66	5.65
1969	3.5	8.2	6.67
1970	4.9	7.18	7.35

Continued

Table 11.2 Continued

Year	US Unemployment Rate	Federal Funds Rate	10 Year Treasury Bond Rate
1971	5.9	4.66	6.16
1972	5.6	4.43	6.21
1973	4.9	8.73	6.84
1974	5.6	10.5	7.56
1975	8.5	5.82	7.99
1976	7.7	5.05	7.61
1977	7.1	5.54	7.42
1978	6.1	7.93	8.41
1979	5.8	11.19	9.44
1980	7.1	13.36	11.46
1981	7.6	16.38	13.91
1982	9.7	12.26	13
1983	9.6	9.09	11.11
1984	7.5	10.23	12.44
1985	7.2	8.1	10.62
1986	7	6.81	7.68
1987	6.2	6.66	8.38
1988	5.5	7.57	8.85
1989	5.3	9.22	8.5
1990	5.6	8.1	8.55
1991	6.8	5.69	7.86
1992	7.5	3.52	7.01
1993	6.9	3.02	5.87
1994	6.1	4.2	7.08
1995	5.6	5.84	6.58
1996	5.4	5.3	6.44
1997	4.9	5.46	6.35
1998	4.5	5.35	5.26
1999	4.2	4.97	5.64
2000	4	6.24	6.03
2001	4.7	3.89	5.02
2002	5.8	1.67	4.61
2003	6	1.13	4.02
2004	5.5	1.35	4.27
2005	5.1	3.21	4.29
2006	4.6	4.96	4.79
2007	4.6	5.02	4.63
2008	5.8	1.93	3.67
2009	9.3	0.16	3.26
2010	9.6	0.18	3.21
2011	8.9	0.1	2.79
2012	8.1	0.14	1.8

Source: US Bureau of Labor Statistics and Federal Reserve Bank of St. Louis Economic Database (FRED).

Figure 11.1 Degree of unionization
Source: BLS Handbook of Labor Statistics and Current Population Survey (various years).

Ian Dew-Becker and Robert Gordon (2005, 2007) look at IRS data on wage incomes, which allows them to avoid a problem with Current Population Survey data, in which incomes above $100,000 may be coded only as 'greater than $100,000'. They find that widening skewness in the upper 10 per cent of the distribution explains the discrepancy between labour compensation and productivity and the fact that labour's share in national income has not fallen in the recent past. They distinguish between 'superstars' in the sports and entertainment industry, high-paid, high-skilled workers in the legal and financial professions and Chief Executive Officers (CEOs) within the top 10 per cent of the distribution, but argue that the combination of these groups have captured the productivity gains in national income.

Bakija, Cole and Heim (2012) map US tax return data to Standard Occupational Codes (SOC) and find that 59.1 per cent of the taxpayers in the top 0.1 per cent of the distribution were either CEOs or financial professionals. The share of national income (inclusive of capital gains) going to this top 0.1 per cent increased from 3.30 per cent in 1979 to 10.34 per cent in 2005, the last year of their dataset. A decomposition of this income share suggests that non-finance executives (CEOs) account for 44 per cent of the increase in this income share while financial professionals account for an additional 23 per cent. So, the biggest change has not been in the relative shares of the income distribution but *within* the wage and salary distribution and primarily at the top of the top 10 per cent of the distribution.

A question, also raised by Kalecki (1954/1991), is this: should these incomes be seen really as wage income or as profit income? Yes, formally it represents wage income rather than dividend or interest or rent or some other type of income we normally see as coming from payments for the use of capital. However, as payment for management-type services, rather than for production or non-supervisory labour, it may be better thought of as coming out of profits. The recipients of this income often receive grants of stock or stock options as part of their compensation (once realized), and bonuses, the size of which has to do with the profits and (stock market) performance of the company. Bivens and Mishel (2013) analyse CBO data to show that the shift between income categories (from strictly labour compensation toward capital and business income compensation) accounts for 27 per cent of the increase in the share of national income going to the top 1 per cent of the income distribution between 1979 and 2007. Bivens and Mishel go on to argue that the growth in incomes at the top of the income distribution is the result of a shift in institutional arrangements (financial deregulation, tax treatment of different types of income, etc.) that has incentivized rent-seeking among the top 1 per cent.

Since the major factor affecting distribution in a Kaleckian framework should be the mark-up, let us see what the data may tell us about that. Table 11.3 provides alternative calculations of the aggregate mark-up.

The first of these measures (NIPA mark-up) is the percentage change in the aggregate mark-up calculated from the series on price per unit labour cost from the National Income and Product Accounts (NIPA) of the US Commerce Department.[3] The numerator in this series is the GDP deflator. The denominator is a broad measure of unit labour costs, which essentially includes all wage and salary expenses per unit of output. The next column (BLS mark-up) is calculated from a measure which describes the difference between the percentage change in the consumer price index for urban consumers and the percentage change in unit labour costs for production and non-supervisory labour. These data come from the US Bureau of Labor Statistics (BLS), from where our Table 11.1 series on productivity and real compensation were obtained. The last column (Mixed mark-up) was calculated from a measure of the difference in the percentage change in the NIPA GDP deflator and the percentage change in the BLS measure of unit labour costs.

Table 11.3 The Mark-up in the United States

Year	NIPA Mark-up	BLS Mark-up	Mixed mark-up
1947	4.1	2.3	1.0
1948	0.1	–0.8	1.2
1949	2.0	2.0	1.8
1950	–1.3	2.1	0.8
1951	–2.5	–1.9	–1.7
1952	–1.7	–2.5	–1.3
1953	0.2	–0.3	–0.3
1954	2.9	0.1	2.3
1955	–2.5	–5.3	–3.4
1956	0.1	0.2	0.1
1957	–0.6	1.1	–0.3
1958	1.4	0.7	1.2
1959	–1.0	–1.5	–1.9
1960	0.4	0.8	0.6
1961	1.0	1.5	1.5
1962	0.4	1.5	0.8
1963	1.2	1.2	1.1
1964	0.5	1.3	1.1
1965	–1.3	0.5	0.0
1966	–0.9	–0.9	–0.8
1967	–0.8	–0.4	–0.4
1968	–2.1	–2.1	–2.1
1969	–1.6	–0.7	–1.2
1970	1.6	2.1	2.0
1971	–0.2	–0.1	0.1
1972	–1.0	1.4	–1.4
1973	–1.6	–1.6	–1.2
1974	3.9	1.1	3.6
1975	–0.2	0.9	0.6
1976	0.0	–0.2	–0.2
1977	–1.1	–0.5	–0.7
1978	–2.0	–0.3	–1.4
1979	–0.9	0.1	–1.3
1980	2.8	1.4	1.5
1981	–0.2	–2.3	–2.1
1982	1.8	4.5	3.4
1983	0.9	2.1	0.9
1984	–0.7	0.6	0.1
1985	–1.3	–0.3	–0.4
1986	0.7	0.1	–0.9
1987	0.6	0.4	–0.3
1988	–0.6	2.5	1.8
1989	–0.4	0.7	–0.6
1990	0.3	–0.1	–0.2
1991	–0.9	1.2	0.7

Continued

Table 11.3 Continued

Year	NIPA Mark-up	BLS Mark-up	Mixed mark-up
1992	0.5	1.1	0.6
1993	2.1	1.3	1.0
1994	0.1	0.7	0.1
1995	1.1	2.0	0.7
1996	0.2	0.6	0.3
1997	–2.3	–1.6	–2.2
1998	–0.6	1.2	0.1
1999	–2.0	–0.5	–2.0
2000	–1.0	1.3	0.2
2001	1.3	2.9	2.2
2002	0.9	1.2	0.2
2003	2.9	2.0	1.7
2004	2.0	1.1	1.2
2005	1.7	0.4	0.1
2006	–1.1	0.4	–0.1
2007	–1.3	1.0	–1.0
2008	0.3	1.1	2.3
2009	3.6	2.7	2.4
2010	0.8	2.6	1.3
2011	–0.2	1.4	1.0

Source: US Department of Commerce, US Bureau of Labor Statistics and Federal Reserve Bank of St. Louis Economic Database (FRED).

As seen in Figure 11.2, The NIPA series shows no significant upward or downward trend. A closer look at this series in levels rather than changes shows a slightly lower mark-up on average in the 1970s and 1980s as compared to the 1950s and 1960s. There is not, however, a significant-enough jump in the mark-up after 1983, we think, which would explain the failure of real wages to keep up with productivity.

The BLS and Mixed mark-ups, however, though not identical, show a measure of the mark-up which is rising in most years from 1983. The BLS mark-up is shown in Figure 11.3.

The mean difference over time between the productivity-wage gap and the Mixed mark-up is equal to zero.[4] The only differences between the BLS mark-up and the Mixed mark-up are due to the differences between the respective price index measure of the Consumer Price Index Research Series (CPI-U-RS) and the GDP deflator.

As seen in Figure 11.4, the much greater correspondence between these two series tells us that the measure of unit labour cost used in the NIPA measure of the mark-up vs. that used in the BLS measure is

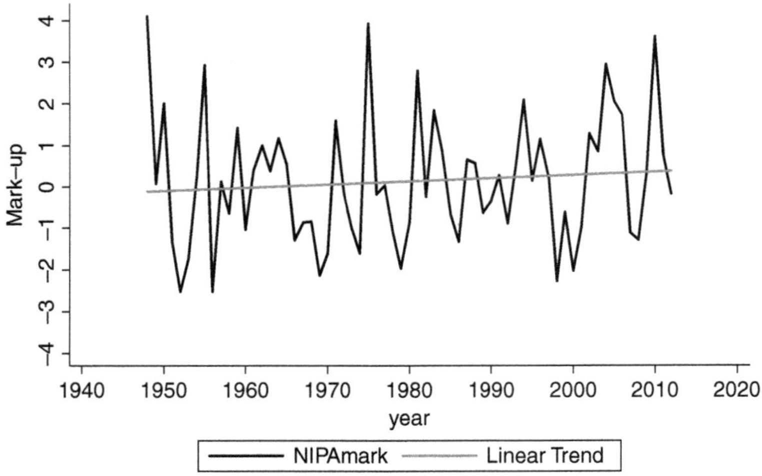

Figure 11.2 NIPA mark-up

Source: US National Income and Product Accounts BEA Table 1.15.

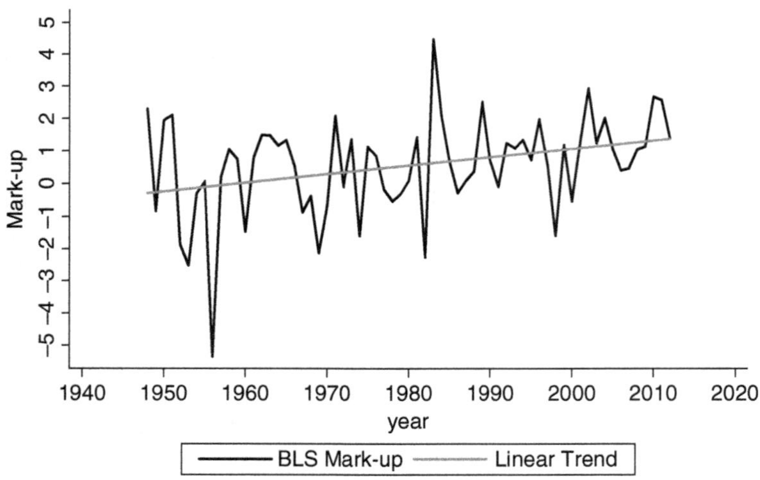

Figure 11.3 BLS mark-up

Source: US Bureau of Labor Statistics and Federal Reserve Bank of St. Louis Economic Database (FRED).

the major source of the differences between the two series. Thus the changes in distribution *within* the wage share explain where the productivity increases that did not go to real wages for production and non-supervisory labour went.

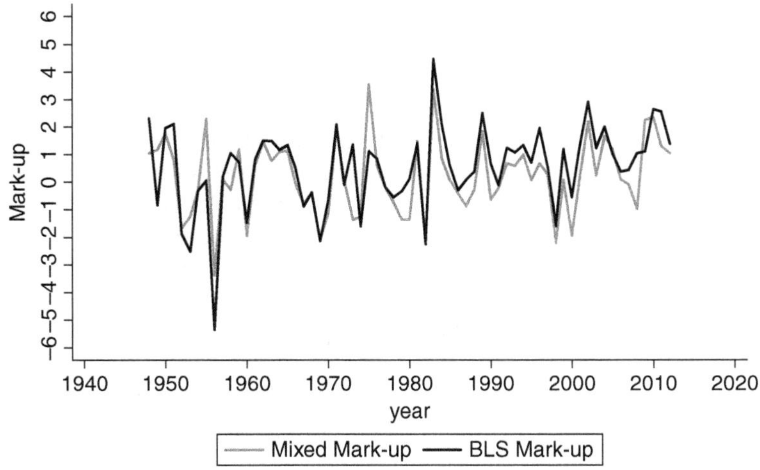

Figure 11.4 BLS and mixed mark-up comparison

Source: US Bureau of Economic Analysis, Bureau of Labor Statistics and Federal Reserve Bank of St. Louis.

11.3 A Kaleckian explanation

We also of course want to ask to what extent this can be explained by the factors appealed to by Kalecki. Should we see it as a rise in overhead labour costs? Can it be explained as a result of the decline in trade union strength?

The story told by Dew-Becker and Gordon (2007), having to do with 'superstar' incomes, needs more explanation. What would allow such a development? In an article in the 10 June – 16 June 2013 issue of *Bloomberg Business Week* on the huge severance packages now available to CEOs in the US (Green, 2013), Robert Thompson, a media professor at Syracuse University, is quoted as saying, 'To most people this kind of money to get fired is inconceivable. But with the budgets of movies and the pay for movie stars at astronomical, almost unthinkable, levels, it creates a bar against which the executives expect to be measured.' Why the rewards going to movie stars are so high and why their contract figures should be relevant to business executive pay are further questions that need to be answered. An argument that is often made is that executive compensation, not to mention severance packages, has to be high to obtain the necessary talent. Whether this is true or not is less important than the fact that it seemingly exists in the minds of boards of directors in the US and that their shareholders go along with this and that the economic forces allow it to continue.

If production and non-supervisory workers had more bargaining power, or if enough companies thought that they had to cut executive pay to stay competitive, presumably this situation would not persist. In a cover story in the same issue of *Business Week* on the membership warehouse outlet Costco (Stone, 2013), which pays its hourly workers an average of $20.89 per hour and covers health insurance for 88 per cent of its employees, it is noted that its CEO in 2012 received a salary of $650,000, plus a bonus of $200,000 and stock options worth perhaps $4 million. This is contrasted to its retailing-giant rival Wal-Mart, which gave its CEO in that year a base salary of $1.3 million, a bonus of $4.4 million, and stock options estimated to be worth $13.6 million, while its average wage for full-time employees is $12.67 per hour with 'more than half' getting health insurance.

Costco also has other lower overhead expenses than Wal-Mart, such as no public relations department, no expensive furniture in its offices, no-frills, warehouse-style retail outlets, and much less advertising. Labour turnover at Costco is significantly lower (5 per cent among those who have been there for more than a year) than elsewhere in its industry, undoubtedly due at least in part to its relative high pay and concern for staff welfare. Turnover is less than 1 per cent in its executive ranks, in spite of not paying the astronomical salaries that some others do. The article states that Costco actually barely gets any profit on many of its products and that 80 per cent of its profits comes from the membership fees it charges its customers, who renew at a rate of close to 90 per cent. Since 2009 Costco's sales have grown 39 per cent and its stock price has doubled, even in the environment of a deep recession and tepid recovery. So it must be making enough in profits to please shareholders.

11.4 Conclusions

Returning to Kalecki's taxonomy of factors affecting aggregate income distribution, it seems to us that the changes in the US since 1983 should be attributed to a rise in the aggregate mark-up due to overhead salary compensation rising at the expense of the real wage income of production and non-supervisory workers. This shows up mostly as changes *within* the wage and salary distribution rather than as a *shift* from the wage share to the profit share of national income, though, as Kalecki wrote, it could well be characterized as a shift from wages to profits.

If we include this overhead salary increase in the wage share, the profit share in the US distribution has not grown to any great extent since 1983, at least up to the Great Recession, which began in late 2007. But if we restrict the wage share to the wages received by production and non-supervisory workers, the profit share has grown. If we do make this restriction, we can attribute the growth we then see in the aggregate profit share to the decline in wage-bargaining strength due to declining unionization, the higher average levels of unemployment we have seen and the fall in the real value of the minimum wage, as appealed to by Mishel, et al. (2012).

The justifications we have given for including executive salaries in profit income can be augmented, we think, by seeing it as resulting from the failure of real wages for production and non-supervisory workers to keep up with productivity gains. Since it is the case that stock prices and dividend payments have not fallen, but have actually grown in real terms (with the exception of the 2007–2009 time period), shareholders overall have not suffered any losses in real income over the period we are examining. Figure 11.5 shows real corporate dividends over the time period.

To be sure, shareholders in some financial companies, and some executives in them, suffered losses, except insofar as they were bailed out by the federal government, in the financial crisis. Stock indexes have

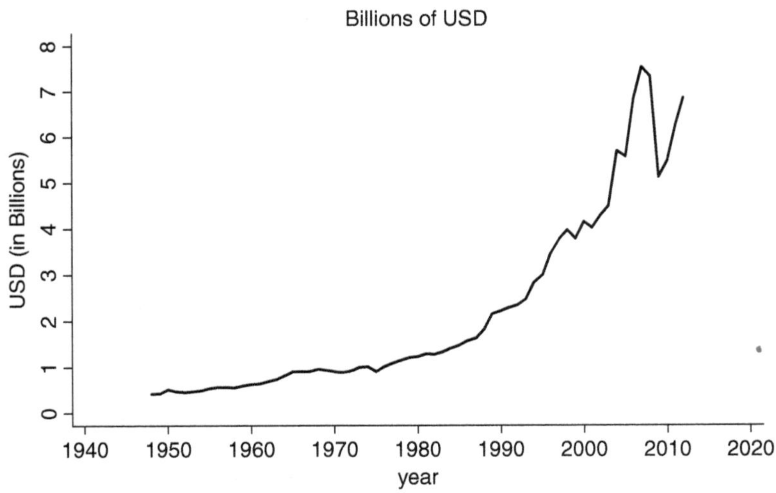

Figure 11.5 Real corporate dividends
Source: US Department of Commerce Bureau of Economic Analysis.

recovered, however, and corporate earnings for the most part have held up due to cost-cutting at the expense of employment in a way that productivity actually rose in the Great Recession. For the most part also, productivity gains in the US economy since 1983 have gone to these higher executive salaries, as we see in our data. It seems to us that the source of these gains is in the reduced ability of production and non-supervisory wages to get the productivity gains, and the ability of companies to pay these larger executive salaries has come from this.

Notes

1. Cf. Jan Toporowski (2000).
2. An earlier version of some of this data and a briefer examination of some these issues can be found in Mott (2010).
3. This ignores the matter of raw materials' prices, which may be of small significance in the US economy. One may ask, what about changes in crude oil prices, which have surely been significant? Even though the U.S. does produce some crude petroleum, it has been a net importer of oil during the period we are examining. The gains from the significant increases in oil prices largely meant a transfer of income from the US to the OPEC countries at the expense of both profits and wages in the US.
4. This is not surprising, since the data from which they arise are taken from a consistent set of BLS data, but it is nice to observe.

References

Bakija, J., A. Cole and B. Heim (2012) 'Jobs and income growth of top earners and the causes of changing income inequality: evidence from U.S. tax return data' *Working Paper* 2012–24, Department of Economics, Williams College, revised April 2012.

Bivens, J. and L. Mishel (2013) 'The pay of corporate executives and financial professionals as evidence of rents in top 1 percent incomes' *Working Paper* 296, Economic Policy Institute.

Dew-Becker, I. and R. Gordon (2005) 'Where did the productivity growth go? Inflation dynamics and the distribution of income' *Brookings Papers on Economic Activity* 2, pp. 67–150.

Dew-Becker, I. and R. Gordon (2007) 'Selected issues in the rise of income inequality' *Brookings Papers on Economic Activity* 2, pp. 169–190.

Green, J. (2013) 'Why fired CEOs go straight to the bank', *Bloomberg Business Week*, 10 June—16 June, pp. 55–60.

Greenhouse, S. (2013) 'Share of the work force in a union falls to a 97-year low, 11.3%' *New York Times*, http://www.nytimes.com/2013/01/24/business/union-membership-drops-despite-job-growth.html?_r=2&, 23 January.

Kalecki, M. (1954/1991) 'Distribution of national income', in J. Osiatyński (ed.), *Collected Works of Michał Kalecki*, Vol. II, Oxford: Clarendon Press, pp. 225–238.

Mott, T. (2010) *Kalecki's Principle of Increasing Risk and Keynesian Economics*, London and New York: Routledge.
Mishel, L., J. Bivens, E. Gould and H. Shierholz (2012) *The State of Working America, 2012*, Ithaca, NY: Cornell University Press.
Stone, B. (2013) 'How cheap is Craig Jelinek?', *Bloomberg Business Week*, 10 June–16 June, pp. 26–28.
Toporowski, J. (2000) *The End of Finance*, London and New York: Routledge.

12 Addressing the 'Great Recession' Using Kalecki's Macroeconomic Analysis

Malcolm Sawyer

12.1 Introduction

The global financial crisis of 2007–2009 and the subsequent 'Great Recession' have often been compared with the 1929–1933 financial crisis starting with the Wall Street crash and the 'Great Depression'. The scale of the 'Great Recession' has for most countries not been as great as that of the 'Great Depression' due to the larger scale of government and the willingness to allow the 'automatic stabilizers' of fiscal policy to work with resulting large budget deficits. But recently the general tenor of debate has swung in the direction of austerity.

Kalecki developed the major elements of his macroeconomic analysis during the 1930s, though he continued to refine his analysis, notably on the analysis of investment (see Sawyer, 1996). However, his major writings on macroeconomic policy were in the period 1943–1946 when he was located at the Oxford University Institute of Statistics and then the International Labour Office in Montreal before appointment in the United Nations secretariat in New York at the end of 1946. In his writings of that period, Kalecki set out clear and compelling arguments on the use of budget deficits and other ways to reach full employment and the social and political barriers to full employment. The present conjuncture has some similarities with the time at which Kalecki was making his major contributions on macroeconomic policies (and of course there are many differences). One broad similarity hinted in the previous paragraph: in the 1930s a peacetime experience of depression triggered by financial crisis only finally alleviated by war then with a now five-year (at time of writing) experience of recession also associated with financial crisis. They are both times of debates on the use of budget deficits. Another which we suggest below is that (associated to some degree with recession) both come after periods of relatively low investment leading to views that investment may tend to be relatively low in the future. It also should be self-evident that the market forces which are reputed to push a capitalist economy to full employment are weak to non-existent, and doubt is cast again on the abilities of market economies to secure full employment.

We suggest that Kalecki's powerful contributions on macroeconomic policies and the possibilities for full employment can be usefully grouped under three headings.

The first starts from the argument that full employment of labour was now technically possible in that it was realized that a sufficient level of aggregate demand was required which would not be readily secured through operation of 'market forces' but could be through the use of fiscal policy and budget deficits. It had in effect been realized that the level of demand set the level of economic activity and that government spending could be the means to ensuring that there was sufficient demand. There can (and often are) capacity constraints such that there is insufficient productive capacity for full employment. Whilst Kalecki often worked with the assumption that there would be excess capacity such that an expansion of demand would lead to an expansion of output and employment, he saw strong characteristics of developing countries being supply-side bottlenecks and lack of capacity, and that capitalist economies in the aftermath of war, for example, would suffer from lack of capacity. Further, Kalecki mentioned trade and foreign exchange difficulties as major constraints on full employment. The most significant obstacles to the achievement of full employment would be the social and political ones. Kalecki saw laissez-faire capitalism as inconsistent with sustained full employment. Kalecki, in rather typical laconic style, concluded by saying that '"full employment capitalism" will, of course, have to develop new social and political institutions which will reflect the increased power of the working class. If capitalism can adjust itself to full employment, a fundamental reform will have been incorporated in it' (Kalecki, 1990, p. 356).

The second (for example, Kalecki, 1944b), was that that there would generally be a need for permanent budget deficits if anything approaching full employment were to be achieved. This view is derived from the intentions to save exceeding the intentions to invest and the lack of any 'market forces' which would bring them into line. This follows from the national income accounts relationship that:

$$G - T = S - I + FA \qquad (12.1)$$

where G is government expenditure, T is taxes (net of transfer payments including interest payments on public debt), S private savings, I private investment, FA financial account surplus (= current account deficit). The public deficit is equal to the private surplus, and intentions to save greater than intentions to invest can only be realized if there is some combination of government budget deficit and capital outflow.

Kalecki criticized those who accepted that budget deficits would rise during economic downswings but who did not accept the arguments for the need for permanent budget deficits. He argued that 'there will emerge out of a consistent anti-cyclical policy a certain more or less stable level of private investment which by itself, i.e. without considerable assistance by loan expenditure of the public authorities, may fall short of the level required to "fill the gap" of savings out of a full employment income'. He then criticized the British government's White Paper Employment Policy as it did 'not propose to use public loan expenditure to push employment up to the level where unemployment, other than frictional is abolished' (Kalecki, 1944b, p. 243).

The third comes from 'Three Ways to Full Employment' (Kalecki, 1944a), where he examined budget deficit, investment stimulation and income redistribution as ways of raising and sustaining high levels of demand consistent with full employment. Other ways could be added, for example export promotion and policies to reduce the propensity to save. Government expenditure (relative to tax revenues), investment and exports (net of imports) are stimuli to the level of demand and hence the level of economic activity and employment. The redistribution of income (from rich to poor, from profits to wages) shifts spending power from those with a relatively low propensity to spend to those with a higher propensity to spend, raising the level of demand. In effect, Kalecki saw these different ways of stimulating demand as routes to sufficient demand to underpin full employment.

A significant consequence of, for example, stimulating investment expenditure is that not only would the level of output and employment rise, but the budget deficit would decline. This can be seen also from considering that, with given tax rates, higher income raises tax revenues and reduces budget deficits. There are, however, limits on these other ways to full employment – promotion of net exports, by definition, cannot be satisfactorily carried through by all countries. There are limits on the stimulation of investment, essentially because of a tendency for the capital-output ratio to rise, which would entail some combination of falling capacity utilization and reducing rate of profit (on capital). 'It must be realized that a permanent budget deficit is not the only way in which lasting full employment can be secured. The same end can be achieved by redistribution from higher- to lower-income grades which tends to increase consumption out of a given national income (because the propensity to save of the rich—especially if one takes into account undistributed profits—is higher than that of the poor' (Kalecki, 1997, p. 243).

Kalecki (1945) argued that securing full employment in the post-war era would require budget deficits in effect to offset the tendencies for intentions to save to exceed those of investment. 'The solution of the problem, of employment after the transition will require a much more unorthodox policy in public finance in the USA than in the UK. The latter will certainly experience serious difficulties in the sphere of foreign trade.... However, the financial problems involved in securing a national expenditure adequate to maintain full employment is likely to be of a much smaller order than in the USA' (Kalecki, 1990, pp. 400–401). In the outturn, there were much higher levels of employment than in the inter-war period, through a combination of higher rates of investment and budget deficits, where expenditure on armaments played a significant role, especially in the USA (Kalecki, 1991, Part 4). It is, however, important to note that, although investment was much more buoyant in the post-war period and growth in the industrialized countries was much faster than in the pre-war period, governments typically ran budget deficits right up to the present day. It is otherwise difficult to explain how debt-to-GDP ratios of the order of 40 per cent of GDP and upwards have continued – the simple algebra indicates that the debt ratio will tend to the deficit ratio divided by the (nominal) growth rate. The need for underlying budget deficits is not a universal law since by reference to Equation (12.1) it can be seen that when investment is high relative to savings and when there are net exports (and hence lending overseas), the budget may well be in surplus. This applies over time (hence an investment boom leads to smaller budget deficit or budget surplus) and across countries where those who have high rates of investment will likely have low budget deficits (and then a negative association between growth of the capital stock and budget deficits and public debt, which is liable to be misinterpreted as low deficits, leads to faster growth, whereas the direction of causation would be the reverse of that).

12.2 Imbalances between savings and investment and budget deficits

Investment was viewed by Kalecki as a relatively volatile component of aggregate demand which drives cyclical fluctuations in the economy.

The general tendency to invest depends on a range of factors such as technological opportunities and degree of monopoly, and these factors shift over time as technology and the intensity of competition shift. Savings are largely undertaken out of profits, and Kalecki often used the working assumption of low or zero savings out of wages. Although saving and investment decisions are often made by firms, and profits are a source of savings and influence upon investment, saving intentions are not matched by investment intentions. When workers undertake saving (often in the form of pension funds), the possible mismatch between savings and investment is intensified in that if savings and investment are to be in balance the firms' demands for external funds have to match the savings undertaken by workers and rentiers.

A first major conclusion which should be drawn from Kalecki's analysis (and indeed Keynes's) is that there are not mechanisms which would readily bring saving behaviour and investment decisions to equality. This contrasts with much of the pre-Keynesian macroeconomics where the rate of interest was often seen as being set to achieve that outcome, a view which continues to impact strongly on mainstream macroeconomics such as the 'new consensus macroeconomics'[1]. Saving and investment are in effect brought into equality through changes in the level of economic activity though recognizing that investment is the driving force. But when there is a general tendency for saving intentions to exceed investment intentions, then there is a strong need for budget deficits to in effect absorb the difference between savings and investment.

Kalecki argued that there would be a need for permanent budget deficits, and not just deficits during some parts of the cycle offset by surpluses elsewhere. He pointed out that the conditions in which a deficit is required are those in which the funding of the deficit does not present difficulties simply because there is an excess of private saving over private investment (which can only be realized if there is a budget deficit). The 'Treasury view', which has come back with a vengeance in the form of the Eurozone 'fiscal compact' as discussed below, was associated with the idea of the government seeking to balance the budget on an annual basis. After the War it was thought that in a downswing of economic activity, tax receipts would fall, opening up a budget deficit, and that attempts to correct that budget deficit through expenditure cuts and tax rate rises would make matters worse, there has been some appreciation of the role of 'automatic stabilizers', and the role of 'big government' in providing a cushion against fluctuations in private economic activity. The 1944 *White Paper on Employment Policy* cemented that view. It argued that 'to the extent that the policies proposed in this Paper affect the balancing of the Budget in a particular year, they certainly do not contemplate any departure from the principle that the Budget must be balanced over a longer period', and there was also concern in reducing 'that part of the public debt which is a dead-weight war debt' (Ministry of Reconstruction, 1944, p. 25). Kalecki (1944b) argued that the White Paper on Employment Policy had 'not presented a programme for lasting full employment which must be based either on a long-run budget deficit policy or on the redistribution of income' (p. 244). The rationale for this view was straightforward: either a budget deficit was needed to mop up with the difference between full employment saving and investment or full employment savings had to be reduced through a redistribution of income (from rich to poor).

12.3 Inequality

Kalecki viewed re-distribution of income as one of the 'three ways to full employment', and one suspects a way which he would have particularly favoured. From an aggregate demand point of view, it is based on the notion that the propensity to spend out of wages is greater than that out of profits, and the poor have higher propensities to spend than the rich[2]. This policy insight of Kalecki remains as valid as ever – and its significance has been amplified by the trends in income distribution over the past three decades or so towards greater inequality, shifts from wages to profits and a less progressive tax system.

The policy measures designed to shift the distribution of income can be readily listed, though of course any attempts at implementation would meet enormous social and political resistance. These policy measures include significant increases in minimum wages, where such exist, and their introduction elsewhere; adoption of 'living wage' ordinances; structuring wage awards in the public sector to increase lower wages faster than higher wages; and enhancing the power of trade unions. These policy recommendations run counter to the 'structural reform' agenda often promoted as the 'cure' for unemployment. In the realm of taxation, recommendations include making the tax system progressive through, for example, capital gains treated as income for tax purpose; removing caps on earnings limits for social security contributions (with no commensurate changes to social security benefits); and enhanced property taxation.

12.4 Investment prospects

Kalecki regarded the third possibility, stimulating investment, as limited: 'private investment must be pushed up to the level sufficient to expand the productive capacity of capital equipment pari passu with the increase in population and productivity of labour' (Kalecki, 1944b, p. 57), but no further, to avoid a rising capital-output ratio and falling rate of profit. (In this Kalecki was incorrect since, for a higher investment-to-output ratio, the capital-output ratio initially rises but then levels out.) He also argued that investment, public and private, should be undertaken to provide capital equipment which would enhance future production ('to provide tools for the production of consumption goods' (Kalecki, 1944b, p. 52)). Investment should not be undertaken simply in order to provide sufficient work to employ the available labour, and indeed more generally that expenditure should be undertaken because it yields benefits. Whilst Kalecki recognized the role which armaments spending ('military Keynesianism') played in generating a high level of economic activity in the post-war period, it cannot be said that he thereby approved of such expenditures! If the effective demand generated by useful private and public investment and indeed other socially useful forms of expenditure failed to provide full employment, 'the gap should be filled by increasing consumption and not by piling up unwanted public or private capital equipment' (Kalecki, 1944b, pp. 52–53).

The post-war period unemployment situation turned out to be much better than the pre-war situation and better than might have been anticipated from the writings of Kalecki. Although lower rates of unemployment were generally achieved in the industrialized world, it was rare for full employment to be achieved. Along with budget deficits and forms of 'military Keynesianism', the rate of investment was substantially higher along with faster rates of growth. These were mutually reinforcing and meant that a higher rate of investment did not lead to rising capital-output ratio and falling rate of profit, which Kalecki had seen as a major limit on the use of investment as a stimulus for demand. A major question now is whether investment rates (relative to GDP) will be higher in the future than during the recession and, more significantly, higher than in the pre-crisis decade. If the investment rate is indeed higher, then the budget deficit requirements diminish and a 'structural balanced budget' may become feasible. But, recognizing the hazards of forecasting in a world of path dependency and fundamental uncertainty, it would seem much more likely that the investment rate will be lower in the future. The processes of financialization have tended to lower investment rates. Hein (2012) argues that 'from a macroeconomic point of view financialization has affected long-run economic developments through the following three channels.

1. With regard to distribution, financialization has been conducive to a rising gross profit share... and to increasing inequality of wages and top management salaries.

2. ... [It has] had partially negative effects on firms' real investment in capital stock and hence on long-run growth of the economy to the extent that productivity growth is capital embodied.

'... it also generated increasing debt-income ratios of private households and thus increasing financial fragility' (pp. 2–3).

It is of particular importance that a higher sustainable investment rate would have to be matched by a higher rate of economic growth, which runs into issues of environmental sustainability. Addressing ecological concerns will require at a minimum a change in the structure of investment in the direction of lower energy consumption.

Kalecki envisaged that private investment might well not match the level of savings in the post-war period and that budget deficits would be needed to bridge the gap between investment and savings. As it turned out, there was much higher investment as compared with the inter-war period, though budget deficits were still needed to underpin high employment rates. Here we are suggesting that the prospects for investment are less buoyant than they were prior to the financial crisis. For many years to come the scars of the financial crisis and its impact on lending and credit creation are likely, the continuing effects of financialization and ecological concerns.

12.5 Social and political constraints

In a famous article, Kalecki (1943) raised many questions on the ability of a laissez faire capitalist economy to achieve and maintain prolonged full employment even though, in the light of the Keynesian 'revolution', the tools to do so were available. In that article, Kalecki introduced an idea which later became known as the political business cycle. Economic activity and employment could be stimulated prior to elections to aid the chances of the governing party being re-elected. But the resulting high level of employment would not last, and at best full employment would only be achieved at the top of the cycle. Following the arguments of Kalecki, many of which have been rehearsed above, we may pose the question as to why at the present time (2013) there has in effect been a refusal by governments, often supported by international organizations such as the IMF and OECD, to use budget deficits and other measures to secure a much higher level of economic activity. All the arguments against the use of budget deficits that have been advanced by politicians and policy makers in the last few years would have been well-known to Kalecki, and he demonstrated them to be false (for consideration of those arguments and their dismissal in the spirit of Kalecki see Sawyer, 2012a,

2012b). Instead of the use of fiscal policy, or indeed of the other 'ways to full employment' which Kalecki enumerated (as outlined above), there have been combinations of austerity programmes, attempts at fiscal consolidation and the adoption of balanced 'structural budgets' as policy objectives. It is also significant that the austerity programmes have been more directed to the reduction of public expenditure than the raising of tax rates – that is 'shrinking the state' and reducing social security and other income transfers. Further, under various headings, there have been policies of 'welfare reform' and advocacy of 'structural reforms'.

The motives of economic 'experts' and journalists, representatives of financial interests and the 'free market' in the promotion of the idea that 'there is no alternative' to austerity and 'structural reforms' were well summarized by Kalecki: 'Among the opposers of this doctrine [that full employment may be achieved by government spending] there were (and still are) prominent so-called "economic experts" closely connected with banking and industry. This suggests that there is a political background in the opposition to the full employment doctrine, even though the arguments advanced are economic. That is not to say that people who advance them do not believe in their economics, poor though this is. But obstinate ignorance is usually a manifestation of underlying political motives' (Kalecki, 1990, p. 349). He further argued that 'the social function of the doctrine of "sound finance" is to make the level of employment dependent on the state of confidence' (p. 350). Any policy which is seen to threaten the state of confidence is then argued to threaten investment and employment. Although the terminology of the 'state of confidence' is not often used, the way in which arguments about how regulation, taxes on corporate profits, etc., will damage investment (particularly in a globalized world) are deployed is consistent with the point made by Kalecki.

Kalecki argued that under sustained full employment 'the social position of the boss would be undermined, and the self-assurance and class consciousness of the working class would grow. Strikes for wage increases and improvements in conditions of work would create political tensions' (Kalecki, 1990, p. 351). He suggested that 'discipline in the factories' and 'political stability' would also be undermined. Much may be read into these words, but I think it is reasonable to suggest that full employment may involve significant wage inflation and a fall in work intensity and labour productivity along with a decline of 'discipline in the factories'. The volume of profits would be higher under full employment (and hence the rate of profit, though perhaps not the share), with money wage rises leading to rising prices (to protect profits) and a squeeze on rentier income. As the threat of dismissal ceases to threaten, work intensity may be lower at full employment, and labour productivity thereby lower than otherwise.

As noted above, Kalecki had concluded that '"full employment capitalism" will, of course, have to develop new social and political institutions which will reflect the increased power of the working class. If capitalism can adjust itself to full employment, a fundamental reform will have been incorporated in it' (Kalecki, 1990, p. 356). The fundamental reforms could range from co-ordinated wage bargaining with broad agreement over the distribution of income between wages and profits which may restrain inflationary pressures through to the development of forms of work organization including worker participation which can achieve high levels of productivity without the threat of 'the sack'.

But, 'the entrepreneurs in the slump are longing for a boom; why do they not gladly accept the synthetic boom which the government is able to offer them?' (ibid., p. 349). Kalecki divided the reasons for 'opposition of "industrial leaders" to full employment by government spending' (ibid., p. 349) into three: 'dislike of government interference in the problem of employment as such' (ibid., pp. 349–350), 'dislike of the direction of government spending (public investment and subsidizing consumption)' and 'dislike of the social and political changes resulting from the maintenance of full employment' (ibid., p.350). Further, he argued that 'subsidizing mass consumption is much more violently opposed by these experts than public investment. For here a moral principle of the highest importance is at stake. The fundamentals of capitalist ethics require that "you shall earn your bread in sweat" – unless you happen to have private means' (ibid., p. 351).

The general thrust of economic policies among European countries in the past three years or so (from early 2010 after the initial flush of allowing budget deficits to rise as the 'automatic stabilizers' kicked in as economies went into recession along with some mild discretionary fiscal policy) has been austerity programmes often with the explicit intent of eliminating the budget deficit on a long-run basis. The austerity programmes have been combined with attempts at major reforms of the welfare state and the labour market. The general direction of those policies has been to reduce any power of organized labour and to put downward pressures on wages and on social security benefits. This is conveniently expressed by British Prime Minster David Cameron at the Davos summit in January 2013: 'How do we succeed when other nations are growing, changing, innovating so fast? A lot of the answers are clear. Deal with your debts. Cut business taxes. Tackle the bloat in welfare. And crucially: make sure your schools and universities are truly world-class. In the UK we've been doing all these things. Less than three years in and we've cut the deficit by a quarter. Our corporation tax rate is the lowest in the G7. In welfare reform we've been radical. In education – revolutionary, busting open the state monopoly and allowing new schools to start up' (Cameron, 2013). The welfare state and social security systems have many purposes, but, in terms of the quote from Kalecki above, shrinking the welfare state reduces 'mass consumption' and seeks to ensure that 'you shall earn your bread in sweat'.

We would argue that within the sweep of policy agendas in the aftermath of the financial crisis there are many elements which are consistent with the arguments of Kalecki in the following sense. There is no need for austerity or for getting rid of budget deficits to the detriment of employment, and this suggests that the promotion of austerity and the other policy initiatives such as 'structural reforms' serves other purposes. This is not to suggest some grand conspiracy, but rather that opportunities are being taken in different ways and forms to seek the creation of a de-regulated, more insecure labour market and reduced social protection.

12.6 Kalecki's analysis and the EMU fiscal compact

The 'fiscal compact' being implemented by the countries of the Economic and Monetary Union (the European Union) is, from the perspective of Kalecki's writings, problematic to say the least. The *Treaty on Stability, Coordination and Governance in the Economic and Monetary Union* (European Union, 2012) (hereafter referred to as the Treaty), of which the 'fiscal compact' is the central part, and the associated so-called 'six pack' of policy measures seek to enshrine balanced budget requirements on all member countries. These involve the imposition of a 'structural budget deficit' rule such that the budget deficit does not exceed 0.5 per cent of GDP with a stricter policy imposed on countries with debt ratio exceeding 60 per cent of GDP to run surpluses to bring down the debt ratio. The deficit requirement is to be written into a country's national constitution or equivalent. The 'structural budget' is a slippery concept, for it is intended to calculate what the budget position would be (for given tax rate and expenditure plans) if the economy were operating at potential output, that is, with a zero output gap. This should not be taken as equivalent to full employment: for example, taking figures from before the financial crisis to avoid the impact of that crisis on potential output and its estimation, for the OECD area as a whole the output gap was +1.8 per cent (so output was about potential), and unemployment was 5.6 per cent[3]. The estimation of potential output is also surrounded with difficulties (see Sawyer, 2013, for further discussion). The significant element, though, of the 'fiscal compact' is that it puts the assessment of the fiscal position in the hands of 'experts', those who make the calculations on the 'structural budget position', and out of the hands of politicians and any relationship with the democratic process. As monetary policy was transferred to an 'independent' central bank, so fiscal policy is transferred to 'experts' to seek to first measure and then enforce 'structural' budget deficits.

The key point which comes from the writings of Kalecki is that there is little reason to think that full employment and balanced budget are mutually compatible. In the context of the 'fiscal compact' this has shifted to whether a zero output gap (actual output equal to potential output) and balanced budget are compatible. The Kaleckian response would have to be that since there is little reason to think that savings intentions and investment intentions would be equal at full employment or at a zero output gap, there is little reason to think that a structural balanced budget is possible. The argument needs to be modified in so far as a country's net exports and corresponding lending abroad can absorb the excess private savings over investment. But that is clearly not a universal option since global net exports must sum to zero. The 'fiscal compact' seeks to impose a 'structural balanced budget' which may often be impossible to achieve (and recall that the 'fiscal compact' is to be imposed on all members of the EMU).

12.7 Concluding comments

Kalecki argued that budget deficits were required to secure sufficient demand to achieve full employment, and he argued persuasively against the arguments used to promote fiscal consolidation. Redistribution of income would be an additional way to raise the level of demand, as would promotion of investment which would, however, be subject to limitations. Although the economic conditions in terms of level of demand which were required for full employment had been established and the tools (budget deficits) which could be used to achieve that were also established, there were close to insurmountable political and social obstacles. The 'fundamental reforms' which Kalecki saw as necessary are more remote than ever. On an analysis from the work of Kalecki, the present directions of policy travel – of fiscal consolidation and lack of any measures to seriously confront inequality – will seriously jeopardize a return to low unemployment.

Notes

1. For a simple version of the new consensus macroeconomics expressed in three key equations see Meyer (2001); for a thorough exposition Woodford (2003); essays on the 'new consensus' can be found in Arestis (2007); for a critique see Arestis and Sawyer (2008).
2. In recent literature, often based on models which would be given the epithet Kaleckian, the distinction is drawn between wage-led and profit-led regimes, where in the former a shift to wages would stimulate demand and growth, whereas in the latter a shift to profits would. The extent to which a rise in profits would stimulate investment is central to the difference between the two regimes. I would interpret Kalecki as viewing profits and changes in profits as having some impact on investment, though working through retained profits and hence savings, and that the balance between investment and savings was such that a rise in profits would raise the gap between saving and investment (the 'incomplete' use of profits). Further, as indicated in the text, there is a limit on investment stimulation linked with the rate of growth of the economy.
3. Figures are taken from OECD *Economic Outlook* November 2009. The comparable figures for the Euro-zone were +1.9 per cent and 7.5 per cent respectively, and for the USA +1.0 per cent and 4.6 per cent.

References

Arestis, P. (ed.) (2007) *Is There a New Consensus in Macroeconomics?*, Basingstoke: Palgrave.

Arestis, P. and M. Sawyer (2008) 'A critical reconsideration of the foundations of monetary policy in the new consensus macroeconomics framework', *Cambridge Journal of Economics*, 32(5): 761–779.

Cameron, D. (2013) 'Speech to the World Economic Forum in Davos' (http://www.number10.gov.uk/news/prime-minister-david-camerons-speech-to-the-world-economic-forum-in-davos/) accessed 24 January 2013.

European Union (2012) *Treaty on Stability, Coordination and Governance in the Economic and Monetary Union*, Brussels: European Union.

Hein, E. (2012) *The Macroeconomics of Finance-dominated Capitalism—and Its Crisis*, Cheltenham, UK: Edward Elgar.

Kalecki, M. (1943) 'Political aspects of full employment', *Political Quarterly*, 14(4): 322–331.

Kalecki, M. (1944a) 'Three ways to full employment', in Oxford University Institute of Statistics, *The Economics of Full Employment*, Oxford: Blackwell.

Kalecki, M. (1944b) 'The White Paper on Employment Policy', *Bulletin of the Oxford University Institute of Statistics*, reprinted in Kalecki (1997).

Kalecki, M. (1945) 'The maintenance of full employment after the transition period: a comparison of the problem in the USA and the UK', *International Labour Review*, 52(5): 449–464, reprinted in Kalecki (1990).

Kalecki, M. (1990), *Collected Works of Michał Kalecki* Vol. 1, ed. J. Osiatyński, Oxford: Clarendon Press.

Kalecki, M. (1991), *Collected Works of Michał Kalecki* Vol. 2 ed. J. Osiatyński, Oxford: Clarendon Press.

Kalecki, M. (1997) 'Studies in applied economics 1940–1967; Miscellanea', *Collected Works of Michał Kalecki* Vol. 7, ed. J. Osiatyński, Oxford: Clarendon Press.

Meyer, L.H. (2001) 'Does money matter?', *Federal Reserve Bank of St. Louis Review*, 83(5), 1–15.

Ministry of Reconstruction (1944), *Employment Policy*, Cmnd. 6527, London: HMSO.

Organization for Economic Co-operation and Development (OECD), Paris. (2009) *Economic Outlook*, – See n. 3.

Sawyer, M. (1996) 'Kalecki on the trade cycle and economic growth' in J. King (ed.) *An Alternative Macroeconomic Theory: The Kaleckian Model and Post Keynesian Economics*, New York: Kluwer, pp. 93–114.

Sawyer, M. (2012a) 'The tragedy of UK fiscal policy', *Cambridge Journal of Economics*, 36(1): 205–221.

Sawyer, M (2012b) 'Fiscal austerity: the 'cure' which makes the patient worse', Centre for Labour and Social Studies (available at http://classonline.org.uk).

Sawyer, M. (2013) 'The problematic nature of the Economic and Monetary Union', in S. Fadda and P. Tridico (eds), *Financial Crisis, Labour Market and Institutions*, London: Routledge.

Woodford, M. (2003) *Interest and Prices: Foundations of a Theory of Monetary Policy*, Princeton: Princeton University Press.

13

Economic Policies for Exit from Crisis, in a Post-Kaleckian Model

Edwin Le Heron[1]

The 2008 economic crisis is the most serious crisis that Western countries have faced since 1929. Many parallels can be drawn and similarities found between these two crises. However, the fall in GDP after 2008 does not reach the level of the 1929 crisis, particularly in the United States. Lessons were learned from the 1929 crisis, and economic policies served to reduce the impact of the recent crisis on GDP. It seems obvious for the monetary policy of central banks. But some proposals, such as the return to a 'constitutional' balanced budget in the European Union remind us of the Treasury view denounced by Keynes at the time.

What have we really learned from the 1929 crisis? Is it a structural crisis, that is, a historical break in the trend? Or is it a cyclical crisis, that is, an abrupt variation in the trend? If the policy mix was weak just after the 1929 crisis, it ultimately involved major structural changes in capitalism as, for instance, the reduced scope left to the financial markets.

In contrast, the 2008 crisis seemed to follow an opposite trend: firstly, a structural change in the 1980s with 'financialization' as a new regulation of capitalism and a major explanation of the crisis and, secondly, powerful monetary and fiscal policies, which proved ineffective in the absence of structural change.

It is enlightening to examine the economists of the 1930s and particularly Michał Kalecki, who questioned the 1929 crisis and proposed to change the rules of capitalism to boost economic growth and employment. In his famous paper on the political economy of employment in capitalism, Kalecki observed that 'Under a laissez -faire system the level of employment depends on the so-called state of confidence.... This gives to the capitalists a powerful indirect control over Government policy: everything which may shake the state of confidence must be carefully avoided because it would cause an economic crisis. The social function of the doctrine of 'sound finance' is to make the level of employment dependent on the 'state of confidence' (Kalecki, 1971, p. 139).

If we insist on a reinterpretation of Michał Kalecki's analysis, the contributions of Nicholas Kaldor and John Maynard Keynes are also important in our modelling. If PK usually stands for Post-Keynesian, it can also stand for Post-Kaleckian or Post-Kaldorian. Moreover, Michał Kalecki certainly seems the most important reference because he discovered Keynes's principle of effective demand on his own in 1933 and had a profound influence on Cambridge economists, in particular Nicholas Kaldor. In this chapter, we will combine some ideas from Kalecki, Kaldor and Keynes.

From Kalecki, we use the mark-up pricing theory, fixed technical coefficient, capacity utilization and two classes of households: workers and capitalists. Of course, the model is a dynamic growth model introducing lags and time. The long run is conceived as a chain of short terms. With the corporate retained profits, we introduce the principle of increasing risk (Kalecki, 1937) both in terms of the borrower and the lender. The long-term interest rate is linked to the level of debt in firms. The risk and the interest rate increase with a lower self-financing and the size of investment. The relevance of income distribution is introduced to the consumption function as Kaldor perfectly summarized (in a discussion on Kalecki) with the sentence (1956, p. 96): 'capitalists earn what they spend, and workers spend what they earn'.

The state of confidence is a fundamental variable, notably through its impact on effective demand. Like Keynes, Kalecki recognized the importance of psychological variables in determining growth and unemployment, especially in a world with radical uncertainty. Moreover, uncertainty is the main explanation for the difference between the behaviour of the entrepreneur who agrees to calculate in the long-term and the behaviour of the speculator who only expects price changes in the short term. This analysis, which is the heart of Chapter 12 in the *General Theory*, is also found in an interesting paper by Kaldor on speculation and economic stability: self-fulfilling prophecy explains the negative impact of speculation on growth: 'What distinguishes speculative purchases and sales from other kinds of purchases and sales is the expectation of an impending change in the ruling market price as the sole motive of action' (Kaldor, 1939, p. 1).

Firstly, I shall build a Post Kaleckian stock-flow consistent (SFC) model (Lavoie and Godley, 2001; Godley and Lavoie, 2007; Le Heron, 2014).

I shall introduce the question of the state of confidence to the private sectors and other features of Kalecki's models. Secondly, I shall simulate the model to study the effects of different economic policies to understand the best way for an exit strategy to the crisis.

13.1 A post-Kaleckian stock-flow consistent growth model

In this section, I develop more specifically the features influenced by Kalecki and the most important matter of the model[2]. The economy contains six sectors: government, firms, households divided into workers and capitalists, private banks and central bank. SFC modelling is based on two tables: the transactions matrix (flows, Appendix 3) and the balance sheet matrix (stocks, Appendix 4). The complete dynamic model (Appendix 2) contains 56 equations.

All production must be financed. However, current production is financed by the working capital of entrepreneurs (retained earnings) and by contracted revolving funds granted by banks at the current rate of interest. These two factors constitute a shock absorber to possible monetary rationing by banks. I am essentially limiting my study to the effects that a fall in the state of confidence of banks and firms might have on new financing for investment and growth of production. Let us proceed to examine the gross supply (φ) and the net supply (ΔL) of finance by banks – that is to say, the new flow of money, as opposed to the existing stock of money (Δ). There is also a stock of money demand equal to transaction, precaution, finance and speculative motives, whereas the desired gross finance demand (φ^d) represents the new flow of financing required by firms for the desired investment (I^d) and for the redemption of the debt (amortization = $amort_L$) minus the undistributed profits (P^u). Thus the internal funds of firms (IF) represent the undistributed profits (P^u) minus the redemption of the debt ($amort_L$). Assuming a closed economy, demand for money can be satisfied by banks via credit. At the end of the period, net financing demand (ΔL_D) can be constrained by net money supply from banks (ΔL). ΔD determines monetary creation in the period, issued from loans (L) to firms and Treasury bonds (B) to Government.

The national income (Y) adds the household consumption (C), investment of the firms (I) and the public expenditure (G). The rate of growth of the national income is gr_y.

$$Y = C + I + G \tag{13.1}$$

$$gr_y = \Delta Y/Y_{-1} \tag{13.2}$$

13.2 Investment of firms

The investment function is the most important one in a growth model. The stock of capital (K) increases with the flow of net investment (I) that is financed by the total of the corporate retained profits of firms and by external funds from commercial banks (gross finance = φ). Firms prefer self-financing (Kalecki, 1937) because borrower's risk begins with external funds. The self-financing of firms corresponds to the net retained profits, that is, the retained earnings (P^u) minus the redemption of the debts of firms ($amort_L$). Firms borrow money from banks to finance investments (loan at variable rate) (L).

$$I \equiv \varphi + IF \tag{13.3}$$

$$IF = P^u - amort_L \tag{13.4}$$

$$amort_L = a_l \cdot L_{-1} \tag{13.5}$$

In this model, I differentiate between net or effective investment (I) and the desired investment of firms (I_D). The banks finance the latter totally or in part according their lender's risk (LR) (see equations 13.21, 13.22, 13.23, 13.27). A rationing in investment financing can exist ($\varphi < \varphi^d$ or $I < I_D$). The desired rate of accumulation (gr_{kD}) is a function of an exogenous state of confidence (γ_0), the capacity utilization rate (u) and the increasing risk of the borrower (BR), which is measured by the rate of cash flow (r_{cf}) and by the financial condition index (FCI). The rate of cash flow is the ratio of retained profits to capital, and the financial condition index captures the sensitivity of investment to the level of indebtedness and to the long-term interest rate. The borrower's risk captures Kalecki's principle of increasing risk. The risk and the long-term interest rate increase with a lower self-financing and the size of investment.

$$I_D = gr_{kD} \,.\, K{-}1 \tag{13.6}$$

$$\varphi^d = I^d - IF \tag{13.7}$$

$$gr_{kD} = \gamma_0 + (\gamma_1 \cdot r_{cf-1}) + (\gamma_2 \cdot u_{-1}) - (\gamma_3 \cdot FCI_{\,-1}) \text{ With } \gamma_i\text{: constants} \tag{13.8}$$

where the rate of capacity utilization is defined as the ratio of output to full capacity output (Y_{fc}):

$$r_{cf} = P^u / K_{-1} \tag{13.9}$$

$$u = Y / Y_{fc} \tag{13.10}$$

The capital to full capacity ratio (σ) is defined as a constant:

$$Y_{fc} = K_{-1} \cdot \sigma \qquad \text{With } \sigma\text{: constant} \tag{13.11}$$

$$FCI = \mu_1 \cdot i_l \cdot L/K \qquad \text{With } \mu_i\text{: constants} \tag{13.12}$$

I measure the output gap ratio using Y_{fc} the output of full capacity and not the capacity that corresponds to the potential output. Distributed profits (P^d) are a fraction of profits realized in the previous period:

$$P^d = (1 - s_f) \cdot P_{f-1} \qquad \text{With } s_f\text{: constant} \tag{13.13}$$

13.3 Two classes of households: workers and capitalists

Income distribution is relevant. I assume that households (denoted H) determine their consumption expenditure (C) on the basis of their expected disposable income ($Y_H{}^a = Y_W{}^a + Y_K{}^a$) and of their wealth of the previous period, consisting entirely of bank deposits. Following the Kaleckian tradition and the Kaldorian equation (1956), there are two classes of households: workers (denoted W) and capitalists (denoted K). Working households earn essentially wages and consume a large part of their income (Y_w) while financial income of capitalist households (Y_k), consisting of distributed profit (P^d) and interest, is largely devoted to saving ($\alpha_1 > \alpha_2$ and $\alpha_3 > \alpha_4$). The consumption decision depends on the social class of the households and determines the amount that they will save out of their disposable income. The financial behaviour of workers is simplified, and they only hold banking deposit accounts that earn interest. The capitalists hold equities and banking deposit. The consumption decision and the level of taxes (T_W and T_K) determine the amount (ΔD) that households will save out of their disposable income (essentially the capitalist households). A small part of the household wealth (D) is consumed.

$$C = C_W + C_K \tag{13.14}$$

$$C_W = (\alpha_1 . Y_W{}^a) + (\alpha_3 . D_{W-1}) \qquad \text{With } \alpha_i\text{: constants} \tag{13.15}$$

$$C_K = (\alpha_2 . Y_K{}^a) + (\alpha_4 . D_{K-1}) \qquad \text{With } \alpha_i\text{: constants} \tag{13.16}$$

$$Y_W{}^a = Y_{W-1} + \theta_h \cdot (Y_{W-1} - Y_W{}^a{}_{-1}) \qquad \text{With } \theta_h\text{: constant} \tag{13.17}$$

$$Y_K{}^a = Y_{K-1} + \theta_h \cdot (Y_{K-1} - Y_K{}^a{}_{-1}) \qquad \text{With } \theta_h\text{: constant} \tag{13.18}$$

$$Y_W = W + (i_{d-1} \cdot D_{W-1}) - T_W \tag{13.19}$$

$$Y_K = P^d + (i_{d-1} \cdot D_{K-1}) - T_K \tag{13.20}$$

Financing by private banks

In this model, banks do not make loans to households. But firms' financing is fundamental in a monetary economy of production. Firms begin by being self-financed then turn to external finance (ΔL_D). Banks only finance projects they consider profitable, but confidence in their judgment is variable and can justify various strategies. Banks examine firms' productive and financial expectations and also their financial structure. This investigation is made according to their confidence in the state of long-term expectations of yields on capital assets, influencing what Keynes referred to as 'animal spirits'. The state of confidence of banks is notably taken into account by an exogenous variable (γ_4). After the study of expected production and of demand of financing that integrates the firm's borrowing risk, bankers can refuse to finance. The state of confidence of banks summarizes these factors.

Banks experience a lender's risk (*LR*) when underwriting finance and creating money. Lender's risk is the sum of three fundamental risks: risk of default, risk of liquidity and market risk. In equations (13.21, 13.22, 13.23, 13.27), the risks of default and of liquidity are taken into account by the gap of the leverage ratio with a conventional leverage ratio. Monetary policy involves a money market risk when fluctuations in the money interest rates occur.

When the lender's risk is at a maximum ($LR = 1$), commercial banks refuse to finance the net investment of firms: $\Delta L = 0$. Desired investment (I_D) faces a serious finance rationing. The flow of net investment is only financed by self-funding, that is, the retained earnings (P^u), minus the amortization of the debt ($amort_L$). Thus the money supply (in stock) can be reduced with the redemption of the debt. If the lender's risk is null ($LR = 0$), desired investment is fully financed: $\Delta L = \Delta L_D$ or $\varphi = \varphi^d$. This corresponds to the endogenous money (horizontalism) of Kaldor (1982).

$$\varphi = \varphi^d \cdot (1 - LR) \qquad \text{With } 0 \leq LR \leq 1 \tag{13.21}$$

$$\Delta L = \varphi - amort_L \tag{13.22}$$

In the model, the lender's risk (*LR*) is measured by the difference between the current leverage ratio and the conventional leverage ratio (amount of indebtedness considered normal), and the short-term interest rate (i_{cb} from the monetary policy) serves as a proxy of the risk of inflation. The higher the current indebtedness of firms (L/K) over the accepted indebtedness, the greater the lender's risk. The accepted indebtedness is conventional, but this conventional indebtedness can increase during a boom and decrease during a crisis: (γ_5) is linked to growth and to the state of confidence (measured by the Index of Business Climate (*BCI*) in this model) and thus endogenous.

$$LR = -\gamma_4 + a_1 \cdot (lev_{-1} - \gamma_5 \, . \, lev_c) + (b_1 \cdot i_{cb}) \qquad \text{With } \gamma_4, a_1, b_1 \text{ and } lev_c\text{: constant} \tag{13.23}$$

$$lev = L/K \tag{13.24}$$

$$\gamma_5 = a_2 \cdot BCI \qquad \text{With } a_2\text{: constant} \tag{13.25}$$

Monetary authorities determine endogenously the key rate on the money market (i_{cb}) following a Taylor rule (Taylor, 1993). While central banks fix the short-term rates, private banks' liquidity preference determines banking rates (short-, medium- and long-term interest rates). The significant rates for growth and financing (loan) are the long-term interest rates (i_l). The link between short-term and long-term interest rates is complex. Macroeconomic banking interest rates (i_l) are the production costs of money plus a risk premium. The first element corresponds to functioning costs (wages, investment, immobilization); to payment costs for monetary liabilities (subjected to the firms' competition for households savings); to the cost of high-powered money determined by the central bank; and to a rate of margin (χ) corresponding to standard profits of banks. The production costs of money are equal to (i_{cb}) plus a relatively constant mark-up (χ).

Risk premiums are not constant because they are the fruits of the banks' liquidity preference, which covers lender's risk (*lr*). There is an increasing risk (Kalecki, 1937) as a consequence of the size of investment and of the level of self-financing. With the prosperity, the size of investment and the leverage ratio rise, involving an increasing long-term interest rate. In the model, I use a similar lender's risk as the one seen previously (Equation 13.23), that is a mix of state of confidence and of leverage ratio plus the expectation of inflation (Π^a). But with the different coefficients (γ_5) and (a_3), (*lr*) can be negative and reduces the mark-up. Therefore the spread between (i_{cb}) and (i_l) is not constant. To explain the short-term interest rate (i_d), i_{cb} and χ are sufficient. On the contrary, (lr) is an important variable in order to explain long-term interest rate (i_l). Banks apply a spread (χ_2) between the key rate and the rate on deposits in order to realize profit.

$$i_l = i_{cb} + lr + \chi_1 \text{ With } \chi_1\text{: constant } \chi_1 > \chi_2 \tag{13.26}$$

$$lr = -\gamma_6 + a_3 \cdot (lev_{-1} - \gamma_5 \cdot lev_c) + \Pi^a \tag{13.27}$$

With γ_6, a_3, lev_c constant and c = convention on the 'normal' debt ratio,

$$i_d = i_{cb} - \chi_2 \tag{13.28}$$

The initial structure of interest rates is as follows: $i_l = i_b > i_{cb} > i_d$

Economic activity also depends on the animal spirits of banks. Finance scarcity can only be the consequence of a deliberate choice. 'Desired scarcity' of financing is the sign of banks' liquidity preference. From an optimal structure of their balance sheet, I can measure the profits of commercial banks (P_b) obtained by monetary financing:

$$P_b \equiv i_{b-1} \cdot B_{-1} + i_{l-1} \, . \, L_{-1} - T_B - i_{d-1} \, . \, D_{-1} - i_{cb-1} \, . \, REF_{-1} \tag{13.29}$$

Fiscal policy of the government

Government expenditures are only final sales of consumption goods. The government collects taxes from workers on wages and from capitalists, firms and commercial banks on profits. The government finances any deficit issuing bonds, so that the supply of treasury bonds (B) in the economy is identical to the stock of government debt. In other words, it is given by the pre-existing stock of debt plus its current deficit (DG). The current deficit of the Government includes the redemption of the National Debt. I assume that private banks give limitless credit to government at the long-term rate of interest (i_l).

To analyse the consequences of a supply shock, I assume a stabilizing effect of the fiscal policy. Public expenditure (G) is always growing at the same rate (gr_y) as the national income (Y) with a lag of one year. Tax revenue is proportional to income and hence varies in line with the public expenditure. With the State debt, the global impact is linked to the key interest rate and, then, to the monetary policy. It looks like a co-ordination between the monetary and the fiscal policies. The final effect of the fiscal policy is measured by the government deficit (DG). Our economy has a self-stabilizing tendency due to the fiscal policy.

$$G = G_{-1} \cdot (1 + gr_{y-1}) \tag{13.30}$$

$$DG = G + (i_{b-1} \cdot B_{-1}) - T - P_{cb} - amort_B \tag{13.31}$$

$$T = T_H + T_F + T_B \tag{13.32}$$

$$T_H = T_W + T_K \tag{13.33}$$

$$T_W = \tau_1 \cdot Y_{W-1} \quad \text{With } \tau_1\text{: constant} \tag{13.34}$$

$$T_K = \tau_2 \cdot Y_{K-1} \quad \text{With } \tau_2\text{: constant} \tag{13.35}$$

$$T_F = \tau_3 \cdot P_{f-1} \quad \text{With } \tau_3\text{: constant} \tag{13.36}$$

$$T_B = \tau_4 \cdot P_{b-1} \quad \text{With } \tau_4\text{: constant} \tag{13.37}$$

Monetary policy of central bank

Following the theory of endogenous money (Kaldor, 1982), I assume that the central bank is fully accommodating. I use a Taylor rule for the modelling of the central bank's behaviour. First, the central bank fixes the key rate of interest (i_{cb}) using a Taylor rule, that is, central bankers react to output gap and inflation gap, and second it provides whatever advances (*REF*) demanded by banks at this rate. Taylor propounded his first instrument rule in 1993, modelling the dual mandate of the Fed. It was founded on the output gap and on the inflation gap. From the Taylor rule, I can summarize monetary policy according to three dimensions: strategy, flexibility and intensity. Strategy represents the mandate and therefore the long-term policy. Flexibility measures the deviation in the short term of the policy from the strategy. Intensity is the weight put respectively on output gap and inflation gap. With the 'Taylor principle', the coefficient on inflation gap must be superior to one to avoid that inflation expectations produce inflation.

I assume that central bank uses a flexible Taylor rule. The key interest rate (i_{cb}) is a negative function of the output gap and a positive function of the inflation gap. Output gap is the difference between the full capacity output[3] (Y_{fc}) and the current output (Y). Output gap in ratio is output over the output gap. Inflation gap is the difference between current inflation and the target of inflation (Π^*). As in the standard Taylor rule, I add a neutral interest rate, exogenously fixed at 2 per cent as Keynes in the *General Theory*. The inflation target is 2 per cent. At the steady state, the key interest rate is equal to 3 per cent. The key interest rate should be 4 per cent for the real key interest rate equals the neutral interest rate ($i_{cb} - \Pi^* = i^* = 2$ per cent) and is equal to zero for the three gaps (output, inflation and interest rate) . But the output gap is always positive, involving a lower key interest rate (3 per cent).

The monetary rule of the central bank is:

$$i_{cb} = i^* + \Pi - \alpha_4 \cdot OG_R + \alpha_6 (\Pi - \Pi^*) \tag{13.38}$$

Inflation

I am assuming that income distribution is constant in the short term. This approach corresponds to the Kaleckian view where the long run is conceived as a 'slowly changing component of a chain of short period situations' (Kalecki, 1971, p. 165).

We adopt Kaleckian mark-up pricing to explain the prices. Mark-up pricing asserts that prices are determined by unit costs, somehow measured, to which a mark-up is added by entrepreneurs. Entrepreneurs set prices after the determination of nominal wages. So entrepreneurs have a profit target and set themselves the real wages and the income distribution. This explains why income distribution is constant, even with inflation. According to Kalecki, the mark-up depends from the degree of monopoly. This degree of monopoly measures the balance of power between entrepreneurs and workers for the nominal wages in the labour market. Then, the theory of price inflation is not explained by a change in income distribution, but by the requirements on the nominal wages of workers. This balance of power is measured by the output gap.

When GDP growth is strong and reduces the output gap, workers may demand higher nominal wages that entrepreneurs transmit without delay to their prices to maintain profit rates (the mark-up is constant). The result is an acceleration of inflation. But with economic crisis and rising unemployment, wages rise more slowly than inflation. Inflation is down as long as entrepreneurs prefer to maintain the same income distribution and lower prices, trying to sell all their production. A deflationary trend may develop. Inflation and deflation arise in the productive sector. Except with significant supply and demand shocks, workers demand an increase in their wages that corresponds to the level of inflation in the steady state. Their inflation expectations are anchored on the inflation target of the central bank: the inflation target of the monetary policy becomes self-fulfilling. So there is a 'corridor of stability' where inflation expectations are anchored on the target (inflation targeting). Leijonhufvud (1973/1981, 112n) coined the notion of a 'corridor', the idea that for small disturbances the inflation rate is stable while for large disturbances it is unstable. The economy has stability inside the corridor, while it will lose stability outside. Such a 'corridor of stability' can provide another way of looking at Keynes's insight that the economy is not violently unstable. When inflation is low and close to its target, I consider that the expectations of inflation are anchored on the target. In this case, inflation does not react to the variations of output gap (OG_R). Inflation depends only on the expected inflation (Π^a) that is anchored on the target: $\Pi^a = \Pi^*$. This makes the Phillips curve tend to horizontal.

But if the variations in output are too important (for instance, close to full capacity output) or, if an exogenous supply shock occurs (for instance, a shock in productivity or in the oil price), inflation is the reaction. Inflation reappears over OG_{Rmini} and disinflation under OG_{Rmaxi}.

Inflation can also occur from exogenous supply shocks, that is, a cost-push (*CoP*), as productivity gains or a sharp rise in oil price. So we introduce this cost-push in relation with the oil price.

To write the equation of inflation, I use the output gap as a ratio:

$$\Pi = \Pi^a + d_1 \cdot (OG_{Rmini} - OG_R) + d_2 .(OG_{Rmaxi} - OG_R) + CoP \qquad (13.39)$$

To simplify, inflation is only used to determine the reaction of the central bank (monetary policy), and thus the changes in the short-term interest rates. All the values (flows and stocks) are nominal values, and there are not fixed prices in the model.

13.2 Experimental trials of economic policies for exit from crisis: the case of France

I assume that financial crisis essentially involves a fall in the state of confidence of economic agents that has subsequently depressed the real economy. The aim is to deal with the channels of transmission of these psychological variables. I want to show that psychological reactions (lower confidence) are sufficient to explain the transmission of financial crisis to the real sector. Moreover, if confidence is the stepping-stone of the crisis, what are the best economic policies to restore confidence? With the sovereign debt crisis in Europe and pressure from financial markets, the usual fiscal policies can become very dangerous to implement. Others solutions must be found that do not worsen the financial situation of States.

Crisis in the state of confidence and inflation

With radical uncertainty, agents' expectations can become self-fulfilling prophecies. As Keynes said, in economics, when the people go out with umbrellas, it rains. Group expectations are the strongest predictor of future events, and the most important expectations are those of entrepreneurs. In the *General Theory*, Keynes stressed the importance of psychological variables in determining economic growth, particularly because of radical uncertainty. The state of confidence of private agents affects the economy through two psychological laws, which are at the heart of the model:

- For entrepreneurs: the marginal efficiency of capital (expected profits) that determines the 'effective demand' and therefore the current production, income and demand of external finance.
- For commercial banks: the liquidity preference that determines 'effective finance'. Indeed, as in our previous works (Le Heron, 2007), we generalize the liquidity preference, understood as a response to increasing risk to commercial banks.

A loss of confidence, which corresponds to a generalized liquidity preference, that is to say the fear of long-term commitment, quickly leads to an economic crisis. Entrepreneurs want to stop investing and banks refrain from lending. With the collapse of effective demand, household incomes decline, resulting *de facto* in a decrease in consumption. Entrepreneurs' vision of the future, but also the confidence that entrepreneurs have in this vision, largely determines the present and therefore what our future will really be. Thus Keynes demonstrated the simultaneous importance, in part contradictory, of animal spirits (spontaneous risk taking) and conventions (confidence in the stability of the present). The crisis is reflected in lower animal spirits and the questioning of conventions.

This reasoning applies to many European countries. But I will illustrate it with the specific French example in my modelling[4]. The rate of growth in France dramatically dropped to –4.5 per cent in the first quarter of 2009. And the unemployment rate rose from 7.6 per cent in May 2008 to 11 per cent at the end of 2012. These experiments are only an attempt to simulate the state of confidence with some established figures of confidence index in order to know if we can find the stylized facts of the current period. I make simulations by imposing changes in the state of confidence corresponding to the period of 2005–2012. To take into account the end of the speculative boom and the current crisis,

I test out the period from January of 2005 (INDEX = 100) until October of 2012 (eight years). I use the different monthly indicators formulated by the French National Institute of Statistics and Economic Studies (INSEE). These indices are calculated from monthly polls on a representative population. I use a seasonally adjusted series. The calculated index of confidence drives our model and impacts GDP and the real economy. I do not try to explain these changes in the state of confidence. I assume that these changes impact the real economy and I have no loop from the real economy (GDP for instance) to the state of confidence of the private sector. The state of confidence of the private sector moves exogenously with the calculated expectations of the private agents. The model is thus 'forward looking'. The radical uncertainty is really taken into account since only the state of confidence of economic agents explains the variations from the model's steady state.

Following Kalecki and Keynes, the state of confidence of entrepreneurs affects the economy through investment and effective demand, but the state of confidence of households (workers) cannot have a strong impact on economic growth since they spend what they earn. Indeed, as in our previous works (Le Heron, 2007), we include the lender's risks and then, depending on their state of confidence, commercial banks can ration the finance requested by firms.

Finally, although our economy is closed, taking into account the international dimension of the crisis in polls conducted among private agents justifies our integration of the global dimension of the real world.

The state of confidence of firms

In a post-Kaleckian framework, firms' expectations are the most important because they explain 'effective demand'. For firms, I use an indicator of the state of confidence of firms (*SCF*) that summarizes more than 18 issues: turning point indicator, recent changes in output, personal production expectations, inventory levels of finished goods, demand and total order books, demand and total export books, personal price expectations, general production expectations, etc. I am taking into account the expectations about the international demand. The changes in the state of confidence of firms (γ_0) impact the desired rate of accumulation. It is a good proxy for the marginal efficiency of capital and the effective demand. Pessimistic expectations of firms depress effective demand and involve a supply shock and then a demand shock.

$$gr_{kD} = \gamma_0 + (\gamma_1 \cdot r_{cf-1}) + (\gamma_2 \cdot u_{-1}) - (\gamma_3 \cdot FCI_{-1}) \qquad (13.40)$$

$$\gamma_0 = a_5 \cdot SCF \tag{13.41}$$

The state of confidence of commercial banks

Following Schumpeter, the bankers are considered entrepreneurs in money. For banks, there is not a specific index on the state of confidence of this sector. I use the French business climate index (*BCI*) that summarizes the business tendency surveys of the different economic sectors, as banks usually do. This indicator of French business climate influences the conventional level of the leverage ratio and the lender's risk. The index changes the coefficients (γ_4), (γ_5) and (γ_6) in equations of lender's risk. Moreover, it changes the level of the conventional leverage ratio (quantity of firms indebtedness considered as normal (lev_c)).

$$LR = -\gamma'_4 + a_1 . (lev_{-1} - \gamma_5 . lev_c) + (b_1 \cdot i_{cb}) \tag{13.42}$$

$$lr = -\gamma'_6 + a_3 \cdot (lev_{-1} - \gamma_5 . lev_c) + \Pi^a \tag{13.43}$$

$$\gamma'_4 = \gamma_4 . a_4 . \text{BCI}, \gamma_5 = a_2 . \text{BCI and } \gamma'_6 = \gamma_6 . a_6 . \text{BCI} \tag{13.44}$$

$$\gamma_5 = a_2 . \text{BCI} \tag{13.45}$$

Inflation and central bank monetary policy

The key interest rate of the central bank (i_{cb}) reacts to the changes in inflation rate through the Taylor rule (Equation 13.38). Inflation is calculated through a hybrid New Keynesian Phillips Curve (HNKPC, Equation 13.39), including expected inflation. The measurement of the forward-looking expected inflation is to extract inflation expectations from the market. We use the information provided by inflation swaps. If inflation expectations are really extracted, a 'risk premium' of inflation is also extracted, that corresponds to the expected volatility of inflation. Econometric studies have attempted to measure this premium that is estimated at around 25 bps (Garcia and Werner, 2010). We assume for simplicity that this premium is constant over the period.

From the second quarter of 2007 to the first quarter of 2008, inflation increased even though the crisis had begun in the United States. To understand inflation during this period, we need to include a cost-push from raw materials (oil price). In the model, cost-push is positive when the price of Brent is above \$80 a barrel and negative below (Figure 13.1).

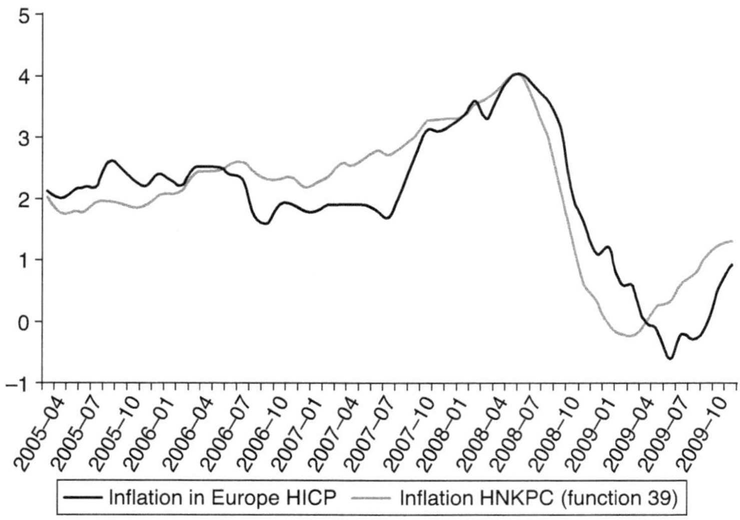

Figure 13.1 Inflation curve

Experiments with inflation and the state of confidence of the French private sector

I put together these processes for an analysis of the state of confidence of the private sectors (banks and firms) in relation to changes in the rate of inflation. In the experiments, the respective importance of the different economic sectors (banks and firms) on the economic situation is not relevant. The objective is only to find the stylized facts. The changes in the state of confidence of banks and firms and in the key interest rate involve supply shocks, and then impact the household income, involving a shock of demand.

The drop in the state of confidence of firms at the beginning of 2008 mainly explains the decline of the growth rate of the economy because it depressed effective demand, that is, the desired growth rate of accumulation of capital. The crisis deepened after August 2008. The rate of utilization of productive capacity fell. However, it is the state of confidence of firms (affecting effective demand) that is the driving mechanism in the economy. The economy is demand-led.

If we compare the observed rate of French real growth (Growth rate compared to the same quarter of previous year, seasonally adjusted, Trim-year GYSA, OECD) and our simulation with the state of confidence of firms, we note a strong convergence (Figure 13.2). Thus, introducing

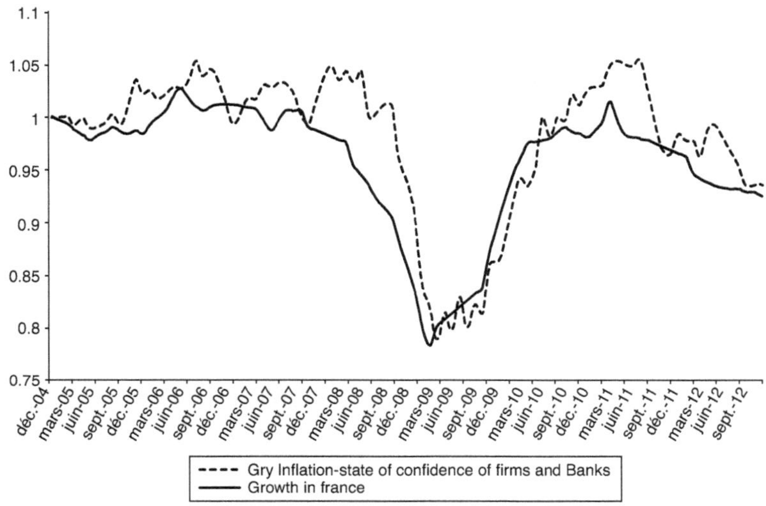

Figure 13.2 Inflation and state of confidence of firms and banks in France: effects on the economic growth

only the recorded confidence of French firms, the model reproduces the reality of the French production crisis and notably the shape of a 'W': a first deep drop in 2008–2009, a good recovery due to the fiscal deficit in 2010 and the first quarter of 2011, then a new drop during the end of 2011 and in 2012, with the end of the fiscal stimulus. With the current public debt crisis and the new Stability and Growth Pact in Europe and its 'Golden Rule', we can expect a new period of recession in 2013. Of course, in real life, the crisis certainly influences the state of confidence and the reverse: they are clearly self-fulfilling prophecies.

In a deep economic crisis, monetary policy tries to avoid deflation, and then the flexible Taylor rule focuses on unemployment. The key interest rate goes down quickly to stop the fall of prices and, also, of asset prices. The influence of output gap on the key interest rate is the same but is lower than that of inflation. Commercial banks have also a responsibility because financing conditions deteriorate. The consequence is a weak rationing of firms' investment financing by private banks ($\varphi < \varphi^d$) during the end of the boom. But during the crisis, the firms reduce drastically their demand for financing, and consequently, there is no credit crunch, even if there is a significant fall in the profits of banks. A credit crunch is not a satisfactory explanation for understanding the transmission channel of this financial crisis to the real world. With the policy mix, the higher government deficit allows an increase in the cash flow of firms. Self-financing increases. Government indebtedness is substituted for firms' indebtedness. The negative impact of the crisis in the banking sector on the government deficit is clear. A loss of confidence in the private sector explains the crisis and pushes the government to 'become optimistic' and to support the effective demand with a huge fiscal deficit in 2008. This is the case of France with a maximum of 8.5 per cent of GDP. With these three variables (inflation, state of confidence of firms, state of confidence of banks), we obtain a good approximation of the crisis in France (Figure 13.2). The channel of confidence is an important explanation of the recent crisis.

Contrary to the neo-classical synthesis (IS-LM), to New-Keynesians or to usual the usual Post-Keynesian Stock-Flow Consistent (PK-SFC) models, the slope of the yield curve is not constant. The spread between the short-term and the long-term interest rate is not constant. First, the model shows the same evolution as the stylized facts of the last crisis: a rise of this spread, which corresponds to higher lender's risk, at the time of the key rate decreasing at the central bank. Second, the central bank lowered its key interest rate faster than inflation, particularly to boost the prices of capital assets. We find that the real long-term interest rate decreased more slowly than other rates, which reduces the effect of expansionary monetary policy.

Policy to overcome the crisis?

Fiscal policies

First, we implement three kinds of fiscal policies at the beginning of 2011. The normal pattern of the model is a slightly countercyclical fiscal policy that is not very different from the French current policy. A second hypothesis corresponds to a more powerful fiscal stimulus, using the Keynesian multiplier to stabilize growth. Finally, the last policy reflects European requirements: a return to a balanced budget. Studies and practical cases (Greece, Spain) suggest that fiscal multipliers are currently high in many European economies. One important implication is that fiscal tightening could raise the debt ratio in the short term, as fiscal gains are partly wiped out by the decline in output. Although this effect is not long-lasting and debt eventually declines, it could be an issue if financial markets focus on short-term changes in the debt ratio, or if country authorities engage in repeated rounds of tightening in an effort to get the debt ratio to converge to the official target.

The model cannot take into account the effects of fiscal policy on the interest rates of the sovereign debt. Indeed, the interest earned by banks is spent and therefore, there is no negative effect on growth. It is different in real life, where confidence can be strongly reduced. If we do not take into account the risk of a speculative attack and its impact on confidence, fiscal stimulus is effective (Figure 13.3). The growth rate remains positive, employment is maintained and, finally, government debt stays under control, thanks to better tax income.

Income distribution policies

Second, we can use our post-Kaleckian model to examine two kinds of income policy currently proposed in Europe. First, we can make a more equal income distribution, lowering the tax rate on workers and increasing the tax rate on capitalists. However, we stabilize the tax rate of households as a whole at 28 per cent of GDP. This income policy on households is no cost for the State budget. The initial rate on workers and on capitalists was 50 per cent of their income, that is, 22.5 per cent of GDP for the workers and 5.5 per cent for the capitalists. The tax rate on workers is reduced to 40 per cent, representing a decrease of about 3.5 per cent of GDP. The increase in the tax rate on capitalists exactly offset declining taxes on workers (Figure 13.4). The growth rate is higher with the better income distribution, and the economic situation is much better. Government debt is significantly lower, which avoids the risk of a speculative attack on sovereign debt. This policy is most effective.

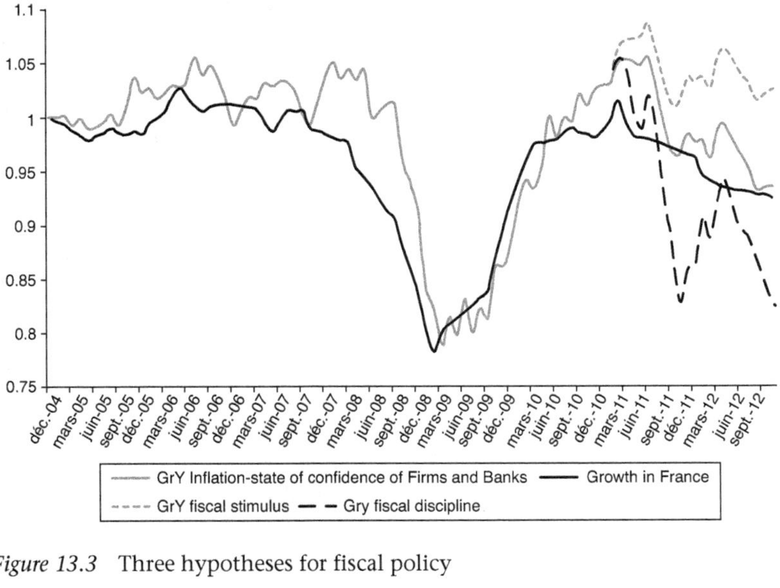

Figure 13.3 Three hypotheses for fiscal policy

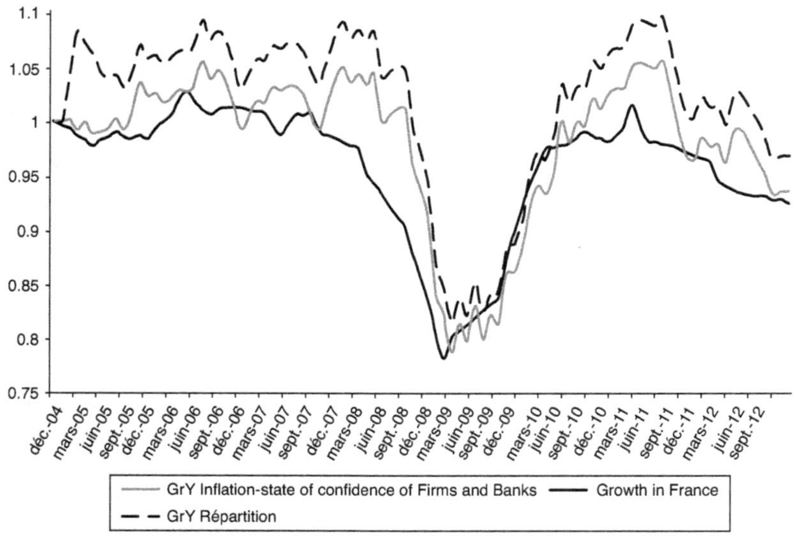

Figure 13.4 Better income distribution: effects on economic growth

Second, as has been demanded of Greece, we can impose lower wages, representing a decrease of 2.5 per cent of GDP. Lower wages, by depressing the effective demand, worsens the crisis and the fiscal deficit. Wage cuts will never be the solution to the public debt crisis, even in an open economy. The increase in exports can never offset the decline in domestic demand and in growth rate (Figure 13.5).

Of course, if we find that these income policies cannot prevent the crisis, better income distribution allows better growth and reduces the fiscal deficit, as opposed to lower wages.

13.3 Conclusion

To better understand the latest financial crisis and its generalization to the real world, I have taken into account the behaviour of private banks, the financial risks of firms and banks, and the psychological variables along with the state of confidence of private sectors. Kalecki, Kaldor and Keynes give an adequate framework for this. I can argue that confidence and self-fulfilling expectations are fundamental transmission channels of a financial crisis to the real world in a global society. If a fiscal stimulus is effective to maintain sufficient growth without increasing the deficit too much, the risk of a speculative attack on sovereign debt, leading

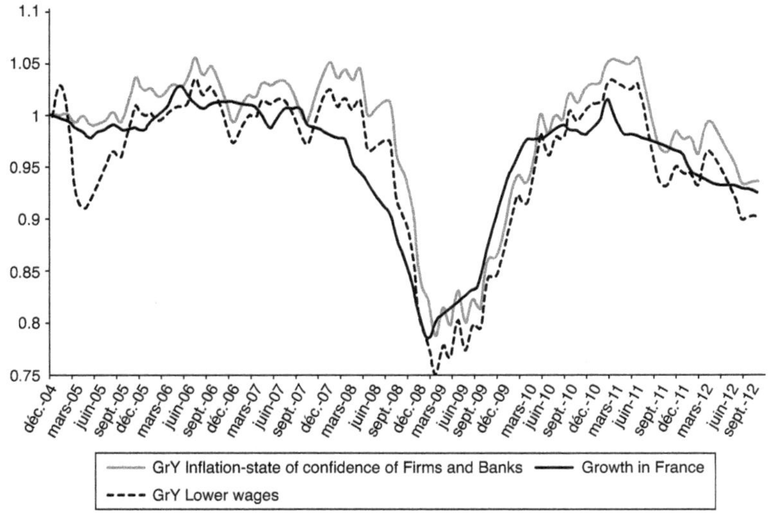

Figure 13.5 Lower wages: effects on economic growth

to a sharp rise in interest rates and destroying business confidence, is high. Because of the importance of financial markets in the financing of European states, this policy can be dangerous.

A better income distribution today is therefore the best solution to restore confidence and economic growth without worsening public debt. The choice of lower wages would reproduce the worst mistakes of the 1929 crisis.

Notes

1. My grateful thanks to Ross Dickie, who helped me with the translation.
2. Further explanation may be found in Le Heron and Mouakil (2008) and Le Heron (2009), for a Post-Keynesian model, and in Le Heron (2014) for a closed Kaleckian stock-flow consistent model with different experiments.
3. I totally rejected the New Keynesian potential output that is founded on a Non-Accelerating Inflation Rate of Unemployment (NAIRU).
4. This model is a mathematical model of a closed modern economy, but it is not fully calibrated on the French economy. We use the E-views 5.5 software. December 2004 is in fact the stationary state of the model.
5. We have defined the 32 variables of the transactions matrix introducing 24 new variables and we now have the same number of equations (56) and unknowns. Furthermore, we have managed to use the M + N – 1 = 12 accounting identities (Latin numbering) issued from the transcription of the transactions matrix.

Appendix 1. Glossary of variables

Y National income
Y_{fc} Output of full capacity
gr_y Growth rate in the national income
Π Inflation
Π^a Expected inflation
Π^* Inflation target
N Employment
N_{fe} Full employment
OG Output gap
OG_R Ratio of output gap
Un Unemployment
r_{un} Rate of unemployment
CoP Cost push

Central bank

P_{cb} Central bank profits
REF Reserve requirements (CB refunds)
H High-powered money
i_{cb} Central bank key interest rate
i^* Neutral interest rate

Commercial banks

L Loans
P_b Banks profits
V_b Net wealth of banks
i_d Interest rate on deposits
i_l Interest rate on loans
i_b Interest rate on treasury bonds
FCI Financial Condition Index
LR Lender's risk
lr Lender's risk for long-term interest rate
$_{4, 5}$ State of confidence of banks
lev Leverage ratio
$amort$ Debt redemption

Firms

I Net investment
I_D Investment demand
W Wages
K Stock of capital

V_f	Net wealth of firms
u	Capacity utilization rate
gr_k	Growth rate in the stock of capital
gr_{kD}	Desired growth rate in the stock of capital
ΔL	Net finance
φ	Gross finance
φ^d	Desired gross investment
IF	Internal Funds
$amort_L$	Amortization of loans
P_f	Firms profits
P^d	Distributed profits
P^u	Undistributed profits
r_{cf}	Borrower's risk (ratio of cash flow)
γ_0	State of confidence of firms

Government

G	Government expenditure
DG	Government deficit
g_{dg}	Constant ratio of government deficit
P_{cb}	Central bank profits
T	Taxes
T_H	Taxes on Households
T_W	Taxes on workers
T_K	Taxes on capitalists
T_F	Taxes on firms
T_B	Taxes on banks
B	Treasury bonds
$amort_B$	Amortization of bonds

Households

C	Consumption of households
C_W	Consumption of workers
C_K	Consumption of capitalists
D	Bank deposits
D_W	Bank deposits of workers
D_K	Bank deposits of capitalists
Y_W^a	Expected disposable income of workers
Y_K^a	Exp. disposable income of capitalists
Y_H	Disposable income of households
Y_W	Disposable income of workers
Y_K	Disposable income of capitalists

Appendix 2 The complete model

$Y = C + I + G$		National income
$gr_y = DY/Y_{-1}$		Growth rate of national income
$OG_R = Y_{fc} - Y / Y_{fc}$	Output gap ratio	
$Y_{fc} = K_{-1} . \sigma$	With σ : constant	Output of full capacity
$K = K_{-1} + I$		Stock of capital
$I \equiv \varphi + IF$		Net investment
$IF = P^u - amort_L$		Self financing
$amort_L = a_l \cdot L_{-1}$		Internal Funds
$I_D = gr_{kD} . K{-}1$		Demand of investment
$\varphi^d = I^d - IF$		Desired gross investment
$gr_{kD} = \gamma_0 + \gamma_1 . r_{cf-1} + \gamma_2 . u_{-1} - \gamma_3 \cdot FCI_{-1}$	With γ_i: constant	Desired growth in the stock of capital
$r_{cf} = P^u / K_{-1}$		Ratio of cash flow
$u = Y/Y_{fc}$		Capacity utilization rate
$FCI = \mu_1 \cdot i_l \cdot L/K$	With μ_1: constant	Financial Condition Index
$W = Y / (1 + \rho)$	With ρ: constant	Wages
$P_f \equiv Y - W - T_F - i_{l-1} . L_{-1}$		Firms profits
$P^d = (1 - s_f) . P_{-1}$	With s_f: constant	Distributed profits
$P^u \equiv P_f - P^d$		Non-Distributed profits
$C = C_W + C_K$		Consumption of households
$C_W = (\alpha_1 . Y_W{}^a) + (\alpha_3 . D_{W-1})$	With α_i: constant	Consumption of workers
$C_K = (\alpha_2 . Y_K{}^a) + (\alpha_4 . D_{K-1})$		Consumption of capitalists
$Y_w{}^a = Y_{W-1} + \theta_h . (Y_{W-1} - Y_W{}^a{}_{-1})$	With θ_h: constant	Expected disposable income of workers
$Y_k{}^a = Y_{K-1} + \theta_h . (Y_{K-1} - Y_K{}^a{}_{-1})$	With θ_h: constant	Exp. disposable income of capitalists
$Y_H = Y_W + Y_K$		Disposable income of households
$Y_W = W + i_{d-1} . D_{W-1} - T_W$		Disposable income of workers
$Y_K = P^d + i_{d-1} . D_{K-1} - T_K$		Disposable income of capitalists
$D_W \equiv D_{W-1} + Y_W - C_W$		Bank deposits of workers

$D_K \equiv D_{K-1} + Y_K - C_K$		Bank deposits of capitalists
$D = D_W + D_K$		Bank deposits
$T \equiv T_H + T_F + T_B$		Taxes
$T_H = T_W = T_K$		Taxes on households
$T_W = \tau_1 \,.\, W_{-1}$	With τ_i: constant	Taxes on workers
$T_K = \tau_2 \,.\, P^d{}_{-1}$		Taxes on capitalists
$T_F = \tau_3 \,.\, P^u{}_{-1}$		Taxes on firms
$T_B = \tau_4 \,.\, P_{B-1}$		Taxes on commercial banks
$\Delta B = DG$		Treasury bonds
$i_b = i_l$		Interest rate on treasury bonds
$G = G_{-1} \,.\, (1 + gr_{y\,-1})$		Government expenditure
$DG \equiv G + i_{b-1} \cdot B_{-1} - T - P_{cb} - amort_B$		Government deficit
$amort_B = a_b \cdot B_{-1}$		Amortization of Government debt
$\varphi = \varphi^d \,.\, (1 - LR)$		Gross finance
$\Delta L = \varphi - amort_L$		Net finance
$LR = -\gamma_4 + a_1 . (lev_{-1} - \gamma_5 \,.\, lev_c) + b_1 \cdot i_{cb}$	With γ_4, a_1, b_1, and lev_c : constant	Lender's risk
$lev = L / K$		Leverage ratio
$\gamma_5 = a_2 \cdot BCI$		Changes in conventional leverage
$i_l = i_{cb} + lr + \chi_1$	With χ_1: constant	Interest rate on loans
$lr = \gamma_6 + a_3 \cdot (lev_{-1} - \gamma_5 \,.\, lev_c) + \Pi^a$		Lender's risk for long-term interest rate
	With γ_6 and a_3, lev_c constant = convention on leverage ratio	
$i_d = i_{cb} - \chi_3$		Interest rate on deposits
$P_b \equiv i_{b-1} \,.\, B_{-1} + i_{l-1} \,.\, L_{-1} - T_B - i_{d-1} \,.\, D_{-1} - i_{cb-1} \,.\, REF_{-1}$		Banks profits
$H = \eta \,.\, D$		High powered money (bank reserves)
$P_{cb} \equiv i_{cb-1} \,.\, REF_{-1}$		Central bank profits
$i_{cb} = i^* + \Pi^a - \alpha_4 .OG + \alpha_5 (\Pi - \Pi^*)$		Central bank key interest rate
$REF \equiv REF_{-1} + \Delta H + \Delta B + \Delta L - P_b - \Delta D - amort$		Reserve requirements (CB refunds)
$amort \equiv amort_B + amort_L$		Amortization of debt
$\Pi = \Pi^a + d_1 .(OG_{Rmini} + OG_R) + d_2 \cdot(OG_{Rmaxi} + OG_R) + CoP$		Inflation

Appendix 3. Transactions matrix

Operation \ Sector	Govt	Firms		Households		Private banks		Central Bank		Σ
		Current	Capital	Workers	Capitalists	Current	Capital	Current	Capital	
Consumption		$+C$		$-C_W$	$-C_K$					0
Government expenditures	$-G$	$+G$								0
Net investment		$+I$	$-I$							0
Wages		$-W$		$+W$						0
Taxes	$+T$	$-T_F$		$-T_W$	$-T_K$	$-T_B$				0
Interest on Treasury Bonds	$-i_{b-1} \cdot B_{-1}$					$+i_{b-1} \cdot B_{-1}$				0
Interest on loans		$-i_{l-1} \cdot L_{-1}$				$+i_{l-1} \cdot L_{-1}$				0
Interest on bank deposits				$+i_{d-1} \cdot D_{W-1}$	$+i_{d-1} \cdot D_{K-1}$	$-i_{d-1} \cdot D_{-1}$				0
Interest on CB advances						$-i_{cb-1} \cdot REF_{-1}$		$+i_{cb-1} \cdot REF_{-1}$		0
Profits of firms		$-P$	$+P^u$		$+P^d$					0
Profits of banks						$-P_b$	$+P_b$			0
Profits of CB	$+P_{cb}$							$-P_{cb}$		0
Δ HPM							$-DH$		$+DH$	0
D T Bonds	$+DB$						$-DB$			0
D Loans			$+DL$				$-DL$			0
Amortization	$-amort_B$		$-amort_L$				$+amort$			0
Δ Bank deposits				$-\Delta D_W$	$-\Delta D_K$		$+DD$			0
D CB advances							$+DREF$		$-DREF$	0
Σ	0	0	0	0	0	0	0	0	0	0

Appendix 4. Balance sheet matrix

Sector / Assets	Government	Firms	Households	Private banks	Central Bank	Σ
Capital		+ K				+ K
HPM High-powered money				+ H	− H	0
Treasury Bonds	− B			+ B		0
Loans		− L		+ L		0
Bank deposits			+ D	− D		0
CB advances				− REF	+ REF	0
Net wealth	− B	+ V_f	+ D	+ V_b	0	+ K

References

Garcia, A. and T. Werner (2010) 'Inflation risks and inflation risk premia', *ECB Working paper*, No. 1162, Mars.

Godley, W. and M. Lavoie (2007) *Monetary Economics: An Integrated Approach to Credit, Money, Income, Production and Wealth.* London: Palgrave Macmillan.

Kaldor, N. (1939) 'Speculation and economic stability', *The Review of Economic Studies*, 7(1): 1–27.

Kaldor, N. (1956) 'Alternative theories of distribution', *Review of Economic Studies*, 23(61): 94–100.

Kaldor, N. (1982) *The Scourge of Monetarism*, Oxford: Oxford University Press.

Kalecki, M. (1937) 'The principle of increasing risk', *Economica*, 4(13): 440–447.

Kalecki, M. (1971) *Selected Essays on the Dynamics of the Capitalist Economy*, Cambridge: Cambridge University Press.

Keynes, J.M. (1936/1973), *The General Theory, The Collected Writings of John Maynard Keynes, Vol. VII*, London: Macmillan.

Lavoie, M. and W. Godley (2001) 'Kaleckian growth models in a stock and flow monetary framework: a Kaldorian view', *Journal of Post-Keynesian Economics*, 24(2): 277–312.

Le Heron, E. (2007) 'The dynamic analysis of monetary policy shock on banking behavior', in J. McCombie and C. Rodriguez (eds) *Issues in Finance and Monetary Policy*, London: Palgrave Macmillan, pp. 79–99.

Le Heron, E. (2009) 'Fiscal and monetary policies in a Keynesian stock-flow consistent model', in J. Creel and M. Sawyer (eds), *Current Thinking on Fiscal Policy*, London: Palgrave Macmillan, pp. 145–175.

Le Heron, E. (2014) 'Confidence increasing risks, income distribution and crisis in a Post Kaleckian stock flow consistent model', in R. Bellofiore, E. Karwowska and J. Toporowski (eds), *Economic Crisis and Political Economy, Volume 2 of Essays in Honour of Tadeusz Kowalik*, London: Palgrave.

Le Heron, E. and T. Mouakil (2008) 'A post Keynesian stock-flow consistent model for the dynamic analysis of monetary policy shock on banking behavior', *Metroeconomica*, 59(3): 405–440.

Leijonhufvud, A. (1973/1981) 'Effective demand failures', *Swedish Journal of Economics*, reprinted in Leijonhufvud, *Information and Coordination. Essays in Macroeconomic Theory*. New York: Oxford University Press.

Mouakil, T. (2006) 'Instabilité financière et méthode stocks-flux: analyse critique de l'hypothèse de Minsky', PhD, University Montesquieu Bordeaux, 4 November.

Robinson, J. (1982) 'Shedding darkness', *Cambridge Journal of Economics*, 6(3), September 1982: 295–296.

Taylor J. (1993) 'Discretion versus policy rules in practice', *Carnegie-Rochester Conference Series on Public Policy*, 39: 195–214.

Tobin, J. (1958) 'Liquidity preference as behavior toward risk', *Review of Economic Studies*, 25(1): 65–86.

14
Firm Heterogeneity, Finance and Development: A Kaleckian Perspective

Jago Penrose

14.1 Introduction

This chapter will argue that the insights of Michał Kalecki and Josef Steindl into the differences between 'large' and 'small' firms suggests that firms are heterogeneous in their financing, funding (replacing short-term with long-term liabilities) and liquidity management strategies, and that the financial structure of firms and the nature of the investments they conduct will vary according to the financial institutions available to them. Therefore, the impact of financial development on an economy will depend both on the dynamics of institutional change and the composition of the enterprise sector.

Kalecki, and following him Josef Steindl, argued that the ability of firms to make use of finance as a means of survival and a source of investment was, in part, a function of firm size. Small firms struggled to attract capital, risked being overleveraged and lacked the means to diversify their sources of revenue to increase chances of survival. Large firms, on the other hand, could rely on retained earnings for investible funds and were better able to diversify their activities to ensure survival, often at the expense of lower rates of profit.

In developing countries Kalecki identified a shortage of capital stock as one of a number of constraints on economic development. Building capital stock in a less developed country (LDC) was made more difficult by the small size of the entrepreneurial class, as well as their propensity for unproductive spending and investment. This was one of the reasons that led Kalecki to propose a leading role for the state in guiding investments. This chapter suggests that Kalecki's insights into the differences between large and small firms, when combined with Keynesian approaches to the role of the finance sector, can provide a useful framework with which to understand the relationship between financial development and the firm sector. This implies that as an economy builds its finance sector firms will not respond uniformly.

14.2 The financial structure of large and small firms in the work of Michał Kalecki and Josef Steindl

Kalecki distinguished between firms in two main ways. First, in terms of the type of industry they inhabit, and second, in terms of access to finance. Whether a firm inhabits a 'competitive' or 'oligopolistic' industry determines the sort of pricing policy open to it: mark-up pricing or demand-determined pricing. The policy adopted is a function of the good or service produced, its price elasticity of demand and of market institutions. The ability to mark up prices enables a firm to generate and sustain retained earnings. This in turn determines a firm's access to external finance as well as the size of investment it can undertake. Here Kalecki introduced the concept of 'increasing risk', in which the greater the ratio between debt and equity the greater the risk of a firm's insolvency, and the more expensive is external credit. Large firms can both access more credit and make larger and less risky investments:

> A firm with large entrepreneurial capital could obtain funds for a large investment whereas a firm with small entrepreneurial capital could not. Differences in the position of firms arising out of differences in their entrepreneurial capital are further enhanced by the fact that firms below a certain size have no access whatever to the capital market. (Kalecki, 1971, p. 106)

Expansion is dependent on 'the accumulation of capital out of current profits'. Firms can then make new investments without 'encountering the obstacles of the limited capital market or "increasing risk"' (ibid., p. 107). Savings from current profits can be directly invested in the business and make possible larger loans. The amount of a firm's entrepreneurial capital will determine the 'amount of rentier capital' the firm can access in the capital market:

> The limitation of the size of the firm by the availability of entrepreneurial capital goes to the very heart of the capitalist system. Many economists assume, at least in their abstract theories, a state of

> business democracy where anybody endowed with entrepreneurial ability can obtain capital for starting a business venture. This picture of the activities of the 'pure' entrepreneur is, to put it mildly, unrealistic. The most important prerequisite for becoming an entrepreneur is the *ownership* of capital. (Kalecki, 1971, p. 109)

Josef Steindl (1945) developed Kalecki's ideas in *Small and Big Business: Economic Problems of the Size of Firms*. In a critique of Marshall's representative firm, Steindl argued that firms need not be restricted by the size of a single industry and that large firms have an inherent advantage over smaller firms. Steindl took issue with Marshall's assertion that because 'the rise from unpropertied worker to small entrepreneur and from then to big entrepreneur is possible' and 'ability always finds capital [and] inability loses it' there will be a 'broad movement from below upwards' (Steindl, 1945, p. 9).

Steindl tested Marshall's propositions in a statistical analysis of the US economy. He found little to support Marshall: the 'rate of growth of corporate enterprises will have to be several thousand fold to reach the size of large firms' (Steindl, 1945, p. 36). This takes time and the 'high death rate' makes it unlikely. He also found in favour of the impact of the principle of 'increasing risk' on the growth of firms. Inadequate net worth among small firms, a costly long-term credit market and so reliance on short-term credit, coupled with the finding that large firms have less difficulty accessing all forms of credit, are sufficient for Steindl to proclaim there is no evidence for a 'broad movement upward'. He had come to a similar conclusion in an analysis of the Austrian economy in the 1930s where he found that small firms struggled to grow beyond a certain size (Steindl, 1965).

Steindl argued that large firms come into existence either as newly formed joint-stock companies or through merger. The former 'presupposes' wealthy entrepreneurs and the latter, whilst an observable fact, includes takeovers, often themselves an expression of oligopolistic power. The high turnover of small firms and the large capital required to establish large firms led Steindl to the conclusion that there is an 'elastic supply of small entrepreneurs' and a small and 'inelastic supply of large entrepreneurs'.

For Kalecki large size gives firms the opportunity to make large investments and so accumulate large amounts of entrepreneurial capital and to access, if required, larger loans on more favourable terms. However, firms will tend to limit the use of the capital market because 'of the increasing risk involved in expansion' (Kalecki, 1971, p. 106). The more a firm borrows the greater the danger of insolvency in the event of failure. Large firms with more retained earnings than they care to invest in fixed assets, or who wish to hedge against failure, might instead invest a proportion in securities, meaning that in the event of failure they will still be able to draw some income (Kalecki, 1971). Since small firms suffer from inadequate internal reserves, they must maintain a selection of liquid assets as security or expose themselves to the possibility of insolvency. Kalecki argued that firms that did attempt to access proportionately large amounts of external capital would struggle. Those, for example, floating a bond issue 'which was too large in terms of its entrepreneurial capital', would find it undersubscribed. Raising the interest rate paid would only cause investors to doubt the firm's solvency' (Kalecki, 1971, p. 106). Smaller firms attempting to undertake projects with high costs of production and distribution are 'driven to supplement their own capital by extensive short term borrowing at unfavourable terms' (ibid., p. 106).

Steindl (1945) analysed the impact of holding financial assets on the rate of profit on equity. Steindl utilized the *gross* and *net gearing ratios*, the latter being the proportion of business capital to equity and the former being the proportion of total assets to equity. He showed four things. First, that with high gearing ratios firms will make more spectacular losses in the event of failure. Second, both the gross and net gearing ratios decrease with size. Third,

> The consequences of a high gearing ratio for small firms are reinforced by two further factors: the smaller firms often *rent* buildings etc. (which would normally be owned by big ones), which means nothing else but a borrowing of these capital items *in natura*. The rent provides a fixed charge, like interest, with similar effects on the risk. More important, the relatively greater indebtedness of the small firms takes for the most part the form of short-term debt. This makes the risk even greater (if no renewal of credit is obtained the firm will have to engage in forced selling).' (Steindl, 1945, p. 45)

Fourth, larger companies are more likely to invest in interest-bearing securities, further offsetting any risk they bear. Large firms will therefore receive part of their income in dividends that will be only a part of a company's total profit. As a result,

> very big companies have greater stability from a large income from dividends which is, however, lower than the profit rate in a successful company, especially in times of good business. (Steindl, 1945, p. 47)

All of this suggests that a distinguishing feature of the large firm that emerges from the work of Kalecki and Steindl is that it has greater autonomy than the small firm, and is better able to respond to exogenous shocks. Such firms are able to respond by managing *more* than their real economy operations.

14.3 Funding and financing

A comprehensive survey of post-Keynesian literature on the financial sector is beyond the scope of this chapter. Two insights will be highlighted: the distinction between funding and financing investments, and the possibility of the overcapitalization of firms.

Keynes (1937) first discussed the importance of the funding of investments:

> The entrepreneur when he decides to invest has to be satisfied on two points: firstly, that he can obtain sufficient short-term finance during the period of producing the investment; and secondly, that he can eventually fund his short-term obligations by a long-term issue on satisfactory conditions. (Keynes, 1937, p. 217)

Banks finance investments by advancing credit to firms. Firms then seek to fund their liquidity requirements in asset markets. Savings is a crucial requirement for the latter, rather than the former (Studart, 1995). Credit expansion is then a function of the demand for finance, the willingness of banks to lend and any exogenous constraints (by the central bank or government) on bank lending, and saving is primarily dependent on the level of income. There can only be a 'financial constraint' if, for some reason, banks refuse to advance firms credit (Davidson, 1996, p. 101). Nevertheless, bank financed investment and growth can lead to increased financial fragility and instability (Studart, 1995), particularly since firms holding short-term debt in need of refinancing will be dependent on future conditions of credit.

14.4 Capital market inflation and over-capitalization

Stock markets provide firms with the opportunity to both access long-term finance and the opportunity to fund existing investments. This enables firms to reduce their reliance on bank debt for both finance and funding, and, in principle, facilitates larger investments at lower risk. However, the concept of 'funding' investments implies the firm sector's interaction with asset markets is directly related to real economy operations. Firms 'only issue capital up to the point where the return from their commercial and industrial activities would exceed the cost of financing that capital' (Toporowski, 2008). However, firms also issue capital beyond this point and invest the excess capital in liquid rather than fixed assets. Toporowski (2008) defines this 'excess capital' as the excess of a company's liabilities over its productive capital, that is, the plant, equipment, materials and stocks of unsold products and semi-fabricates that a firm holds. 'If the return from these assets is less than is necessary to pay the cost of the excess capital, the margin between them is a "cost of liquidity"' (ibid.). There are a number of benefits of such a strategy. Liquid assets provide firms with extra collateral, or firms can 'buy and sell companies in balance sheet restructuring that may be profitable as long as capital markets are inflating' (ibid.). Capital market inflation, induced by increases in domestic credit or foreign inflows, can provide such firms with potential profits that may even be greater than the costs of liquidity.

14.5 Large and small firms, finance and economic development

As a Polish economist writing through the Great Depression, the Second World War and the Cold War, Kalecki saw three 'worlds', each with its own unique set of problems. The greatest problem for the first or developed world was unemployment, and so maintaining a sufficient level of effective demand. Low levels of demand were a consequence of underutilized productive capacity in the firm sector. The third or underdeveloped world had a different set of challenges. Although, for Kalecki, the ultimate aim remained the same, to tackle under- and unemployment, the issue was not idle productive capacity but insufficient capital stock. The general objective of economic development was therefore investment in productive capacity (Kalecki, 1933). As might be expected from his work on developed economies, Kalecki argued that finance need not be a constraint on economic development: investment finances itself (Kalecki, 1933).

Just as in developed economies, it is the inadequacy of the private sector that necessitates the intervention of the state. However, unlike in mature capitalist economies, it is not shortfalls in private investment that calls for intervention, but the small size and lack of dynamism of the entrepreneurial class. At this point Kalecki and Steindl's observation, that firms are essentially heterogeneous in their ability to undertake large investments and in the means available to them to manage their own survival, can provide useful insights. It should also be noted that for both Kalecki and Steindl investment projects are lumpy. Relatively large amounts of capital are required to undertake some investments, and, given that small firms have limited retained earnings and constrained access to credit, such capital can only be accessed by large firms. Steindl went so far as to suggest that there are differential lines open to different 'size classes' of entrepreneurs and as large entrepreneurs 'are restricted in number' then 'a hierarchy of profit rates will be established, with a *smooth* increase of profit rates as size of the enterprise, measured in capital, increases' (Steindl, 1945, p. 12). Lines with the 'greatest scale economies available' will offer entrepreneurs capable of exploiting them a 'more than "normal" profit'.

Kalecki appeared to assume a developed and functioning banking system in developing countries. However, the ability of small firms to access credit is also predicated on the existence of secondary markets for banks to dispose of collateral in the event of default. The diversification of larger firms into securities and other assets to manage their survival also assumes functioning asset markets. The absence of functioning finance and banking systems does not, however, preclude the need for firms to access finance, fund investments or diversify sources of revenue. It does, however, suggest that the types of investment undertaken by firms and the survival strategies they undertake will depend on the level of development, either because of the absence of certain opportunities or the need to compensate for the absence of markets and financial services.

One way to think through the implications of this for understanding financial development is to develop a simple model based on national accounting identities. Kalecki's model, assuming that households don't save, wages finance consumption and firm saving is equal to profits, may be demonstrated using the saving identity:

$$S = \mathrm{I} + (G - T) + (X - M)$$

Distinguishing capitalist (S_C) and workers saving (S_W), capitalists' saving is as follows:

$$S_C = I + (G - T) + (X - M) - S_W$$

Profits must equal capitalist saving and consumption (C_C) so,

$$P = S_C + C_C = \mathrm{I} + (G - T) + (X - M) + C_C - S_W$$

Since capitalists can only determine their levels of consumption and investment, not profits, capitalists' consumption and investment define profits. It is the decision of firms to invest that leads to the accumulation of savings.

Using this simple framework it is possible to see how the initial composition of the firm sector might affect the outcome of financial development on an economy. Beginning with a stationary state in which investment in each period is financed entirely by savings from the previous period, and in which it is assumed that either workers do not save, or that workers' savings is entirely passed on to firms, and all savings is used by firms, it is possible to show an economy may grow slowly. Jan Kregel (1989) developed just such a model to illustrate that in a closed economy populated entirely by 'small proprietorships' financed by their single owner's equity, and in which all profits are invested and workers do not save, the rate of growth will depend on the 'distribution of income as determined by a Kaleckian degree of monopoly within the limits of subsistence' (ibid.). If assumptions are relaxed slightly and workers save, then firms will need to borrow to finance investment in excess of net profits. However, bank lending to small firms will then be limited by the value of the firm's assets that can be pledged as collateral. If workers' savings exceed the value of assets owned by firms accepted by banks, then there would still be a deficiency of demand. The larger the average size of firms, then the more likely the economy will grow over time. The evolution of the debt-equity ratio will 'depend on the relative size of profits and workers' savings in national income' (Kregel, 1989). If savings exceed profits, then the debt-equity ratio will tend toward unity. However, it is likely lending will cease long before this point is reached as lender's risk becomes too high, and as the interest rate correspondingly rises above the internal rate of return of investments, both increasing the reluctance of entrepreneurs to borrow and also increasing the incomes of lenders, and so increasing the savings rate further (ibid.).

Larger firms in possession of greater collateral may be able to access credit. However, they will also limit the size of their investments relative to own capital so as to ensure they are not overexposed. The availability of funding opportunities has a further bearing on the size and type of investment. In the absence of financial markets, larger firms may choose to diversify sources of cash flow and limit the size and riskiness of investments, in the process limiting borrower's risk. Diversified sources of cash flow from real economy activities also have the potential to provide a more stable source of financing for investments.

Although limited savings need not constrain expansion (assuming a certain level of development of the banking sector), its availability still plays a vital role in funding investments, and so managing borrowers' and lenders' risk and tempering unwelcome tendencies to financial instability. Financial markets thus play a crucial role as the *loci* of funding, and providing information for firms issuing securities, underwriters and those wishing to purchase securities (Studart, 1995). In less developed financial systems with smaller and thinner asset markets, firms become reliant on bank loans for their liquidity needs. However, loans themselves are more likely to be short-term since banks are reluctant to take on the risks of long-term investments (Studart, 1995). Such a situation can lead to financial instability, as firms become excessively leveraged and vulnerable to interest rate fluctuations, as well as shocks to other sources of income.

During periods of capital market inflation firms may choose to become 'over capitalized' and hold a greater portion of current assets – particularly cash and short-term financial assets. This, in turn, provides opportunities for speculation and accessing further loans, which may serve either to provide the firm with a portfolio of revenue-generating liquid assets and so provide extra levels of stability or contribute further to capital market inflation and, in the event of a market downturn, increase the firm's financial instability.

Over time an economy may develop an enterprise sector with distinct categories of firms with regard to the finance and banking sector. Small firms, generating all or the majority of their revenue through one primary activity, with limited access to credit or finance markets, will generally make smaller, less capital-intensive investments. Mortality rates among smaller firms will be higher. Larger firms, able to generate greater revenues, will be able to make larger investments depending on profit margins and so available retained earnings. However, to ensure sufficient cash flow to manage commitments and an uncertain business environment, they may also refrain from capital-intensive investments and diversify their investment portfolios.

The introduction of institutions that enable firms to 'fund' investments may facilitate more capital-intensive investments, particularly by larger firms. The opportunity to exchange short-term debt for equity will reduce commitments and decrease both borrower's and lender's risk. Those same institutions will also provide firms with the opportunity to better manage a portfolio account of liquid assets.

14.6 Conglomerates in Southeast Asia

The literature on the corporate history of Southeast Asia (particularly, Indonesia, Malaysia and Thailand) illustrates the role of large domestic firms in economic development and provides some insight into the destabilizing impact of such firms' response to the emergence of financial markets. As Indonesia, Thailand and Malaysia experienced relatively high rates of economic growth over several decades, it is also possible to track the responses of firms to the development of both banking and financial markets.

A majority of studies argue that the majority of large Southeast Asian conglomerates achieved large size because the state either explicitly granted them with access to relatively risk-free rents, or, more implicitly, opted against regulating rent-seeking behaviour[1]. The literature is then divided as to whether such firms' subsequent strategies were pragmatic responses to the absence of formal asset markets that would provide funding opportunities to large firms operating in relatively unstable economic environments or straightforward rent seeking.

Yoshihara (1988) provided the classic argument that large conglomerates not only pursued monopoly rents, but did so deliberately in low-technology sectors requiring low levels of investment, giving rise to 'Ersatz Capitalism', an economic model that limits productive investment, technological development and growth. Jamie Mackie (2002) and Akira Suehiro (2003), on the other hand, argued that whilst there were (and are) problems with the practises of large, politically connected conglomerates, their behaviour was primarily a response to the conditions and institutional environment in which they operated. In the absence of effective competition and modern institutions, the diversified conglomerate form designed to maximize cash flow and build a portfolio of assets was an effective strategy. In Indonesia, for example,

> [M]ost Indonesian conglomerates are highly diversified. This makes good sense in an uncertain economic or political environment, as a means of spreading risks, but it has hindered serious industrial commitment, and long-term investment strategy. Liem Sioe Liong... controls a vast and heterogenous business empire, a rambling collection of enterprises. Cash flow and control of assets seem to be his primary aims, not corporate strategy or market dominance, and this is true of the other Indonesian conglomerate heads. (Mackie, 2002, p. 181)

Brown (2006), in a seminal analysis of the 'corporate economy' in Southeast Asia, argued that the majority of the corporations he studied used 'size and diversified growth as a proxy for the fundamental risk of high debt burdens' (p. 334). Larger firms diversified because they were highly leveraged. Diverse sources of cash flow lowered the risk of having to renege on repayments.

Other studies demonstrate changing strategies as business environments and, particularly, financial institutions developed. Wailerdsak (2008), in a survey of corporate structures and strategies in Thailand, argued that firms did respond to a changing environment by focussing on core strengths and limiting their holdings of financial assets following the Asian crisis. Studies of individual corporations pointed to similar changing strategies as financial institutions developed (Sato, 1994 and 2002).

Even so, responses to financial development were not always benign. The most brazen, but not uncommon, strategy to secure cash flow was to establish or purchase a controlling share in lending institutions (Suehiro, 1989). A number of firms, for example, exploited lax regulation and government contacts to establish banks whose primary purpose was to provide liquidity to firms within the group. Brown (2006) highlighted the importance of banks to corporate strategies in Indonesia:

> [C]orporate empires often had a family bank. Bank Central Asia (BCA), the largest private commercial bank in Indonesia, formed the core bank in the Salim Group. It was a major recipient of state revenues, foreign aid and foreign direct and portfolio investments, and had access to offshore banks as well as to diverse and innovative sources of finance such as derivatives. This capital abundance intensified corporate economic concentration.... A further feature of concentration is the high percentage of loans to single individuals, or select groups of conglomerates. (Brown, 2006, p. 11)

He goes on to discuss in detail the tendency of conglomerate-owned banks to lend primarily to subsidiaries.

Stock markets were also a means to further build the diversified conglomerate. Once stock markets became firmly established, and in some cases inflated with foreign capital inflows, many conglomerates built large stock and real estate portfolios that were designed to generate speculative profits rather than a diversified source of cash flow (Habir, 1999). Brown (2006) discussed the impact of inflows of portfolio capital into Southeast Asian markets in the 1980s and 1990s:

> The large concentrated positions of portfolio capital in targeting specific sectors of the economy (property, finance and currency markets), their herding and manipulative activities, not only increase

> speculation but assist in creating large diversified corporations in Southeast Asia, which are reluctant to specialise because diversification provided revenues, reduced risks and concealed problems of quality in subsidiaries and connected firms. (Brown, 2006, p. 149)

This brief survey of the corporate history of Southeast Asia suggests that many large firms' initial source of entrepreneurial capital was politically determined rents, and in the absence of a developed financial sector, such firms managed risk through diversification into relatively risk-free activities that provided cash flow to meet commitments and retained earnings for investment. Financial development, or more specifically, liberalization of banking systems and capital markets, did provide the means to fund investments and better manage liquidity. However, it could also provide a means to generate cash flow and profit from the manipulation of a portfolio of financial assets, particularly in periods of capital market inflation. This suggests that Kalecki's and Steindl's insights into the heterogeneity of firms with regard to their relationship with the financial sector can provide a perspective into the changing behaviour of firms, and the firm sector as a whole, as financial development unfolds.

Note

1. See, for example, Doner (1992), Gomez (2002), Studwell (2007), Yoshihara (1988), Suehiro (1996), Hutchcroft (1994) and Hewison (1997).

References

Brown, R.A. (2006) *The Rise of the Corporate Economy in Southeast Asia*, London: Routledge.

Davidson, P. (1996) 'Reality and economic theory', *Journal of Post Keynesian Economics*, 18(4): 479–508.

Doner R. (1992) 'Politics and the growth of local capital in Southeast Asia: auto industries in Philippines and Thailand' in R. McVey (ed.), *Southeast Asian Capitalists*, Ithaca: Cornell Southeast Asia Program.

Gomez, E.T. (2002) *Political Business in Southeast Asia*, London: Routledge.

Habir, A. (1999) 'Conglomerates: all in the family?' in D.K. Emmerson (ed.), *Indonesia beyond Soeharto*, New York: M.E. Sharpe.

Hewison, K. (1997) 'Thailand: capitalist development and the state', in G. Rodan, K. Hewison and R. Robison (eds), *The Political Economy of Southeast Asia: An Introduction*, Oxford: Oxford University Press.

Hutchcroft, P. (1994) 'Booty capitalism: business-government relations in the Philippines' in A. Macintyre (ed.), *Business and Government in Industrialising Asia*, Ithaca: Cornell University Press.

Mackie, J.A.C. (2002) 'Changing patterns of Chinese big business in Southeast Asia' in R. McVey (ed.), *Southeast Asian Capitalists*, Ithaca: Cornell Southeast Asia Program.

Kalecki, M. (1933) *Outline of a Theory of the Business Cycle. Selected Essays on the Capitalist Economy*, Cambridge: Cambridge University Press.

Kalecki, M. (1971) *Selected Essays on the Dynamics of the Capitalist Economy*, Cambridge: Cambridge University Press.

Kalecki (1993) – See p. 7.

Keynes, J.M. (1937) 'The ex ante theory of the rate of interest', *Economic Journal*, 47: 663–668.

Kregel, J.A. (1989) 'Operational and financial leverage, the firm, and the cycle: reflections on Vickers' money capital constraint, *Journal of Post Keynesian Economics*, 12(2): 224–236.

Sato, Y. (1994) 'The development of business groups in Indonesia: 1967–89', in T. Shiraishi (ed.), *Approaching Suharto's Indonesia from the Margins*, Ithaca: Cornell University Southeast Asia Program.

Sato, Y. (2002) 'The Salim Group in Indonesia: the development and behaviour of the largest conglomerate in Southeast Asia', in H. Hill (ed.), *The Economic Development of Southeast Asia*, Vol. 3, Cheltenham: Edward Elgar.

Steindl, J. (1945) *Small and Big Business: Economic Problems of the Size of Firms*, Oxford: Basil Blackwell.

Steindl, J. (1965) – See p. 4

Studart, R. (1995) 'The efficiency of financial systems, liberalization, and economic development, *Journal of Post Keynesian Economics*, 18(2): 269–292.

Studwell, J. (2007) *Asian Godfathers: Money and Power in Hong Kong and Southeast Asia*, New York: Atlantic Monthly Press.

Suehiro, A. (1989) *Capital Accumulation in Thailand 1855–1985*, Chiang Mai: Silkworm Books.

Suehiro, A. (1996) *Capital Accumulation in Thailand, 1855–1985*, Chiang Mai: Silkworm Books.

Suehiro, A. (2003) 'Determinants of business capability, in Thailand' in K.S. Jomo and B. Folk (eds), *Ethnic Business and Chinese Capitalism in Southeast Asia*, London: Routledge.

Toporowski, J. (2008) 'Minsky's induced investment and business cycles', *Cambridge Journal of Economics*, 32(5): 725–737.

Wailerdsak, N. (2008) 'Companies in crisis', in P. Phongpaichit and C. Baker (eds), *Thai Capital: After the 1997 Crisis*, Bangkok: Silkworm Books.

Yoshihara, K. (1988) *The Rise of Ersatz Capitalism in Southeast Asia*, Singapore: Oxford University Press.

15
The Kalecki-Steindl Theory of Financial Fragility

Jan Toporowski

Kalecki and Steindl modelled the financial fragility of companies through a circular flow of income analysis, extending the treatment of inter-sectoral flows that Marx put forward in Volume II of *Capital* to include household saving as a leakage from firms' revenues and firms saving representing the financial accumulation of capitalist firms. Household saving causes financial fragility by reducing that financial accumulation. In Kalecki, this relation was put forward as an element in the 'trend' of economic development. Steindl made it of more immediate macroeconomic concern because it induces 'enforced' indebtedness among companies. The chapter extends this analysis by showing how recent asset inflation may have reduced this source of financial fragility, albeit at the expense of the indebtedness of households.

This chapter is a contribution to economic methodology, history of economic thought and the analysis of current financial developments. It shows how economic concepts can be refined and developed beyond their original purpose for use in a better understanding of economic developments with which the original authors of those concepts could not have been familiar. It traces the origins of household saving as a factor in the macroeconomics of Kalecki through to its role in precipitating financial crises. Finally, the paper shows how in circumstances of asset inflation, the character and significance of household saving changes.

The paper is structured as follows. Section 15.1 presents the role of household saving in Kalecki's business cycle theory. Section 15.2 shows how Steindl created a theory of financial fragility out of household saving. Section 15.3 shows how asset inflation reduces household saving and thereby shifts financial fragility from the firm sector to the household sector.

15.1 Household saving in Kalecki's analysis.

Kalecki's analysis is based on the reproduction (or as we would nowadays call them, circular flow of income) schemes put forward by Marx in Volume II of *Capital*. In his analysis, Marx argued that surplus value is turned into money by the expenditure of capitalists: 'it is the capitalist class itself that throws the money into circulation which serves for the realisation of ... surplus value incorporated in ... commodities' (Marx, 1974, p. 338). Whereas Marx emphasized capitalists' consumption as the way in which capitalists 'realise' their surplus value, Kalecki was able to show that the realization of profit was chiefly done through capitalists' expenditure on investment, as well as their expenditure on their own consumption. (Marx's analysis, and its link with that of Kalecki, is most clearly discussed in Trigg, 2006, pp. 22–28). This can be easily shown as follows.

According to the standard national income identity, in any given period, total national income (Y) is equal to consumption (C) plus gross fixed capital expenditure, or investment (I), plus the fiscal deficit, plus the trade surplus.

Saving (S) is then equal to Y – C, which is then equal to investment, plus the fiscal deficit plus the trade surplus. Abstracting away from the fiscal surplus and the trade surplus, and in an economy in which there are only capitalists and workers, saving and consumption can be divided up into the saving and consumption respectively of capitalists and workers:

$$C = C_c + C_w;\ \text{and}\ S = S_c + S_w$$

So that:

$$Y - C = S = S_c + S_w = I \qquad (15.1)$$

The surplus or profits of capitalists (P) is also, by definition, equal to their expenditure on their own consumption (C_c) plus their saving (S_c):

$$P = C_c + S_c$$

Since, by (15.1) above, capitalist saving is equal to their investment expenditure minus the saving of workers, it follows that $P = C_c + I - S_w$, which can be rearranged to give the familiar Kalecki profits equation:

$$P = I + C_c - S_w \qquad (15.2)$$

In other words, capitalists' profits are equal to their expenditure on fixed capital, plus their expenditure on consumption, minus workers' saving. Since this is derived from national income identities, the equation itself cannot yield any causal mechanism. This has to be obtained by a consideration of its economic significance:

> What is the proper meaning of this equation? Does it mean that profits in a certain period determine capitalists' consumption and investment, or the other way around? The answer to this question depends on which of these items is directly subject to the decisions of capitalists. Now, it is clear that they may decide to consume and invest more in a certain short period than in the preceding period, but they cannot decide to earn more. It is therefore their investment and consumption decisions which determine profits, and not vice versa. (Kalecki, 1943, pp. 48–49)

In this analysis, workers' saving clearly has a negative effect on profits. It acts as a 'leakage' whereby money spent by capitalists on wages does not return to capitalists in the form of sales of wage goods. With capitalists' saving, the situation is more complex. Kalecki divides such saving up into 'entrepreneurs' saving' or the undistributed profits of companies, and the saving of 'rentiers', or those who own companies and financial assets. Because of their relatively high and stable incomes (except at times of hyperinflation), rentiers have a high propensity to save, and this saving stays relatively constant. Unlike entrepreneurs' saving, which is used to finance investment and is therefore matched by expenditure, rentiers' saving is a steady 'leakage' of income from the circular flow of money that capitalists put into circulation by their expenditure.

In this analysis, rentiers' and workers' saving is the result of what Marx described as 'a stagnation of circulation', whereas entrepreneurs' saving is 'merely the creation of money capital existing temporarily in latent form and intended to function as productive capital' (Marx, 1974, p. 353). With his analysis clearly focussed on an investment-driven business cycle, Kalecki incorporated the rentiers' saving as a factor in what he called the 'trend', that is, the direction of economic growth disregarding 'the pure business cycle' (Kalecki, 1943, chapter 5; Kalecki, 1954, p. 159). He argued that such saving tends to give a negative trend. In his last discussion of rentiers' saving, Kalecki merely assumed that it is small in relation to entrepreneurial saving, or retained profits, and that the two types of saving are proportionate to each other (Kalecki, 1968). This would tend to make rentiers' saving fluctuate with the profits cycle.

Kalecki's classification of rentiers' saving as a trend factor makes such saving a weak foundation for any theory of financial fragility or crisis. A theory of financial fragility or crisis is by definition an explanation of economic breakdown caused or rooted in the financial system. While financial fragility may take time to build up, its adverse consequences should be apparent in the fluctuation of economic variables, rather than their averages or any trend. It was Josef Steindl, Kalecki's friend and associate, who turned his friend's theory of saving into a theory of financial fragility.

15.2 Steindl's theory of financial fragility

Steindl's analysis is more advanced and perhaps more general than that of Kalecki because Steindl looked more broadly at the impact of middle class saving behaviour on the dynamics of the capitalist economy (Steindl, 1952, pp. 113–121). The version that is presented here is the one Steindl later put forward (Steindl, 1982; Steindl, 1989).

Consider the Keynesian saving identity, in which saving (S) is the sum of firms' gross fixed capital formation (I), the fiscal deficit (G – T) and the foreign trade surplus (X – M). If we divide up total saving into Household Saving (S_H) and Firms' Saving (S_F), we get the following identity:

$$S \equiv S_H + S_F \equiv I + (G - T) + (X - M) \qquad (15.3)$$

These are all flow variables over a given period of time. Household saving is broadly related to income. Both Kalecki and Steindl confirmed Hobson's observation that the middle classes and those on higher incomes account for the vast bulk of household saving, for the obvious reason that they have higher incomes than people on lower incomes, and it is easier to save out of higher income.

In the theory of saving, household saving is the residual income of households that is not consumed. In the case of firms, their saving is the residual profit that they have, after their expenditure on the costs of producing their goods and services, and after payment of income commitments to holders of their financial liabilities (i.e., creditors and holders of equity). In other words, firms' saving is the retained profits of all firms in the economy, or what Kalecki called 'entrepreneurs' saving'.

Firms' saving plays a crucial part in the dynamics of the capitalist economy. The vast bulk of capital accumulation by firms is financed out of retained profits. This was first noted by Kalecki, and was confirmed in studies by Locke Anderson, by Victoria Chick and by recent research that I have done with Marilyn Polena (Anderson, 1964; Chick, 1993). Through its influence on capital expenditure, firm saving is a crucial factor in capitalist dynamics, that is, inflation, employment and business fluctuations. This is apparent if Equation (15.1) is re-arranged to give:

$$S_F \equiv I - S_H + (G - T) + (X - M) \tag{15.4}$$

Once again, for the sake of simplicity, the sum of the fiscal deficit and the trade surplus is disregarded. This yields an identity in which Firms' retained profits (S_F) are equal to their gross capital expenditure minus household saving.

An implication of this is the Keynesian formulation that Investment determines Saving. The Steindl formulation given above retains Kalecki's insight that investment determines the retained profits of firms. However, household saving is a financial barrier to retained profits: Firms will only end up with retained profits amounting to the difference between firms' investment and household saving. If household saving exceeds the level of investment, then firms' saving becomes a net financial deficit. In this way, saving at all times equals investment. But the factor which equalizes them in practice is not the rate of interest, as most text-books teach, but the net retained profits or financial deficit of the business sector.

This is illustrated in Figure 15.1 below:

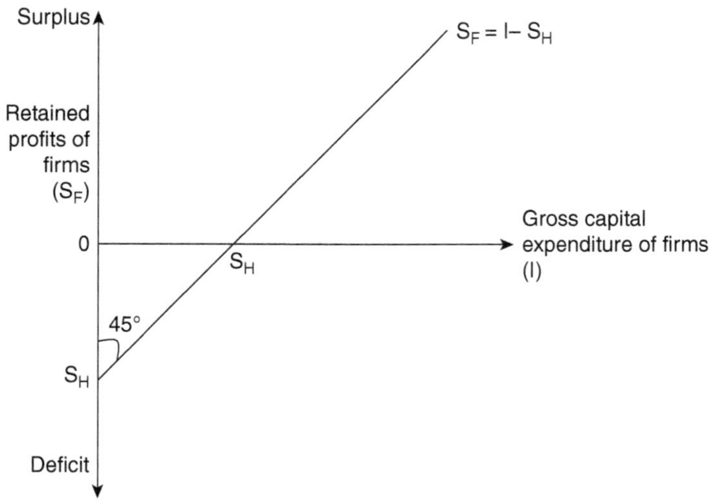

Figure 15.1 Household saving & firms' retained profits in industrial capitalism
Saving = Firms' saving (S_F) +Household Saving (S_H) = Gross Capital Expenditure of Firms (I)

The figure shows the dependence of firms' net cash flow (retained profits – the curve S_F in the diagram) on investment and the level of household saving. On the vertical axis is shown the net financial surplus or deficit of the company sector. On the horizontal axis is shown the level of gross investment in the economy. S_H marks the threshold level of investment that investment must reach if the company sector as a whole is to avoid going into deficit. If investment exceeds that threshold, then firms receive a net cash inflow. If investment falls below the level of household saving, firms as a whole experience a financial deficit.

In Steindl, this relationship between household saving and the financial surpluses or deficits of firms plays a key part in the business cycle. If investment falls below the level of household saving, firms find themselves paying out more in costs, and payments to holders of their financial obligations, than they receive in income. Firms will then borrow to make up the deficit, and the rise in their indebtedness will tend to reduce investment further. Kalecki had argued that this is caused by the 'inelasticity of saving' with respect to investment (Kalecki, 1943, p. 86). In other words, when investment falls, this does not immediately affect the incomes of recipients of higher incomes who account for the bulk of saving. Their continued saving prevents the money that firms throw into circulation, in the process of production, from returning to firms as sales revenue equal or greater than their costs of production and financing. In order to cope with this unexpected financial deficit firms continue to reduce their investment, driving the economy into recession, until household saving falls below the level of investment.

In his pioneering study *Maturity and Stagnation in American Capitalism* Josef Steindl gave a more detailed account of household saving, and showed that it was largely accounted for by rentier incomes and the incomes of the middle classes (Steindl, 1952, pp. 113–121). Rentier incomes are largely received through the intermediation of banks and financial institutions, which stabilize those incomes through diversification. The saving of rentiers is therefore largely unaffected by a rise in the financial deficit of firms. Some humbler investors, whose wealth does not allow them to diversify their portfolios, may find their incomes affected by the financial difficulties of firms. But such investors are marginal in economic and saving terms.

The remainder of household saving is accounted for by the saving of the middle classes, that is, those employed in public administration, education, the liberal professions and, increasingly today, the managerial bureaucracy engaged in the administration of financial, industrial and commercial corporations. This social group is largely disconnected from the industrial business cycle, which does not affect those working in public administration, education and the liberal professions. Even the management of financial, industrial and commercial corporations may, if those corporations are large enough, insulate their incomes from industrial fluctuations by diversifying the business of those corporations.

This high and stable level of middle-class saving forms a threshold that forces firms into unanticipated debt, when their gross capital expenditure approaches that threshold, and then falls below it. Firms respond to such 'enforced indebtedness' by postponing investment (it is much more difficult to reduce the costs of current production) and using the money saved to repay debts. This merely prolongs the industrial crisis because it reduces investment even more below the household saving threshold. Investment is then further reduced. The crisis continues until public sector projects or replacement investment (depreciation) induces a rise in investment.

This prolonged industrial crisis is typical of the difficulties that affected industries in Britain and the United States in the 1950s and the 1960s. At the time, these difficulties were attributed to a lack of competitiveness against industrial producers in East Asia, the greed of trade unions and so on. But the true cause of these crises was the thrift of the middle classes, with memories of their difficulties in the Great Depression.

15.3 The theory of asset price inflation

The situation changed in the 1970s with developments that laid the basis for a new financial cycle. The proliferation of unregulated credit (most notably in the Euro-markets) and the ease with which credit can be expanded against rising collateral values undermined financial regulation and created a new spirit of competition and innovation in banking and financial markets. Legislation greatly expanded the scope of funded pension schemes, in part at least on the grounds that this would direct more finance into industrial investment and thereby revive the industrial fortunes of the UK and the US. As we now know, the industrial revival did not happen, for reasons outlined in the next section. But the inflow of money into pension funds and its placement in financial securities set off a prolonged financial boom. At the same time, the removal of restrictions on housing credit inflated house prices.

With the expansion of the financial markets, and their influence on economic activity beyond merely financing trade and investment, a new phase of capitalist development has emerged in which companies and households have their economic activities increasingly determined by development in capital and asset markets. This section discusses the impact on economic dynamics of this new development. As a preliminary, it is useful to review the market processes that operate in capital markets. Similar processes occur in the market for housing that have more relevance for more households than the processes in capital markets that also affect companies and financial intermediaries.

Capital markets, that is, markets for long-term financial assets, do not fix prices that make supply equal to demand, except in a notional sense. Nor are the prices in financial markets determined by the discounted future returns on any given security since such returns depend on future capital market inflation or deflation. Financial markets typically operate for extended periods out of equilibrium. When the demand for financial securities exceeds the amount of money that holders and issuers of those securities are prepared to take out of the market, prices rise. As prices rise, demand for those assets, far from falling off, is enhanced by a speculative demand for assets to benefit from capital gains. However, prices of securities do not rise equally across all markets. Short-term securities and bonds usually have the price at which they are repaid written into the terms of the bond. As the date of their repayment approaches, their market price converges on their repayment price. The market price of such bonds will only exceed that repayment price by a small margin reflecting any differences between the interest payable on such a bond and the interest payable on equivalent new issues. Excess demand for new securities will therefore inflate most of all equities (common stocks) that do not have any guaranteed repayment value.

Asset and capital market inflation allow debts to be written off against capital gains because collateral can be sold and debts repaid at an overall profit. The mechanism for such write-offs works only as long as the credit system is funnelling more credit into the market to facilitate the asset sales used to repay debts. When that stops, the liquidity of the market collapses and debt deflation sets in. The dependence of capital gains on net credit inflows into a given asset market turns the whole market into a Ponzi scheme. Financial fragility in such markets arises because, while the market may need net credit inflows to sustain a given rate of capital gain, there is no mechanism to ensure that sufficient credit will automatically flow into the market to more than off-set the credit being taken out of the market to write off debts and finance other activities. If capital gains cannot be realized, then the whole mechanism for writing off debts against capital gains breaks down.

The majority of securities are issued by financial intermediaries and bought by other financial intermediaries ('in an era of finance, finance mostly finances finance'). This issue therefore does not constitute any net expansion of credit, or of the balance sheets of non-financial businesses, such as would take out of the markets any excess net inflow of money into those markets. The non-financial sectors that do take money out of the markets are governments and corporations. The finance that governments take out of the markets is limited by their fiscal position (the balance between government income and expenditure). An excess demand for securities, such as was set off by the inauguration of funded pension schemes in the UK and the US therefore impacts most directly on the balance sheet operations of corporations. During the 1980s, corporations that issued securities in the capital markets found that they could issue shares cheaply. In particular, with capital market inflation, shares came to be held not just for the sake of their dividend income, which is paid by the company, but also for capital gains, which are not paid by the company but by other buyers in the market for the shares.

As a result of the excess demand for shares, corporations have issued capital in excess of what they need to finance their commercial and industrial operations. In the past the over-capitalization of companies might have been avoided because it would have involved the 'watering down' of profits (sharing a given amount of profits among more shareholders) or loss of control by the directors of a company who could no longer control the majority of shares at a company general meeting. However, today's shareholders are mostly institutions whose large diversified portfolios are sub-contracted to professional fund managers and rated on financial returns, rather than on their active running of companies. By and large they have too many diverse holdings to take any other than a financial interest in a company. At the same time, new techniques of senior management remuneration have tended to replace profit-related pay with share price-related pay, through stock options. Along with new techniques of debt management, stock option remuneration has removed inhibitions about the over-capitalization of companies: An over-capitalized company, holding its excess capital in the form of liquid assets, is a liquid company and therefore worth more than the equivalent capital tied up in illiquid assets.

Additional capital raised has been used to replace bank borrowing with cheaper long-term capital. Replacing borrowing with shares also has the advantage that pre-tax profits can be made to rise by the reduction in interest cost. Where excess capital has not been used to reduce debt, it has been used to buy short-term financial assets. Alternatively, excess capital is committed to buying and selling companies. Hence the extended festival of merger and takeover activity and balance sheet restructuring that has characterized corporate finance since the 1980s.

One may wonder what happened to the hopes of industrial revival, entertained at the end of the 1970s, when it was argued that funded pension schemes would make more long-term capital available for industrial investment. These hopes have by and large not materialized. Britain and the US, where capital market inflation has been most heavily promoted, remain economies with weak industrial investment and performance, for which the cause is fairly obvious to anyone who has followed recent changes in corporate finance. Large corporations, which account for the vast bulk of private sector investment, now have excess capital and engage more in balance sheet restructuring (buying and selling financial assets; issuing and repaying liabilities). Such restructuring leaves corporations with larger risky financial market exposures, which therefore require the holding of greater amounts of liquid assets (short-term deposits, holding of financial paper). If a company finds itself with too much liquid assets, profits can be immediately increased by using the excess liquid assets to repay debt. Indeed, this is a far more certain way of raising profits than the prolonged and uncertain business of investment in plant and equipment. Industrial regeneration is a dream of engineers, from which companies are awoken by their finance directors to face the irrefutable realities of balance sheet restructuring as the only financially viable way forward for all companies.

The overall effect of company over-capitalization on banks has been to make them more fragile. Before the 1970s, the largest, most reliable borrowers from banks were large corporations. From the end of the 1970s, such corporations found that they could borrow much more cheaply by issuing their own bills (company paper) or directly from the inter-bank market. If banks want to hold company loans, they have to buy them in the market at yields that give banks no profit over their cost of funds in the capital or money markets. The loss of their best customers has turned banks towards fee-related business in derivatives and debt obligations markets, and towards lending into the property market and to other risky customers that banks had hitherto treated with much more caution. The overall effect, from the savings and loans scandals of the early 1980s, to the sub-prime market crisis since 2007, has clearly been to make banking markets much more fragile.

The rise in the value of their real estate and financial assets has induced a change in saving behaviour of the middle classes. Hitherto the middle classes saved more or less passively, along lines loosely related to the Life Cycle Saving Hypothesis, or the New Classical consumption function: Income was put into savings to support future consumption in retirement. Only among the small minority of the wealthy upper classes was wealth used as a substitute for income, with legacies and realized wealth being used to support current expenditure. From the 1980s onwards, active use of their balance sheets to generate cash flow became much more common among the middle classes. Asset inflation in the housing market allowed the emergence of an alternative 'welfare state of the middle classes' based on issuing financial liabilities against rising asset values or the sale of inflated assets. Private health care, fees for education and replacement income in periods of unemployment have increasingly, among the middle classes, been accommodated by borrowing against wealth whose value has conveniently been rising much faster than current expenditure, or selling such wealth.

When assets are no longer largely held long-term, to be realized only on death or retirement, but come to be held more briefly, for capital gain purposes, their turnover inevitably increases. The more common use of debt or asset sales to pay for current expenditure has brought down saving rates in the household sectors of the United States and Great Britain to negligible or negative levels. This in turn has removed the household saving threshold which firms' investment must exceed in order to provide the business sector as a whole with a financial surplus. Now the total amount of firms' capital expenditure is realized as net cash flow in the form of retained profits. This is illustrated in Figure 15.2 below.

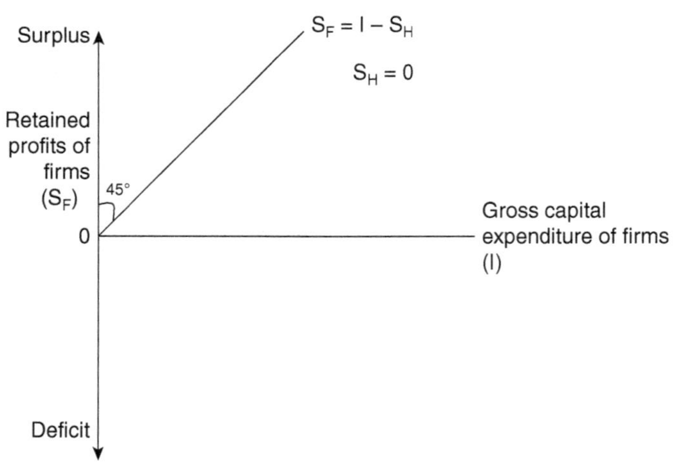

Figure 15.2 Household saving & firms' retained profits in financialized capitalism

The business cycle is now different. Industrial crises no longer play a part in bringing economic booms to an end. Such crises are largely eliminated by the over-capitalization of corporations, which makes it easier for corporations to maintain their liquidity. Industrial crises have now been replaced by a less dramatic under-investment in fixed capital by those companies. Booms are increasingly driven by middle-class consumption, sustained by capital gains extracted from inflating asset markets. The end of a boom is marked by a financial rather than industrial crisis. But the resilience of consumption, which in wealthy countries remains one of the most stable elements of total expenditure, ensures that economic recessions are weak, except where debt crises are exacerbated by political constraints on counter-cyclical policy (in Europe, for example).

15.4 Conclusion

This chapter has argued that, before the crisis of 2008, asset and capital market inflation had brought about relative economic stability by removing the 'congestion' to the circular flow of income induced by household saving. It has not considered the consequences of the decline of industry in the financialized economies, with manufacturing being the main industrial casualty of financial inflation. Nor has this chapter considered the extent to which financial inflation in the US and the UK, by backing their currencies with inflated asset values, has accommodated the macroeconomic imbalances that have resulted from weakening industrial performance in those countries. Essential to the theory of financial fragility is the idea that macroeconomic imbalances do not work themselves out in some reified way, abstracted from or a mere conjuncture of prices in the economic calculations of 'economic agents'. In a credit-based capitalist economy, such imbalances are resolved through the constraints that debts impose upon firms and households. The ultimate financial fragility arrives when financial inflation can no longer be used to write off debt.

15.5 Acknowledgements

I am grateful to Marilyn Polena for research assistance, and to Karel Williams, Victoria Chick and Geert Reuten, participants in a conference on 'Crisis in Financialization' held at the School of Oriental and African Studies, University of London on 30 May 2008 and a seminar on 25 April 2008 at the Research Centre for the History and Methodology of Economics, University of Amsterdam, for comments on earlier drafts of this paper.

References

Anderson, W.H.L. (1964) *Corporate Finance and Fixed Investment: An Econometric Study*, Cambridge, Mass.: Harvard University Press.

Chick, V. (1993) 'Sources of Finance, Recent Changes in Bank Behaviour and the Theory of Investment and Interest' in P. Arestis (ed.), *Money and Banking: Issues for the 21st Century*, London: Macmillan.

Kalecki, M. (1943) *Studies in Economic Dynamics*, London: George Allen and Unwin.

Kalecki, M. (1954) *Theory of Economic Dynamics: An Essay on Cyclical and Long-Run Changes in Capitalist Economy*, London: George Allen and Unwin.

Kalecki M. (1968) 'Trend and the Business Cycle' in *Selected Essays on the Dynamics of the Capitalist Economy 1933–1970*, Cambridge: Cambridge University Press, 1971.

Marx, K. (1974) *Capital: A Critique of Political Economy, Volume II The Process of Circulation of Capital*, London: Lawrence & Wishart.

Steindl, J. (1952) *Maturity and Stagnation in American Capitalism*, Oxford Institute of Statistics Monograph No. 4, Oxford: Basil Blackwell.

Steindl, J. (1982) 'The role of household saving in the modern economy', *Banca Nazionale del Lavoro Quarterly Review*, 140, pp. 69–88, March.

Steindl, J. (1989) 'Saving and debt', in A. Barrère (ed.) *Money, Credit and Prices in Keynesian Perspective*, London: Macmillan.

Toporowski, J. (2000) *The End of Finance: The Theory of Capital Market Inflation, Financial Derivatives and Pension Fund Capitalism*, London: Routledge.

Trigg, A.B. (2006) *Marxian Reproduction Schema: Money and Aggregate Demand in a Capitalist Economy*, London: Routledge.

Index

Anderson, W.H.L., 255
Andrews, P.W.S., 65
Arestis, P., 51
Asimakopoulos, T., 51
Austria, 42
Austrian economics, 17–18, 73, 95

Balcerowicz, L., 174, 175, 180
Barro, R.J., 123
Bhaduri, A., 41, 64, 77
Blanchard, O., 122, 123, 124–126
Brus, W., 119, 162, 174
Burczak, T., 95–96

Caldwell, B.J., 95–96
Chick, V., 255
China, 20, 41, 86
competition, 31, 34, 35, 36, 47, 53, 71, 165, 246, 258
see also monopoly
consumption, 10–25, 32–33, 35–36, 45, 53–54, 64, 120, 121, 133, 135, 140, 146, 216, 253, 261–262, 263
Courvisanos, J., 99–100, 105
credit, 43–44, 45, 60–61, 214, 217–219, 227–228, 230, 243, 247, 249, 258–262

Davidson, P., 51–65
debt, 56–57, 60, 124, 208, 229
Deprez, J., 62
developing countries, 21, 245, 248–250
Dixon, R., 51–52, 57–58, 64
Dobb, M.H., 2, 16, 19, 21–23
Domar, E., 17–18, 25
Dostaler, G., 64
Dow, S.C., 89
Dunlop, J.T., 40, 47, 62–63
Dymski, G.A., 60–61, 159, 179–180
Dynamic Stochastic General Equilibrium, 57, 59

Eichner, A., 58
employment, 16, 25, 29–48, 53, 59–60, 61, 82–88, 111, 112–113, 114, 121, 122, 123, 125, 148–149, 159–160, 169–170, 175–178, 184, 186–187, 198–203, 205–210
European Association for Evolutionary Political Economy, 3
European Monetary Union, 42–43, 125, 127–128, 208–209
European Union, 208–209, 212, 222
exports, 16–17, 29–30, 41–43, 46, 135, 145–147

Fel'dman, G.A., 3, 9–19, 21–25
financial capitalism, 150–153
Finland, 42
fiscal policy, 44–45, 121–128, 142–145, 146, 149, 199–201, 202–203, 208–210, 219–220, 228, 230
Flassbeck, H., 48
France, 222–230
Frankel, J., 126
Freeman, C., 102
Friedman, M., 68, 70

Galbraith, J.K., 24–25, 64
Germany, 42, 48, 122, 149
Godley, W., 65
Greece, 42, 48
growth, economic, 15, 22–23, 25, 70–72

Harcourt, G.C., 51, 65
Harrod, R.F., 17, 25, 58, 74, 76, 77, 100, 120
Hausner, J., 3
Hayek, F.A., 4, 80, 88–96, 174
Hein, E., 204–205
Hicks, J.R., 57, 61, 80

Indonesia, 248
industrialisation, 14–15, 16–17, 22–24, 25
inflation, 44–45, 168, 221–222, 226
International Monetary Fund, 4–5, 124–126, 128, 174, 205
interest, rate of, 3, 35, 38, 39, 43–44, 45, 53, 55–57, 61, 88–89, 114, 122, 148, 149, 215, 216, 218–219, 220–221, 227, 231, 242
investment, 53–56, 72–76, 81, 85, 86–88, 103–105, 110–112, 122–123, 135, 136–137, 140, 145–146, 148–149, 159, 200, 201, 210
Italy, 126, 128

Japan, 85
Jespersen, J., 62

Kahn, R., 2
Kaldor, N., 4, 24, 25, 58, 61, 63, 64, 80, 82–85, 100–101, 213
Kalecki, M.
  biography, 1–2
  Essay on the Business Cycle Theory, 32–35
  Essays on Developing Economies, 21
  Essays on Economic Planning, 22–23
  Essays in the Theory of Economic Fluctuations, 37–38
  Money and Real Wages, 35–37
  'Political Aspects of Full Employment', 159–160, 199, 205–207, 212–213
  'Some Remarks on Keynes's Theory', 108–115
  'A Theorem on Technical Progress', 103–104
  Theory of Economic Dynamics, 102–103, 182–183, 189
  Theory of Growth in a Socialist Economy, 104
  'Three ways to Full Employment', 47, 200
Keynes, J.M., 1, 2, 4, 9, 29–31, 38–41, 44–45, 46, 48, 51–56, 57–65, 69, 71, 83, 108–115, 119–120, 131–132, 155, 163–164, 212, 213, 217, 223, 224, 243
Keynesians, New, 57, 228
Kindleberger, C.P., 167, 179
King, J.E., 51, 52, 58
Klein, L., 120
Kley, R., 93
Kornai, J., 163, 173, 174
Kowalik, T., 5, 157–158, 160–167, 173–175
Kregel. J., 58, 246
Kriesler, P., 26, 51, 59, 63–64
Krugman, P., 1

Lange, O., 119, 162, 174
Łaski, K., 48, 119
Lavoie, M., 52, 57, 58–59, 87
Lazonick, W., 155
Leijonhufvud, A., 221–222
Leontief, W., 112
Lerner, A.P., 44–45, 48
Lewis, W.A., 16, 24
liquidity preference, 53, 60
López, J., 51, 54, 55, 59, 61, 65
Lowe, A., 4, 25, 57, 80–81, 87, 88

Malaysia, 248
Malinvaud, E., 77
Mamica, L., 3
Marglin, S.A., 41, 76, 157
Marshall, A., 31, 40, 69, 83, 241
Marx, K.H., 25, 26, 161, 254
Marxian reproduction schemes, 11, 82–84, 133–134, 252
Meade, J.E., 48
microfoundations, 59, 62
Minsky, H.P., 51, 55, 58, 59, 63
Moggridge, D.E., 113
monopoly, 34, 36, 37, 47, 53, 70, 95, 120, 136, 137, 138–139, 145, 148, 183, 202, 221, 246
Moore, B., 58
Musgrave, R.A., 48

Netherlands, 42, 155
Nove, A., 25, 180

Onaran, O., 155
O'Neill, J., 93–94
Osiatyński, J.E., 2, 3

Pasinetti, L., 77
Patinkin, D., 52
pensions, 152–153
Poland, 20, 32, 166, 173–178
Polanyi, M., 91
profits, 5, 26, 29, 31–34, 35–36, 39, 40–41, 44, 45, 46, 47, 51, 53–54, 55, 83–84, 85, 86, 131–155, 162, 172, 201, 204, 206–207, 242, 245–246, 253–254, 256–257, 262–263

Reddaway, W.B., 77
Ricardo, D., 123
Robertson, D.H., 123
Robinson, J.V., 2, 20–21, 31, 51, 63, 64, 77, 103–104, 114, 119–120
Rogoff, K., 124, 127, 128
Romer, P.M., 101–102

Sachs, I., 119
Samuelson, P.A., 77, 137
Sardoni, C., 62
Sawyer, M.C., 51, 60–61, 114
Say's Law, 30, 52–53
Schumpeter, J.A., 30, 99, 103, 225
Sen, A., 19–20
Simon, H., 61
Socialism, 4, 23, 57, 80, 80, 94, 96, 100, 158, 162–166, 173–174, 178
Solow, R.M., 77, 100–101, 149
Soviet Union, 9–11, 18, 86
Sraffa, P., 2, 76
Steindl, J., 6, 70, 100, 239, 241–243, 244–245, 252, 255–258
Stiglitz, J., 127
Stockhammer, E., 155
Swan, T.W., 77
Sweezy, P.M., 86–87

Tarshis, L., 47
technical progress, 4
Thailand, 248
Thirlwall, A.P., 58
Thompson, 193
Toporowski, J., 244

United States of America, 53, 60, 102, 149, 166–172, 184–196, 201, 257, 263
Unsal, E.M., 17, 26

Velupillai, V., 65

wages, 25, 29–48, 59, 61, 69, 76, 81–82, 112–113, 122, 138–141, 172, 182–195, 194–195, 202, 203, 204–205, 230
Wątecki, J., 35, 37
Weintraub, S., 58, 61
Wicksell, K., 114

CPSIA information can be obtained
at www.ICGtesting.com
Printed in the USA
LVHW050315171218
600705LV00010BA/801/P

9 781137 428271